COBA

A Classic Maya Metropolis

This is a volume in

Studies in Archaeology

A complete list of titles in this series appears at the end of this volume.

COBA

A Classic Maya Metropolis

William J. Folan
Centro de Investigaciones Históricas y Sociales
Universidad Autónoma del Sudeste
Campeche, Campeche, Mexico

Ellen R. Kintz
Department of Anthropology
State University of New York College
Geneseo, New York

Laraine A. Fletcher
Department of Anthropology
Adelphi University
Garden City, New York

1983

ACADEMIC PRESS

A Subsidiary of Harcourt Brace Jovanovich, Publishers

New York   London
Paris   San Diego   San Francisco   São Paulo   Sydney   Tokyo   Toronto

ACADEMIC PRESS, INC.
111 Fifth Avenue, New York, New York 10003

United Kingdom Edition published by
ACADEMIC PRESS, INC. (LONDON) LTD.
24/28 Oval Road, London NW1 7DX

Library of Congress Cataloging in Publication Data

Folan, William J.
    Coba, a classic Maya metropolis.

    (Studies in archaeology)
    Bibliography: p.
    Includes index.
    1. Coba (Ancient city) 2. Mayas--Urban residence.
3. Cities and towns, Ruined, extinct, etc.--Mexico.
4. Mexico--Antiquities. 5. Indians of Mexico--Urban
residence. I. Kintz, Ellen R. II. Fletcher,
Laraine A. III. Title. IV. Series.
F1435.1.C63F63 1982   972'.67   82-8895
ISBN 0-12-261880-7

PRINTED IN THE UNITED STATES OF AMERICA

83 84 85 86   9 8 7 6 5 4 3 2 1

The authors dedicate this volume to Nicolás Caamal Canche, Jacinto May Hau, and the citizens of Coba both past and present. May their efforts toward our understanding of the past illuminate our journey into the future.

Contents

List of Figures

List of Tables

Foreword

The formulation of the Coba Archaeological Mapping Project stems from our association during the late 1950s with the National Geographic Society–Tulane University Dzibilchaltun project in Yucatan, Mexico, under the direction of the late E. Wyllys Andrews IV. At that time we were involved in excavation and mapping activities in and around Dzibilchaltun in an effort to understand better what was occurring there before, during, and after the flourishing of such cities as Uxmal, Kabah, Sayil, and Labna to the south, and at Tikal in the Peten region of Guatemala.

We were intrigued by the many research possibilities presented by Coba, with its large groups and numerous roadways jutting into the hinterlands. Our interests were reinforced by the detailed writings of J. Eric Thompson, Harry E. D. Pollock, Jean Charlot, and Alfonso Villa Rojas. These left us with the sense of a mighty sociopolitical unit that had apparently been imbued with great economic powers, but was now far from fully understood.

Although we saw each other only occasionally during the 1960s, and never had the opportunity to visit the ruins of this grand metropolis, the thought of "doing Coba" remained with us. Finally, at dinner one evening in 1972, while attending the annual meetings of the American Anthropological Association in Toronto, we laid out our goals for Coba. It was during the same meeting that we learned from Fernando Cámara Barbachano, then Sub-Director of Mexico's Instituto Nacional de Antropología e Historia (INAH), that INAH would look favorably upon our collaboration with them on a project to be formulated for Coba by the Instituto under the direction of Norberto González Crespo, then director of the Centro Regional del Sureste in Mérida, Yucatan.

Our plans for Coba were influenced mainly by settlement pattern work already done at Dzibilchaltun, by Andrews IV, Stuart, Folan, and Kurjack, similar work at Tikal, and analysis of settlement patterns in the Nootka Sound area of the Canadian Northwest Coast, carried out with the support of Parks Canada and the Canada Council.

We were determined to map as much of Coba as INAH and our financial support would allow. Our major goal was to understand better the composition and organization of a Classic Maya urban area and to relate it to others within the boundaries of a larger region, as well as to other regions in the northern and central parts of the Yucatan Peninsula at different times during the Classic period. To this end we had decided to apply Side Looking Airborne Radar techniques to the Coba area to provide us with a better idea of its extent and content; Adams, Brown, and Culbert later demonstrated the applicability of this technique in the Southern Maya Lowlands.

Following a great deal of preliminary planning, we formulated a proposal. After submission of the proposal to INAH and its final acceptance by INAH's Consejo de Arqueología, the National Geographic Society agreed to fund our part of the greater Coba project. For this we thank Dr. Melvin Payne, then President of the National Geographic Society and chairman of the society's Committee for Research and Exploration, and the late Dr. Matthew W. Stirling. Two graduate students, Laraine A. Fletcher and Ellen R. Kintz of the Department of Anthropology, State University of New York at Stony Brook, joined the project and wrote doctoral dissertations based on their Coba work. Lynda M. Florey Folan, Valery Fadziewicz, and Morgan Ray Crook, of West Georgia College, also assisted in the survey.

All in all, the Coba project has been fruitful, although we spent less than half as much time in the field as we had originally planned. So far, however, more than a dozen papers have been published or submitted for publication in Mexico and the United States, in both Spanish and English, or have been presented at different meetings on both sides of the border. What you will read between these covers should be considered only a stepping stone toward learning more of the ancient Maya and their ways both at Coba and in the rest of southern Mesoamerica as well. This volume is intended to represent the latest but certainly not the final word on these subjects.

William J. Folan
George E. Stuart

Preface

The analysis of data presented in this volume establishes Coba as a major regional capital during the Late Classic period. Our goal in this project, however, went beyond substantiating the importance of Coba. Rather, in this volume we offer a holistic contribution to settlement-pattern research that includes prehistoric and ethnohistoric as well as ethnographic data on the ancient and contemporary Maya. We believe that our approach to settlement-pattern studies has made it possible to present a broader and more accurate understanding of the composition, size, and organization of a Classic Maya metropolis than has been developed previously and is thus pertinent for students of the social sciences interested in the development and accomplishments of preindustrial societies through time. At a minimum we wanted to document the manner in which the residents of Coba extended themselves and their activities over the landscape. We also offer an interpretation of Maya class structure, thereby producing what Pedro Armillas would term a *paleosociological* study of Maya society.

Although excavation of Coba was minimal, we have been able to offer a diachronic developmental model for Coba based on surface material, hieroglyphic texts, and relevant ethnographic information, as well as on data such as settlement-pattern analyses derived from comparable Maya cities in Yucatan and the Peten. Although the early centuries of this model are somewhat speculative, we have developed a fairly representative vision of what occurred in Coba and its regional state, at least from Early Classic times onward.

It has been our intention to take what Armillas has classified as *landscape archaeology* closer to the edge of its considerable possibilities. In this manner we hope that this study will enable others to operate from a firmer, more imaginative base when carrying out similar future analyses. It is to this end that we have dedicated ourselves from the conception of this study to its conclusion.

Acknowledgments

The Coba Archaeological Mapping Project is directed by William J. Folan and George E. Stuart, with the collaboration of Laraine A. Fletcher and Ellen R. Kintz. The project was funded by the National Geographic Society, Committee for Research and Exploration, to whom we are grateful for economic aid.

Our project was carried out in collaboration with the Instituto Nacional de Antropología e Historia (INAH). The Director of the combined projects was Norberto González Crespo, former Director of INAH's Centro Regional del Sureste. The Director of INAH's field operation in Coba was Piedad Peniche Rivero; she was assisted by Antonio Benavides C., then of the Escuela Nacional de Antropología e Historia, Fernando Robles C. of the same Institution, and several other students of INAH and the Escuela de Ciencias Antropológicas de la Universidad de Yucatán.

We wish to thank Guillermo Bonfil Batalla, Fernando Cámara Barbachano, Enrique Valencia Valencia, Eduardo Matos Moctezuma, and Piedad Peniche Rivero of INAH for helping make our project possible. Nicolás Caamal Canche and Jacinto May Hau and the citizens of Coba are to be thanked especially for their cooperation during the 20 months of fieldwork that was essential for recording the data contained in this book. It is to them that we dedicate this volume.

The authors of this monograph would also like to recognize George E. Stuart's efforts toward the conceptualization and development of the Coba Archaeological Mapping Project as well as his help in obtaining financial aid from the National Geographic Society that was essential for Fletcher and Kintz to complete their sections of this volume. We also thank him for his efforts in the completion of the final draft of the Coba maps by the Cartographic Division of the same organization. Thanks also go to John B. Garver, chief cartographer; Richard J. Darley, senior associate chief cartographer; John F. Shupe, associate chief cartographer; Charles L. Miller; Roland R. Nichols; Kevin P. Allen; George P. Bounelis; William E. Carmel, Jr.; Susan B. Malcolm; and Stephen P. Wells.

Additional financial support was provided by the Research Foundation and the Department of Anthropology of the State University of New York at Stony Brook, the Computing Center and the Instructional Resources of the State University of New York College at Geneseo, and the Geneseo Foundation.

Lynda M. Florey Folan and Valery Fadziewicz contributed to the success of the project in the field. Florey Folan participated not only in the mapping of Coba but also in the final preparation of the manuscript. Fadziewicz spent a good deal of his time in Coba taking most of the photographs accompanying this text as well as assisting in mapping activities.

We appreciate the efforts of Rosa Ken Uh for her considerable contributions toward our well-being during the 20 months some of us lived in Coba. She was a gem that shone on numerous occasions.

The Folans are grateful to Dr. Ernesto Guzman Espinosa and family, Dr. Manuel Valencia Romero and family, and the late Dr. Jorge Castillo Maldonado, as well as to Raúl Cervera Sauri, Joaquín Muñoz Cabrera, and Andres Gongora Cásares and his wife Socorro Jiménez for their kind attentions and care during the Coba and other projects with which some of us have been associated on the Yucatan Peninsula during the past 25 years.

William Folan expresses his gratitude to Adrian Valadéz García and Sylvia Gómez Tagle, who generously released parts of an unpublished manuscript on Coba for inclusion in Chapter 2 of this volume. Burma H. Hyde is to be recognized for making several astute observations toward improving the content and organization of the manuscript; Nicolas A. Hopkins and J. Kathryn Josserand are to be thanked for their encouragement and advice during its final preparation.

Likewise, Humberto Lanz Cárdenas, Rector, La Universidad Autónoma del Sudeste, Campeche and Román Piña Chan, Coordinator of the Centro de Investigaciones Históricas y Sociales, of the Universidad Autónoma del Sudeste, are to be acknowledged for their help and encouragement during the final months of work on the manuscript.

Ellen Kintz thanks Lawrence Peterson, Pamela Adams, and Melanie Stanford, students at the State University of New York College at Geneseo, for assisting in the preparation of the Coba maps; Raymond Mayo, Instructional Resources, SUNY College at Geneseo, for assisting in the preparation of the figures; Lee Bryant and Don Ash, Computing Center, SUNY College at Geneseo, for assistance in utilizing the computer; Ronald Pretzer,

Photographer, Instructional Resources, State University of New York College at Geneseo, for the production of the photographic prints taken by Valery Fadziewicz in Coba (1975, 1976, 1980); and Pauline Johnson, for typing the preliminary revisions of this manuscript.

Laraine A. Fletcher acknowledges the assistance of Ellen R. Kintz and of Donald Ash, Jr., Director of the Computer Center of State University of New York College at Geneseo, toward the completion of the statistical analysis of the Coba–Mayapan comparison.

To all the people unnamed by us who have made our efforts possible, may you receive at least some satisfaction from the contents of this tome in that space does not allow us to name and thank all of you individually. But, as always, any errors or omissions in this work are the exclusive property of its authors.

COBA

A Classic Maya Metropolis

Chapter 1

Archaeological Investigations of Coba: A Summary

William J. Folan

THE DEBATE OVER URBAN STATUS

The debate over the urban status of Classic Maya settlements is a controversy well known to those familiar with Mesoamerican archaeology (Arnold and Ford 1980; Ashmore 1981a; Bullard 1960; Folan 1975, 1976; Folan *et al.* 1981; Haviland 1966, 1969, 1970a,b; Kurjack 1974; Sanders 1962, 1963; Sanders and Price 1968; Willey 1956a,b). The debate has been central to the assessment of the social, political, and economic organization of Maya civilization. Our analysis and interpretation of the survey of approximately 6000 structures and features at Coba, Quintana Roo, Mexico, contribute toward the resolution of this controversy.

Settlement in Maya urban areas has been characterized as limited in numbers. Research efforts at Tikal (Carr and Hazard 1961; Puleston 1973) and Dzibilchaltun (Andrews IV 1968; Kurjack 1974), however, have now demonstrated the large size and high density of populations resident in these Classic Maya centers. Our analysis of the structures and features at Coba indicates that during the eighth century an estimated 20,000 structures housed a population of approximately 55,000 inhabitants. Coba thus qualifies as one of the largest cities in the Maya and Mesoamerican area during the Late Classic period (see Table 14.1 for periods of cultural development at Coba).

Establishing an operational definition of ancient cities has been problematic (Haggett 1965; McTaggert 1964–1965:221; Sanders 1973:354–359; Sanders and Price 1968; Schaedel 1970; Wheatley 1971:386–399) partly because the

1

population of cities has varied greatly through time and space. Whereas most preindustrial cities (with such notable exceptions as Teotihuacan in the Central Mexican Valley during the Early Classic) were small, ranging from approximately 5000 to 10,000 inhabitants (Pounds 1969) or from 2000 to 20,000, with an average size of 5000 (Mumford 1961:62), many cities of the industrial era have populations greater than 1 million. The size of the classic Greek *polis,* as quasi-urban and urban settlements, ranged anywhere from 200 to 20,000 inhabitants (Pounds 1969). It is suggested that the population of Roman *civitates* in Britain ranged from 500 to 17,000 and those of Gaul from 600 to 35,000 (Hammond 1972:178–183; Pounds 1969).

Thus, although population is a necessary consideration in the determination of urban status, it is not an overriding factor. Walton has suggested that there has been an exaggerated focus on size; instead, he feels that a theory of urbanism should be "based on the economic integration of society" (1978: 26–27).

By the criteria of economic and social complexity, Coba again qualifies as an urban center. Our analysis in the pages that follow demonstrates the complex social organization of the population (see Chapter 4) and presents the evidence that Coba served as the capital of a regional state that held sway over a great many secondary and tertiary cities and towns in an 8000-km² area stretching from the Caribbean coast to the southeastern limits of the neighboring state that had the mighty metropolis of Izamal as its capital (Folan 1975, 1976, 1978a, 1980a) (see Chapter 2).

INVESTIGATIONS OF COBA

The complete record of early explorers who visited Coba has yet to be compiled. One historic account of the conquest of Yucatan relates a stopover in what the author identifies as Coba. This stopover may have occurred when the Spaniards were in transit from Conil to the north coast of the peninsula (Cogolludo 1957).[1]

The first verifiable contact with Coba was that by a group of intrepid travelers headed by Srs. J. P. Contreras and D. Elizalde, who arrived in Coba circa 1886. They sketched a few of the main buildings, such as La Iglesia and Ixmoja, as well as what may represent a small group of thatched dwellings inhabited by Maya horticulturists (Benavides 1976a:28).

The Austrian archaeologist Teobert Maler arrived at the ruins in 1891 (Maler 1932). He photographed the vaulted room crowning the Ixmoja Temple[2] and described the Coba core area (in Thompson *et al.* 1932:8).

---

[1]It may have been in Coba where the Spaniards were first referred to as "eaters of *anonas,*" or the custard apple (*Annona cherimola*).

[2]This structure was apparently first recorded as Monjas by the Cura Garcia of Chemax (in Stephens 1963:232, vol. 2).

Coba probably was inhabited intermittently during at least the later part of the nineteenth century. This is attested to by a newspaper account that described orange trees in Coba, written sometime in the 1890s (Don E. Dumond 1977: personal communication).

Don Rafael Regil of Mérida later visited Coba in 1897. In addition to the numerous architectural features that he reported, he also saw a mound in the middle of a lake. (Although J. Eric Thompson *et al.* [1932:8–9] did not see this mound during his trips to Coba, he believed that it was quite possible that the Maya could have built a structure in the middle of the lake, and perhaps the ruins were only visible during periods of exceptional drought.)

Thomas Gann (1926:103–128) reached Coba in February 1926.[3] Gann described Lakes Coba and Macanxoc and several principal and secondary structures, *sacbeob*,[4] and stelae situated in and around the core area. He described some buildings as being of Tulum style.

Intensive archaeological exploration and recording took place primarily from 1926 through 1930 when Carnegie Institute of Washington scientists such as J. Eric Thompson, Harry E. D. Pollock, and Jean Charlot (1932) mapped a great deal of the central core area, including the *sacbe* system. They also recorded numerous stelae.

At about this same time Professor Alfonso Villa Rojas followed and recorded the 100-km long *sacbe* connecting Coba with the great Classic center of Yaxuna located a few kilometers to the southwest of Chichen Itza, Yucatan (Villa Rojas 1934).

Following these efforts, E. Wyllys Andrews IV (1938) visited Coba during the late 1930s and discovered several additional *sacbe*-related features. Michael and William Coe (1949) spent a few days at Coba during the latter part of the 1940s. They also contributed toward our knowledge of Coba and its *sacbeob*. Carlos Navarette, María José Con, and Alejandro Martínez Muriel (in press) continued formal research on the Coba *sacbeob* in 1972. The remainder of the major undiscovered *sacbeob* was recorded in the summer of 1974 by William J. Folan, George E. Stuart, and Lynda M. Florey Folan, with the collaboration of Nicolás Caamal Canche and Jacinto May Hau of Coba. It also was during the same time period that Folan, and Florey Folan, Caamal, and May followed and described the 20-km-long *sacbe* between Coba and Ixil (Folan 1977a; Folan and Stuart 1974).

Antonio Benavides C. (1976a) and Fernando Robles C., now of the Instituto Nacional de Antropología e Historia (INAH), began to map the primary discovered, recorded, numbered, and named arteries and termini of the Coba *sacbe* system during the summer of 1974, while Folan, Caamal, Fletcher, Kintz, May, and Florey Folan made a detailed sketch map of approximately 30% of

---

[3]Gann noted that John L. Stephens was the first to mention its name in 1842, although Stephens did not visit the city (see Gann 1963:232, vol. 2).

[4]*Sacbeob* are causeways. The singular form is *sacbe*.

the urban area between 1974 and 1976. Meanwhile, George Stuart and Gene Stuart continued to record stelae inscriptions and murals discovered by INAH personnel within the central core (Folan and Stuart 1974; Stuart 1975; Stuart and Stuart 1977).

Piedad Peniche Rivero, INAH's field director during the summer and fall of 1974, is responsible for the excavation and consolidation of the Ixmoja Temple and El Templo de las Pinturas as well as other associated structures and features in Coba (Peniche and Folan 1976). Antonio Benavides C. (1976b) and Fernando Robles C. stabilized La Iglesia and El Cono during the 1975 season under the direction of Norberto González Crespo, then director of IN-AH's Centro Regional del Sureste.

Test pitting and ceramic analysis has been carried out by Fernando Robles C. (1980), while further mapping has been done by Baltazar González F. (1975), Tomás Gallareta (1981), Teresa Ramayo Lanz (1978) of the Escuela de Ciencias Antropológicas de la Universidad de Yucatan, Jaime Garduño (1979) of the Escuela Nacional de Antropología e Historia, and Fernando Cortés de Brasdefer (1981a,b) of INAH.

The Coba–Ixil *sacbe* was retraced in 1976 by Robles (1976a) who also partially mapped and test pitted the ruins of Ixil under the direction of Norberto González Crespo of INAH.

THE COBA MAPS

One of the principal goals of the Coba Archaeological Mapping Project was to define the settlement patterns of a Maya metropolis (Folan and Stuart 1974). During the 1974–1975 season, William J. Folan, Nicolás Caamal Canche, Jacinto May Hau, and Lynda M. Florey Folan surveyed 13 zones in the urban area, mainly by transversing areas bounded by *sacbeob*. Subsequently, Caamal, Fletcher, Kintz, and May produced a map that detailed the relationships between structures and features and the complex system of house-lot walls in Zone I, the northern test zone of Coba (Figures 1.1, 1.2, and 1.3, and maps).

The datum point for Zone I was a stake 25 m north of the altar atop the "Crucero Mound" at the junction of Sacbe 1 and Sacbe 3. Zone I, measuring slightly less than 4 km² north to south, is bounded by Sacbe 27 on the east, Sacbe 3 on the west, the shore of Lake Macanxoc on the south, and extends to the terminus of Xmakaba in the north (Figure 1.3 and maps of Zones I and VI).

To ensure as complete coverage of the area as possible, we employed a system similar to the transect method employed by Puleston at Tikal (Puleston 1973:68–78). A Brunton compass and tripod were used to maintain the east–west lines between the *sacbeob,* and a 30-m fiberglass tape was used to measure distances. *Brechas* were cut and stations established every 30 m. Although we had planned to take stadia rod readings for contours, this pro-

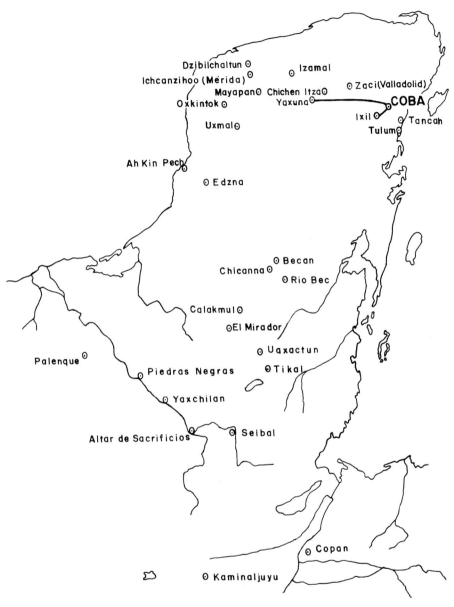

FIGURE 1.1 The Maya area.

cedure was dropped due to budget and time restrictions (Figures 1.4, 1.5, and 1.6).

Ubiquitous linear features crisscross the entire zone and sometimes appear as scarcely more than scattered stones. These features were some of the most challenging to plot; the plotting could not have been accomplished without

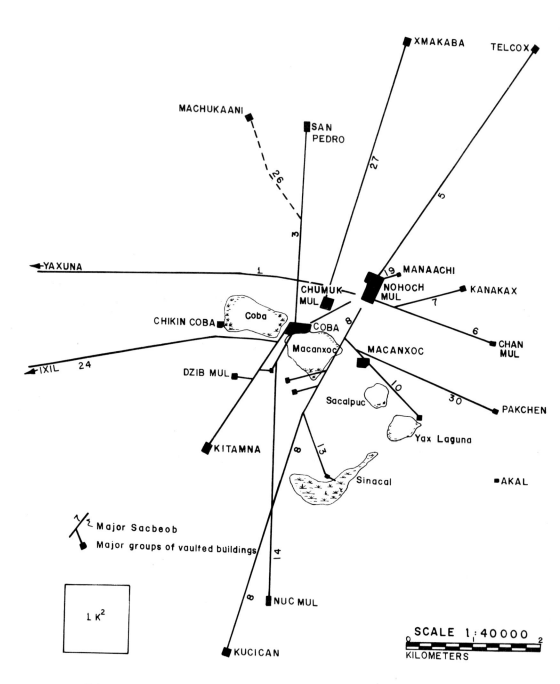

FIGURE 1.2 Major groups and *sacbeob*, Coba, Quintana Roo. Distances and directions are approximate. (Adapted from a map by G. Stuart in Folan 1975.)

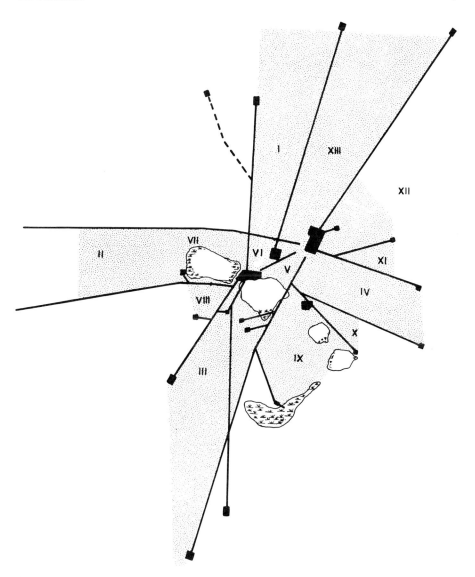

FIGURE 1.3 Zones surveyed and code numbers, Coba, Quintana Roo.

the assistance of Caamal and May and the expertise they had gained by surveying with Folan (Fletcher and Kintz 1975: personal communication).

Very few buildings or features were overlooked using this method. If the completeness of the Tikal survey was approximately 95% (Puleston 1973:75), the total coverage for Coba is as good if not better. It is thought to represent accurately the distribution of prehistoric architectural remains, particularly in Zone I. This is especially true because the visibility factor seems to be more

FIGURE 1.4 Opening brechas. (Photograph by V. Fadziewicz.)

favorable in Coba than at Tikal. Puleston found that those platforms overlooked during mapping at Tikal were low, barely visible, or invisible features.
This does not seem to be the case in Coba where although the majority of the
platforms fall into two modal categories (50 cm and 1.0 m, with range of 20
cm to 3.0 m in height), such low features as the foundations of round, apsidal,
and rectangular rooms are visible, on the ground surface.

The maps of Zone II to the west, Zone III to the south, and Zone IV to
the east have been drawn from Folan, Caamal, and May's field notes
(1974–1976). These are sketch maps with relationships between structures and
features located *relatively* in space. For example, buildings and features located on a single line in these maps are shown more or less as they are in
association with each other, but buildings on *different* lines should not be
considered as occurring in exactly that relationship to each other. It seems
appropriate to mention here that the Chikin Coba section of the western zone
is not included on the Zone II map nor is Uitzil Mul at the base of the Zone
III map as these areas were mapped by INAH personnel (Benavides 1976a).

FIGURE 1.5   Platform perimeter seen through undergrowth. (Photograph by V. Fadziewicz.)

Despite the incongruities mentioned, the architectural and other features (wells, catchment basins, metates,[5] etc.)on all maps document the complexity of the residential precincts at Coba. Data on these structures and features were coded on approximately 7000 computer cards, and the Statistical Package for Social Sciences (SPSS) was used for data analysis.

TOPICS OF THIS STUDY

Our efforts in Coba have considerably increased our knowledge of Maya urban centers. They have also contributed toward a better understanding of the hydrology, paleoclimatology, flora patterns, and soils of Coba (see Chapter 3) and its extension and overall organization (see Chapter 4). We have been

[5] Metates are not drawn to scale in the Coba maps. However, all other features are drawn to a 1:1000 scale.

FIGURE 1.6   Surveying in a milpa. (Photograph by L. Florey Folan.)

able not only to estimate the size of Coba (see Chapter 13) and its configuration, but also the manner in which its principal parts functioned internally as units and with each other to form a functioning urban center (see Chapter 4).

These accomplishments have been made possible through the recording and classification of linear features in Coba that delimit social units, such as household groups, as well as areas of intensive horticultural activities within the urban area (see Chapter 6). Residential structures, including their metates and *solares* (Chapter 7), have been recorded and analyzed to determine the organization of the Classic Maya family. This information is also applied toward discovering evidence of cottage industries and guild formations among the ancient Maya (Chapter 10) as well as for determining Maya class structure (Chapters 4 and 11). To carry the analysis one step further, a quantitative analysis has been made of all architecture from Zone I to the north of Coba to discover the formation and limits of neighborhoods and wards (Chapter 12).

Thus, a considerable amount of effort has been expended to learn more about the population of Classic Maya centers such as Coba. Furthermore, it is believed that a calculation of the population resident in the ancient city of Coba at a given time will provide a more complete representation of the center for those interested in Mesoamerica in general, and the Maya in particular.

Chapter 2

The Importance of Coba
in Maya History

William J. Folan

TRADITIONAL HISTORY OF COBA

Coba[1] has been inhabited from Late Preclassic times to the present (Robles 1980). Although the numerous stelae discovered in Coba provide us with a series of dates beginning in the early seventh century, historic accounts of the city are scarce. Local tradition, however, has it that a group of people referred to as the *pus'ob,* or dwarfs, are responsible for the stelae that dot the core area of the city. Reportedly, these people drowned in a self-inflicted, mythical deluge that brought an end to the fourth creation of the Maya world (Thompson 1976:332).

Following the *pus'ob* and other unnamed groups of people inhabiting Coba, the Itza (Chontal-speaking Maya from the present-day states of Campeche and Tabasco) arrived in Coba in the ninth century. Members of the Canul family, who probably formed part of the Chontal group, claimed Coba as their territory. Itza association is found in the name of Lake Sacalpuc to the south of Coba. The Sacalpuc lineage is closely linked with Itza migration

---

[1]Coba is an obscure term that may describe the abundance of water supplied by the lakes in the area or another water-related meaning (Benavides 1976a:26: Thompson *et al.* 1932:5, 198) Edmonson (1982:30, 53) translates Coba as *"chachalaca* water." The first term refers to a bird (*Cissolopha yucatanica*) common to the region, and the last refers to the region's lakes. Coba is also known locally as Oxkinca (Folan 1976). Edmonson (1982:30) identifies Ix Bach Can *"chachalaca snake"* from the Books of Chilam Balam of Tizimin as being a name for Coba, probably reflected in the current usage of Ixcabaca by people living near Ixil (Folan 1976).

11

originating on the east coast of the peninsula at an indefinite date. The protohistoric Itza are said to have left Coba for Chichen Itza, but not before their Rey Macehualo built a Kusan Sum, or celestial roadway in the form of a blood-filled umbilical cord linking Coba, Tulum, and Zaci (Valladolid). A similar kinship link connects Zaci and Ichcansihoo, the present site of the historic city of Mérida (Folan 1975; Miller 1974; Tozzer 1907). Likewise, another connects Dzibilchaltun with Izamal (Folan 1981b).

The only other group of people reportedly associated with Coba are the Mexicanos who migrated to Coba from the Mexican highlands after the arrival of the Itza. These Mexicanos came to Yucatan mainly during the ninth century onward as merchants and warriors. They are said to have maliciously cut the celestial roadway between Coba and Zaci (May Hau 1975: personal communication). The name of the Uitzil Mul Group in Coba is probably associated with their importance there. Another event that occurred in Coba and for which we have some historic evidence suggests that Valladolid seated its last calendrical count at Coba in A.D. 1800 (Edmonson 1978, 1982).

Certain individuals also are linked with Coba. Among these are Kinchil, or Lord Sun Sailfish, whose family represented the ruling lineage in Coba at least during the latter years of its existence. Kukulcan, the Precious Serpent, after whom the largest intrasite *sacbe* terminus is named, is also associated with Coba, as is Ah Kin Coba. The former is a Mexican deity and historic personage and the latter originally may have left Coba to become a priest within the walls of Mayapan, the capital of Yucatan during the thirteenth through the fifteenth centuries. Hunac Ceel Cauich, the ruler of Mayapan, may have arrived in Coba after the final collapse of this important city (Folan 1976; Edmonson 1980: personal communication regarding chronology).

The tutelary deity of Coba is Ah Muzen Cab (Edmonson 1982:26). This individual is related mainly to the production of honey and is depicted in Coba by the Diving God adorning the upper facade of the Ixmoja Temple in the core area and on at least one urn. Here, honey producers of the region gathered in the past to give thanks for their production (May Hau 1982: personal communication).

The Maya Merchant God M, known as Ek Chuah, is represented on murals within the city and on ceramic figures. He is closely associated with the Itza. This deity is often times depicted in the Maya codices as a traveler carrying a bag of copal. In addition to commerce, he is strongly associated with cacao, an article of trade for which the Coba area was once well known (see Thompson 1976:306–308).

Chiribiras, a goddess possibly known to the Itza, is presently associated with the large temple mound at the eastern edge of Lake Coba. Better known to the prehispanic Maya as Ix Chebel Yax, she is the wife of Itzamna, the Creator God, who may be represented in Coba by the large *lagarto* ("lizard") said to reside in Lake Coba.

COBA AS A REGIONAL CENTER

The manner in which the Maya and Cobaeños organized themselves territorially, what they produced within these territories, and the way in which they carried out their intra- and interregional exchange activities has been of interest to students of Maya culture since the earliest contact. It has been established that the Postclassic Maya lived in cities and divided their territory into provinces, and that they produced and traded numerous items among themselves and outsiders. Recent studies by Piña Chán (1978), Folan (1977c, 1979), Potter (1973), Rathje *et al.* (1978), and Simmons and Brem (1979) have considerably sharpened our focus on these important traits and their contributions to our understanding of both the Northern and Southern Lowland Maya (Folan 1980).

In an unpublished manuscript entitled *The Puuc: Uxmal, Kabah, Sayil and Labna* (Folan 1977c), the existence of two major political systems—North and South—has been hypothesized for the Lowland Maya because virtually none of the Northern Maya hieroglyphic texts include references to the great southern cities and, apparently, the multiple Southern Lowland texts do not mention cities to the north. Thus, based on such diverse attributes as great physical size and population, degree of participation in the carving of inscriptions in stone, and location with respect to the Gulf of Mexico or the Caribbean, Folan (1977c, 1980) has selected Coba in Quintana Roo, Tizimin in the northeast, Izamal in the north, Dzibilchaltun to the northwest, Oxkintok to the west, and Edzna in Campeche as the most probable contenders for major regional capitals during the Classic period in the Northern Lowlands. All these cities are located within 50 km of a coast, which places them in the advantageous position of benefiting from products associated with the interior as well as from the sea and shore. These resources would include crops and natural products, along with shell foods and, in some cases, salt deposits, and those products obtained from contacts with land-based and seafaring merchants who traveled the interior and coast. Such commerce has been carried on from earliest times to the present.

Later, as also happened in the Southern Maya Lowlands, some of the centers lost importance toward the end of the Late Classic, to be replaced by more powerful cities that had acquired great populations, territories, and riches through alliances and warfare. Oxkintok was replaced by Uxmal (with Kabah, Sayil, Nohpat, and Labna as secondary centers) and Dzibilchaltun by Tihoo, where the modern capital of Mérida is now situated.

The capitals were apparently determined by varying climatic patterns affecting the peninsula and its population from earliest times to the present (Folan 1977c, 1980a; Folan *et al.* 1980). (The recent settlement-pattern studies by Garza and Kurjack [1981], at least in part, bear out the validity of this distributional model.)

Regional capitals benefited from their geographic positions and new acquisitions as well as by using, in some cases, "agent-of-trade" cities located between them and the shore. These intermediary cities acted as links or middlemen in the increased and, perhaps, not-as-peaceful commercial activity that had been taking place in Yucatan (Hirth 1978; Rathje *et al.* 1978:148). The primary goods that were used in exchange were the great quantities of honey, wax, cloth, and slaves obtained from the coastal areas and interior of the peninsula. These goods were traded for items coming from the Mexican highlands, the shores of the Gulf of Mexico, and the coasts of, for example, Guatemala and Honduras. Goods from these areas included cacao, precious feathers, polychrome pottery, jade, and obsidian. In this manner, Tancah served as a port for Coba with an unknown center linking these two Classic centers; Río Lagartos was the port for Tizimin, with Loche as a go-between; Dzilam served as a port for Izamal, with Temax as a link; and Progreso for Tihoo, with Dzibilchaltun between them. Punta Desconocida may have served as a port for Uxmal with Oxkintok or Chunchucmil as an agent-of-trade, and Ah Kin Pech (at or near the modern city of Campeche) probably served as a port for Edzna, perhaps through China during the Late Classic period (Figure 2.1).

Even though the identification and localization of major Maya regional centers in the Southern Lowlands has been known for a considerable period of time, the reason, or reasons, behind their development, distribution, and redistribution have been obscure. In an attempt to demonstrate the differential distribution and development of Maya regional centers in the Southern Maya Lowlands, Joyce Marcus (1973) has suggested a quadrapartite distribution of the Southern Maya world based on hieroglyphic texts. These texts strongly suggest that such major centers as Calakmul (south), Copan (east), Palenque (north), and Tikal (west) represented the directional capitals of the Southern Maya Lowlands during one point in the Classic. But for unknown reasons, Copan and Palenque lost their roles as capitals by A.D. 849, with Seibal and perhaps Motul de San José assuming this position. Alternatively, Rathje (1973) has modeled the distribution of Maya centers in the Southern Lowlands on relative ecological variety and access to primary resources, such as obsidian for forming blades and hard stone for manos and metates. Thus, the ecological and primary resource-rich buffer zone of the Peten was thought to be inhabited before the ecologically poorer and resourceless core zone (Figure 2.2). In this way, buffer zone centers such as Altar de Sacrificios would have been settled before core zone centers such as Tikal, and early population pressures in the buffer zones would have been the principal cause of the movement of people into the core zone in search of land.

In yet another approach, Folan (1979, 1980a) suggested that the core zone of the Peten was settled by the Southern Lowland Maya due to the richness of its soils (Adams 1977b:316; Puleston 1978:228; Sanders 1973:354) and because it was central to transportation and communication with both the North-

FIGURE 2.1   Regional centers, ports, and agent-of-trade cities in the Northern and Southern Maya Lowlands. (Map based on Folan 1977c and 1980.)

ern Maya Lowlands and the Maya Highlands. It also had access to the transport facilities provided by the Gulf of Mexico and Honduras. Evidence indicates that even the 30-day round trip on foot from Tikal to the Pacific coast was not considered overly lengthy by the core zone Maya who sought to reach the rich trade routes of the Pacific shore. Historic Maya, for example,

FIGURE 2.2   The Central Maya Lowlands, showing approximate location of the core and buffer zones according to W. Rathje (1973: Figure 50).

commonly traveled this distance between more northern cities (Román Piña Chán 1978).

Folan also has suggested (1979, 1980a) that there exists a rhythm to shifts in Maya settlement loci in the Northern Maya Lowlands over the millennia, with notable movements in population concentration from the inland interior zone to the coastal zone and then back (Figure 2.3). It is thought that the earliest major centers in the Northern Maya Lowlands are found in the interior zone of the Yucatan Peninsula in such places as Mani (Brainerd 1958) and Toh (Folan 1972b, 1979), a model now being confirmed in Loltun by Veláz-quez Valadéz (1980). This was the most fertile zone of the peninsula before the exploitation of coastal areas was widespread. At a later date, the Yuca-tecan Maya moved toward and into the coastal zone where they built several important regional centers within 50 km of the Gulf of Mexico and the Ca-ribbean Sea. Then, reversing this trend, Late Classic people built centers far-ther inland. This tendency seems to continue in both the northwest and the northern area of Yucatan, where major Postclassic centers are situated still farther inland. An exception to this pattern during the Late Postclassic is ap-

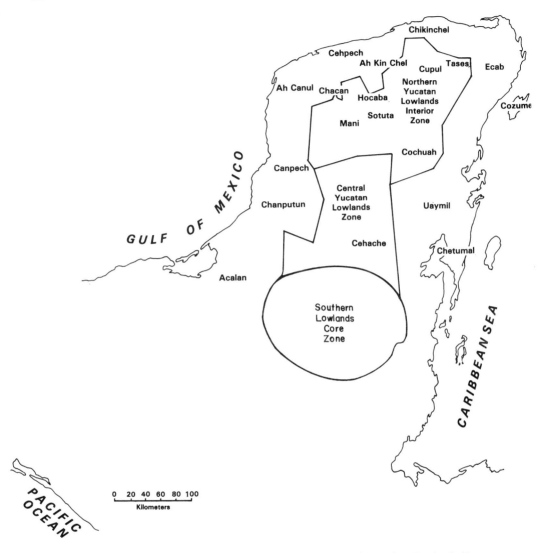

FIGURE 2.3   The Maya area, showing the coastal and interior zones in the Northern Lowlands (Folan 1980) and the Southern Lowland core area (Rathje *et al.* 1978: Figure 72).

parent on the east coast of the peninsula where a considerable amount of development is notable (Folan *et al.* 1980; Folan 1981d).

THE IMPACT OF CLIMATIC CHANGE

The reason behind shifting centers probably is climatic and sea level change affecting the Yucatan from earliest times (Figures 2.4 and 2.5). All factors indicate a warm, dry Preceramic period before appearance of the Olmec, a cool–

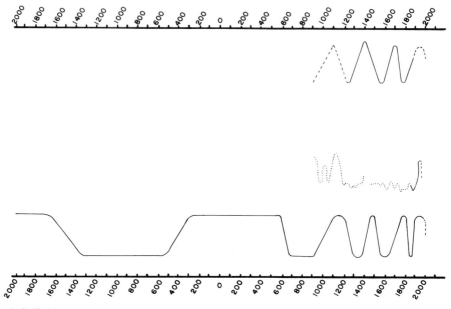

FIGURE 2.4   A schematic graph of climatic conditions from Olmec through recent historic times.
(a) A working graph of Yucatecan climatic conditions as interpreted from the *Books of Chilam*. Although this and the bottom graph do not indicate the severity of weather conditions, the upper registers represent a warmer-drier climate for Yucatan and the lower a cool-wetter climate.
(b) Bergthórsson's record (1969:Fig. 1) of climatic conditions in Iceland illustrating the number of severe years, interpreted by Bryson and Murray (1977:Fig. 4.2).
(c) Warm and cool trends prevalent in the Maya areas, interpreted from Denton and Karlén's (1973:Fig. 1) chart with the years A.D. 1700–1900 taken from Eddy (1977:88).

wet climate during the rise of the Olmec from approximately 1500 to 400 B.C., followed by a warmer-drier period from approximately 400 B.C. to A.D. 600. From A.D. 600 to 900, a cooler-wetter climate prevailed, making possible the florescence of the Maya Classic at places such as Coba and Tikal. After this period of tremendous growth, the warmer-drier period that followed evidently contributed to the downfall of the Maya Classic and the subsequent rise of Toltec-controlled Chichen Itza to the north. It is thought that these climatic conditions brought about an increase in the salt trade on the northern and western coasts of the Yucatan Peninsula. Concurrent with the fall of Chichen Itza and the rise of Mayapan was the cooler-wetter interval that finally ended about the time of the collapse of the hegemony of Mayapan and the consequent Balkanization of the peninsula. This was followed by the entry of the Spaniards into the peninsula and their conquest of the Northern Maya during a warm-dry period of drought. Lack of rainfall was the cause of food shortages occurring around the fall of Tihoo to Spanish technical superiority (Folan 1977b, 1981b; Folan and Hyde 1980; Folan *et al.* 1980; Gunn and Adams 1981).

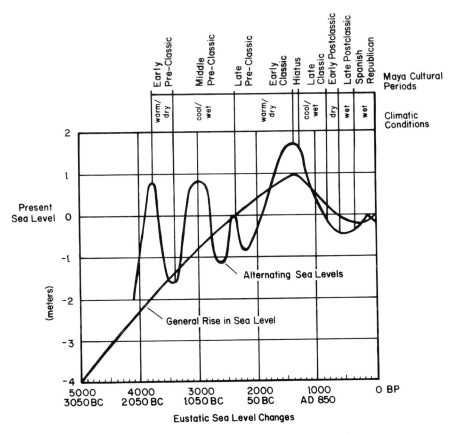

FIGURE 2.5 Climate and sea-level chart developed by Jack D. Eaton (Folan *et al.* 1980).

That climatic change took place through time and space does not mean that it affected everyone, everywhere, in the same way on a year-to-year, season-to-season basis. Some regions would have benefited more from additional rainfall than others.

In summary, we believe that shifting climatic conditions did affect the development of cultures through time, making it possible to prosper more during certain climatic episodes in some places than others. For example, although E. Wyllys Andrews V (Andrews IV and Andrews V 1981:3–4) does not think that the major hiatus in the cultural–historical sequence of Dzibilchaltun from circa A.D. 200 to 700 was caused by climatic change, this period of decreased activity as well as Dzibilchaltun's expansion between circa A.D. 700 and 900 may well have been due, in part, to climatic factors (Folan 1981b).

Furthermore, although the relatively high humidity on the east coast of the Yucatan Peninsula favored habitation by the Maya living there, it perhaps would not have been as beneficial to the Toltecs living in Chichen Itza in the northern part of the peninsula. This could have been due to the origin of the

Toltecs in the drier climes of the Mexican highlands, making the relatively dry northern and western coasts of Yucatan more attractive to them than to the Maya. (In fact, the Maya may have abandoned the arid northern and western parts of the peninsula to the Toltecs instead of having been driven off.) The drier climate benefited the Toltecs in extracting salt and drying fish, activities that would have been less successful on the eastern coast of the peninsula. Here, it was more humid, and fewer salt beds would have made it more difficult to prepare fish for local consumption and exportation. These conditions, however, would have made farming more productive here than on the northern and western coasts, thus providing the means for the Maya to continue their traditional culture. This situation could well explain the comparative absence of the Toltec in this part of Yucatan, where the Maya continued living during Preclassic, Classic, and Postclassic times until the conquest of Yucatan, through the colonial period, the War of the Castes, and into recent times (Folan 1981d).

The following chapters further describe Coba and the surrounding region in great detail as a sociopolitical, economic, and ecological unit and demonstrate how its multiple components formed comprehensive systems that made possible the development and existence of this regional center, primarily during the period of its maximum development in the Late Classic.

Chapter 3

Physical Geography
of the Yucatan Peninsula

William J. Folan

INTRODUCTION

The ruins of the ancient city of Coba are situated in the northeastern sector of the Yucatan Peninsula at 87°40′ longitude W and 20°30′ latitude N. Part of the ruins are within the confines of present-day village of Coba, which is under the jurisdiction of the municipality of Cozumel, Quintana Roo, Mexico (Figure 3.1).

The lowlands occupied by the Maya are essentially divided into northern and southern areas. Ecological variations between and within each of these two zones is noteworthy with respect to the placement of ancient settlements. Coba is particularly interesting in this context because it is situated on a line that marks the ecological transition from the dry evergreen formation of northern Yucatan and the wet, tropical rain forest to the south.

The following description of the ecological setting of the Yucatan is presented to introduce the complex nature of the geology, soil configuration, hydrography, flora, fauna, and climate of the Yucatan. Of interest here is how these ecological variables affected the development of the Maya, and Coba in particular.

GEOLOGY

The geologic structure of the Yucatan Peninsula is made up of the foreland of the folded mountains of northwestern Central America (Maldonado-Koerdell 1964). The low northern portion of the peninsula (maximum elevation is only 40 m above sea level [West 1964:70]) is supported by an intrusive platform overlain with Pliocene calcareous rock (primarily limestone, marl, and gypsum) (Maldonado-Koerdell 1964). The platform rose out of a shallow sea and tilted westward and northward during the Pleistocene. The western and northern portions of the platform are submerged, and are characterized by shoals and coral reefs. This area, the Campeche Banks, was inhabited in pre-Columbian times and is today (as it was then) exploited for its rich marine resources. The area above sea level forms a subdivision of the Atlantic–Gulf Coastal Plain physiographic province (Isphording 1975; Wilson 1980:7).

To the south, the land is characterized by highly karsted Miocene and Eocene limestone ridges elevated to 130 m. The flat northern landscape contrasts with the hilly southern Campeche area that marks the advanced stage of karst topography that includes the Peten of northern Guatemala. The eastern side of the peninsula is formed of low limestone ridges and swamp areas following a north-northeastern–south-southwestern fault pattern, the northernmost line of Old Antilla.

The ancient Maya regional center of Coba is located in this eastern sector and is characterized by an abundance of small depressions, hills, large lakes, and linear depressions (Wilson 1980:7).

Unlike the Puuc Hill area to the west, the Coba area is characterized by limestone karst topography and low elevations, with a landscape of pitted, sharp limestone and outcrops of bedrock. The area has extensive deposits of *sascab* (calcareous sand) and features characteristic of karstic topography.

Mining and Quarrying in the Maya Lowlands

Mining has been a much-neglected aspect of Maya culture although a great many mines and quarries have been located in most Maya cities in both the north and the south. As far as the north is concerned, there were only a few substances mined in any quantity by the ancient Maya. The most important of these, beside salt (Eaton and Ball 1978; Andrews 1977), is the *sascab* (calcareous sand) used by the Maya for the fill of buildings when in block form and, when in granular form, was mixed with lime (often produced by burning chunks of *sascab*) to make mortar. Granular *sascab* was also used, for example, to pave the many *sacbeob* in the Coba area (Folan 1975, 1977a, 1980b). Both Lakes Coba and Macanxoc have been modified by mining and quarrying activities to obtain *sascab* and stone for construction purposes (Folan 1976, 1978c, 1981b).

A second important resource that was mined is chert. The bare, fluted limestone deposits are pitted and scarred by solution depressions and small ridges, often edged with the sharp chert used in ancient times for projectile points and cutting tools.

Following *sascab* and chert, another important product obtained by the

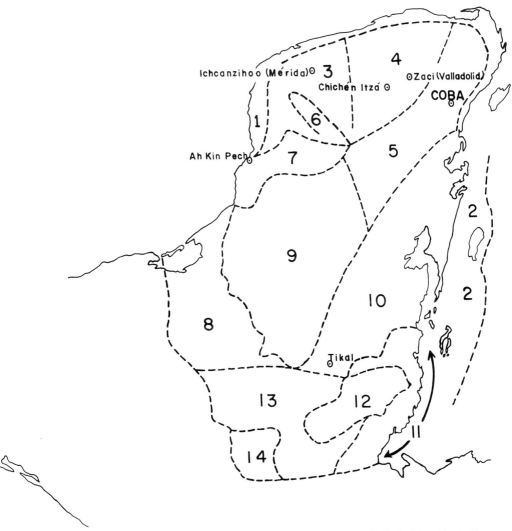

FIGURE 3.1   Physiographic districts of the Yucatan Peninsula: (1) coastal; (2) Caribbean Reef; (3) Mérida district; (4) Chichen Itza district; (5) Coba district; (6) Puuc or Sierrita de Ticul; (7) Bolonchen district; (8) Rio Candelaria-Rio San Pedro district; (9) Rio Bec; (10) Rio Hondo; (11) southern Belize coastal plain; (12) Maya mountains; (13) Flores and (14) the Pasión district. (Map and text adapted from Eugene Wilson 1980:8.)

Maya from the ground was the clay used to produce millions of ceramic vessels. As far as is now known, much of this clay came from closed mines in the neighborhood of ceramic production centers such as Ticul in the central part of the peninsula (Arnold and Bohor 1977).

Beside these, a fourth resource that played a fairly important role in Maya life is *saklu'um,* or attapulgite. Attapulgite forms the principal element in many commercial products presently sold in drugstores and used to cure diarrhea. It was eaten by pregnant women and given to children who were inclined to eat dirt. It was probably widely traded as one of the principal elements along with blue indigo in the production of Maya blue, a coloring compound sacred among the Maya. Attapulgite was also employed in the production of ceramics (Folan 1969b, 1978c; Arnold and Bohor 1975).

MINING AND QUARRYING AT COBA

Coba is dotted by both *sascab* mines and quarries from which over 200,000 m³ of material has been removed. The most common type is the open pit mine and quarry worked to a depth of approximately 1.5 to 2.0 m over an area that may vary from only a few square meters to as many as the 60,000-m² quarry situated to the east of the core area. It is thought that so much *sascab* was quarried in and around Coba that quantities may have been reduced to lime not only for local use but export as well.

A second type of mine is a closed mine produced when *sascab* deposits were encountered beneath particularly hard limestone caps. In such cases, the miners proceeded by tunneling under the limestone cap covering the *sascab* deposit. Sometimes these horizontal tunnels reached a length of 30 m or more and a width of approximately 5 m without support other than that provided at the sides of the tunnel and by the curvature of their roof which, in some cases, produced one of the few cannon-shaped vaults in the Maya area. Often, these tunnels were widened by removing *sascab* from the sides while leaving sections of the *sascab* matrix as pillars to help support the roof (Folan 1978c).

The best-known and understood closed *sascabera* in the Coba area is situated near the core area of the site not far from the southern terminus of Sacbe 3. The formation of this *sascabera* apparently began as an open mine and quarry in the eastern section of Lake Coba under a thin layer of cap rock that was quarried off as building materials for nearby structures. This activity produced an open-pit mine and quarry that continued in all directions for a considerable distance. In the northern section, the *sascab* deposit continued under a thicker and harder limestone crust, making further exploitation impossible without tunneling. This activity thus produced a 1000-m² closed mine supported by 31 hourglass-shaped pillars. A small, shallow well is located near the mine's entrance (Folan 1978c) (Figures 3.2 through 3.9). This mine was worked with the use of hard stone tools with cutting edges as well as wooden wedges. Although none of these tools was found during survey work in the mine, the impressions left by their use on the working face, pillars, and roof of the mine made possible their comparison with other hafted tools found archaeologically inside and outside other mines (Figure 2.19). Beside these tools used to mine the *sascab,* clubs of a hard local wood were used to reduce chunks of *sascab* to granular form.

The specialized corvée laborers mining the *sascab* removed it from the mine in baskets, scooping it up by hand or with the aid of sea- or turtle-shell implements. It has been calculated that one worker cut *sascab* in each of the six main tunnels forming the Coba mine. Each worker could cut and transport as much as 0.33 m³ of *sascab* a day from the mine to an area around La Iglesia. Thus, a total of 1500 m³ of *sascab* could have been mined and removed from the enclosed *sascabera* in an estimated 4500 man-days. Cessation of mining activities may have coincided with the end of major construction in the Coba Group, although the mine could have been worked from time to time later to provide the material for general maintenance and repair work in the immediate area.

Once an open mine and quarry was abandoned, rain-washed soil quickly covered its bottom, thus producing an environment suitable for intensive gardening as demonstrated by the contemporary Maya who raise corn, beans, squash, chile, and numerous fruit trees in relic *sascaberas*. These conditions also could have been improved by the addition of hand-carried earth to freshen the soil already trapped in the *sascaberas* much like modern residents of Coba and other areas collect earth to develop and seasonally freshen their kitchen gardens. Sometimes relic *sascaberas* become water-filled as in the case of Lakes Coba and Macanxoc.

In and near Coba, kitchen-type gardens as well as milpas and cash crops such as cacao could have been produced in relic *sascaberas* (and elsewhere) due to the richness of the soil and the proximity of the *sascabera* floor to the phreatic water table. Thus, perhaps, the Coba *sascaberas* formed part of the "certain hollows and caves (plantations of fruit trees) and cacao trees and certain lands (which had been purchased for the purpose of improving them in some respect)" that were not held in common by the Maya (Gaspar Antonio Chi *in* Tozzer [1941:23]).

In addition to being used for horticultural and arboricultural activities, relic open *sascaberas* were also closely associated with apicultural production. It is rare that either domestic or wild beehives are not today found in a *sascabera* close to a habitation area perhaps due to the relative lushness of the vegetation in the *sascaberas* and the presence of one form of water source or another.

SOILS

The most elaborate development of Lowland Maya civilization occurred in two environments with clearly distinct soil resource bases.

1. The Maya inhabited the northern Yucatan Peninsula, where dry climate, flat relief, and porous limestone bedrock produced Rendzina and Terra Rossa soils.
2. The Maya were also concentrated in and around the Peten. This area

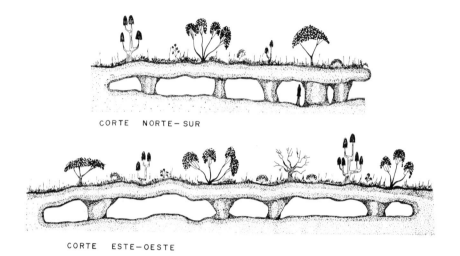

CORTE NORTE–SUR

CORTE ESTE–OESTE

FIGURE 3.2 North-south and partial east-west section of the *sascabera* showing the distribution and shapes of several columns, the roof, and floor. (Section by Caamal *et al.* in Folan 1978c:Fig. 3).

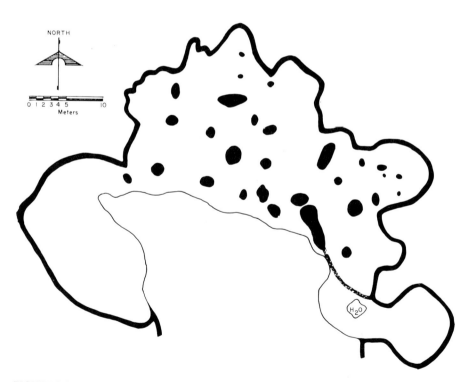

FIGURE 3.3 Plan view of the *sascabera* showing its general shape and distribution of the columns supporting its roof. The area to the south of the closed mine represents a small section of the open *sascabera* fronting the closed mine (Plan by Caamal *et al.* in Folan 1978c:Figure 2).

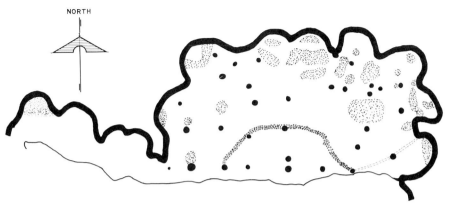

FIGURE 3.4   A folk sketch of the *sascabera* showing the distribution of mining debris. Neither the pillars nor other features are drawn to scale. (Plan by Caamal and May in Folan 1978c:Fig. 4).

is a tropical rain forest with leached zonal soils interspersed with calcimorphic and hydromorphic groups as well as Lithosols (young soils whose chemical composition is similar to that of the bedrock from which they are formed). The zonal soils are formed by calcification, laterization, or podsolization.

Mollisols

In Yucatan and Quintana Roo, Mollisols are the most common soil type. Mollisols are found where calcareous parent material is subjected to weathering in climates ranging from cool to hot and from semiarid to humid. The Mollisols of the Peten and Yucatan were the major soil resources for many Classic and Postclassic Maya settlements (Isphording 1975; Stevens 1964: Figures 3, 4). Although many flat areas lack surface drainage, the soil is well-drained through the porous limestone substrata (Wilson 1980:34–35). Mollisols called *Terra Rossa* cover much of the northwestern part of Yucatan. Rendzina soils cover the flat, limestone platform (Isphording 1975).

Hydromorphic Soils

Hydromorphic soils, including Groundwater Laterites as well as Bog and Half-Bog groups, are found in both permanently and intermittently flooded areas. These large areas are also found in the eastern and central areas of Quintana Roo and occur frequently in the forests and savannas of the Peten. Such soils may occur even without flooding where a perched water table saturates the lower-soil horizons.

Where flooding does not entirely preclude agricultural land use, the productive capacity of the hydromorphic soils is limited by the intensely leached, highly acidic, and sticky soil.

FIGURE 3.5 *Sascabera interior.* (Photograph by V. Fadziewicz.)

FIGURE 3.6 *Sascabera* with an hourglass-shaped support. (Photograph by V. Fadziewicz.)

FIGURE 3.7 *Sascabera* with a barrel-shaped support. (Photograph by V. Fadziewicz.)

FIGURE 3.8 *Sascabera* with tool scars in face of deposit. (Photograph by V. Fadziewicz.)

FIGURE 3.9 *Sascabera* with tool scars in roof of mine. (Photograph by V. Fadziewicz.)

As Morley (1956) pointed out, poor, lateritic soils are the major problem for cultural development in the humid tropics.

Simple drainage works could extend the usable agricultural area (Stuart 1964:298–302, Figure 7), and this seems to have been carried out in much of the Maya area (Adams *et al.* 1981; Turner and Harrison 1978).

Lithosols

Black calcareous Lithosols are characteristic of soils in the Coba area. The Lithosols are derived from soft limestone on terrain that varies from rolling hills to steep slopes and is essentially karstic in eastern and central Peten. The parent rocks are at depths of usually less than 50 cm and rock outcrops can cover more than 15% of the surface. The major Classic Maya civic–ceremonial centers, including those in Coba and in the Peten, appear to have been situated in or between the soil area classified as Rendzina and black calcareous Lithosols resembling Rendzina.

Alluvial Soils

Alluvial soils, rich in mineral nutrients, develop most widely along the Pasion, Usumacinta, and other large rivers of the Peten, Campeche, and Tabasco regions in the Maya area. In the humid tropics, young, alluvial soils offer better possibilities for farming, and many of the Maya cities such as Yaxchilan that flourished for centuries were located in such zones.

Maya Terminology

Systematic study of the soils of the Yucatan Peninsula was begun by the Maya themselves (Stevens 1964:303). Ortiz (1950) adopted Maya terms, compatible with modern soil classification terminology, as the names of families and series within the Terra Rossa, Rendzina, and other intrazonal soil groups. Stevens's (1964) summary of the soils of Yucatan is based on the works of Aguilera (1959), *Diccionario de Motul* (1929), Ortiz (1950, 1957), R. Robles (1959), and Steggerda (1941).

The Maya term *tzekel* (land very stony and poor for sowing) is used to group all the thin, residual soils of Yucatan into one family (Ortiz 1950). The Maya term *kankab-tzekel* (very stony, reddish earth) represents the undifferentiated soil series transitional between the shallow *tzekel* family and the deeper soils of the *kankab* series (Ortiz 1950). Next to the *tzekel*, the *kankab-tzekel* soils are the secondmost extensive in the Yucatan state; like the *tzekel*, they are transitional among Lithosoils, Rendzina and Terra Rossa. The *kankab* soil series, distinctly Terra Rossa as evidenced by its reddish color, has a clay texture, granular structure, and high content of available calcium throughout the profile, even after laterization.

The *kankab–kat* (potter's red earth) series is a red clay soil overlaying a yellow clay subsoil (Ortiz 1950). It is sufficiently laterized to be grouped with the Terra Rossa soils. The *ek–lum* (black earth) series consists of a clay topsoil varying from gray to black in color, overlaying yellow clay washed with gray-black clay. The series probably belongs to the yellow podsolic group in association with intrazonal Planosol or Half-Bog soils (Stevens 1964:303).

Ortiz (1950:285–286) states that these soil families and series were generally so rich that little or no fertilizer was necessary except for the addition of phosphorous in one sample of the family *kankab–tzekel,* manganese in the *chichen–kankab* series, with potassium being the nutrient element critically deficient in most of the soils of Yucatan. He noted, however, that the burning of fallen bush presumably frees some of the potassium and phosphorous otherwise locked into insoluble compounds.

Soil forms such as *kankab* are the result of decaying vegetation and decomposition of abandoned settlements. It is regarded as very good soil for the cultivation of corn and other common crops, but its loose structure and fine texture causes it to become very dry when rains are delayed and causes harvest loss.

Sascab, another Maya term used to describe Yucatec soils, consists of highly calcareous, yellowish-gray, occasionally reddish, substratum deposits underlaying many soils (see above).

HYDROGRAPHY

The Yucatan Peninsula is characterized by two extensive hydrographic zones: (1) the dry northern section lacking surface streams and (2) the wet southern section, which includes the Peten of Guatemala where surface drainage and large lakes are found, as are thick soil accumulations and dense vegetation cover.

The Yucatan is characterized by underground drainage, creating a karstic topography (Doehring and Butler 1974). The drainage features of the peninsula have determined the location of settlements in the area since ancient times and now affect the general health standards of the population due to the widespread distribution of fecal coliform bacteria in the water table.

Lakes in the Yucatan

In the Peten, and in central and eastern Quintana Roo, lakes are elongated, possibly as a result of the collapse of several sinkholes or faulting. Chichancanab in northcentral Quintana Roo, Lake Bacalar near the Caribbean coast in Quintana Roo, and Peten lakes (Macanche, Yaxha, and Peten), and Lakes Macanxoc and Coba in the project area are examples of these lakes. Small edible tropical fish are found in some of these lakes.

Hydrography of the Northern Yucatan Peninsula

The low northern and northwestern coasts of the Yucatan exhibit a series of long barrier beaches enclosing extensive lagoons and tidal swamps. Diego de Landa (1941) was among the first to describe these inordinately long barrier beaches, lagoons, and salines of the northern coast of the Yucatan. Schott (1866) wrote the first scientific treatise on these landforms, later described by C. Edwards (1954). In preconquest times, various points within the shallow lagoons were utilized for producing salt by natural evaporation of sea water or the washing of salt-impregnated mud (Eaton and Ball 1978). Salt from these lagoons was an important trade item of the ancient Maya (Andrews 1977; Chapman 1957; Eaton 1978; Roys 1943) and continues to be produced today by virtually the same process.

The east coast of the peninsula is different from the northern shore. On the northeastern coast, the limestone platform forms a low-cliffed shoreline with headlands interspersed by beaches. The Postclassic ruins of Tulum are situated on such a headland. Farther to the south, the coast is embayed, probably due to the fault structure. The longest barrier coral reef in the Atlantic tropics lies off the eastern shore, extending intermittently 650 km from the northeastern corner of the peninsula south to the Gulf of Honduras (West 1964). This area represents a rich zone of marine resources exploited by ancient populations, as well as present-day inhabitants.

Cenotes   North of a line drawn approximately northeast from the Champoton River in Campeche to the Caribbean shore opposite Cozumel Island, cenotes (deep sinkholes) are the major water source. Cenotes show considerable variation in size and shape, but a cylindrical form with nearly vertical walls is most common. In the northcentral and northeastern part of the Yucatan, nearly all important ancient Maya settlements (and many of the present-day villages) were located near the edge of a cenote or cave where water could be obtained. Seepage through underground channels is the source of fresh water in some cenotes. In others, water is stagnant and layered in terms of temperature and chemical composition, indicating a lack of subsurface flow due to aging (Pearse *et al.* 1936). Biological investigations by Pearse *et al.* (1936) of several cenotes of northern Yucatan noted the presence of several species of small, perch-like fish (cichlids), a tropical catfish (*Rhamdia*), and various crustacea, which were part of the ancient Maya diet.

Aguadas   Water also accumulates in *aguadas,* which are shallow, usually permanent ponds. Surface depressions fill with water and a layer of impermeable clay seals the fissures in the underlying porous limestone. Old cenotes, filled with silt and organic debris, may eventually become *aguadas.* The inhabitants of ancient Maya settlements, particularly in the Puuc Hill area, constructed artificial ponds to collect rainwater to supplement water sources (Wilson 1980).

Minor hydrographic features of the northern part of the peninsula include wells, *haltuns* (natural hollows in outcropping limestone that temporarily fill with rainwater), and *ojos de agua* (freshwater springs) located along the northern coast. Some of these more important springs are near Conil, Sisal, and Dzilam on the northern coast and, according to sixteenth-century chroniclers, were used in pre-Spanish times by coastal inhabitants for their water supply (Landa 1941:187).

Hydrography of the Southern Yucatan Peninsula

The southern section of the peninsula is also characterized by subsurface drainage. It is noted for its lakes and swamps, disappearing streams, and sluggish (often intermittent) headwaters of rivers that drain either to the Gulf of Mexico or to the Caribbean Sea.

Another hydrographic feature, the *akalche,* is common in the Peten and in eastern Yucatan. These low, wooded, clay-filled depressions are covered with a thin sheet of water only during the rainy period. They vary in size from a few meters to 4.5 km in diameter (Sapper 1896, 1899), and even much larger.

Hydrography of Coba

Several features recorded in Coba indicate the maximization of all water resources: the dikes surrounding many of the lakes and water holes, the numerous check dams crisscrossing almost the entire city, the catch basins located in most areas, cenotes, and wells. Beside these features, there appears to exist a man-made connection between Lakes Coba and Macanxoc in the form of several narrow culverts through the Coba–Kitamna *sacbe*–dike that link both of these lakes in conjunction with what appears to be a short canal between the Coba–Kitamna *sacbe* and the eastern shore of Lake Coba. There may also be another canal associated with Lake Coba, located on its western shore where it unites Lake Coba and a small pond a few meters to the west.

FLORA

Rain Forest

According to various authors, vegetation surrounding Coba can be categorized as a two-story semievergreen seasonal forest with only the ramon trees, established on the archaeological monuments, forming a climax forest situation (Barrera Marín 1976; Barrera Marín *et al.* 1976; Wagner 1964:222; Wilson 1980).

The tropical rain forest, in general, consists of at least three (and sometimes as many as five) stories of woody plants, one or more of which at or near the top of the forest forms a closed canopy. In broad and well-drained valleys or on gently undulating land, the forest grows to a height of 50 m. The larger trees stand above the canopy and more or less shade the second story from direct sunlight. In forests with an abundance of ramon trees (*Brosimum alicastrum*), the upper-story emergents are chiefly mahogany, the mastic trees (*Sideroxylon*), and the wild fig. In the middle story, edible, fruit-bearing *Achras, Talisia,* and many other genera are found as well as *Brosimum,* which is the dominant species (as dense as 240/ha). The lower-tree story contains, among other genera, a hackberry *Celtis,* the laurel *Ocotea,* and many palms including *Opsiandra.* Lianas, especially of the begonia family, are abundant. Orchids, the aroid *Anthurium,* and Spanish moss (*Tillandsia*) are common epiphytes (Wagner 1964:228) (Figure 3.10).

Another striking characteristic common to all tropical forests, and seldom found outside this formation, is the profusion of growth in addition to the large trees. In every instance, palms form a substantial part of the understory; sometimes, the palm-like *Carludovica* is present as well. In some stands of palm, the distinctive cycad *Zamia* (a cross in appearance between a palm and a fern), appears.

Ficus and *Coussapoa* (strangler figs) are among the common smaller trees. The middle layers of trees usually contain the fast-growing *Cecropia* and *Didymopanax,* and the giant leaves of *Calathea, Heliconia,* and *Costus.* The

FIGURE 3.10 Miscellaneous vegetation fronting La Iglesia, Group B in Coba. (Photograph by V. Fadziewicz.)

closed canopy of trees blocks sunlight and inhibits growth of vegetation on the forest floor. The spacious arrangement of the tree trunks at ground level actually give the rain forest an empty appearance (Wagner 1964:230).

Secondary Vegetation

The secondary vegetation referred to in the Peten as *acahual* has also been described in Yucatan by Lundell (1934) and Bartlett (1956). The succession varies considerably from one area to another, depending on the manner of disturbance and the climatic and edaphic conditions. In the early stages, the assemblage of plants in older clearings tends to include species capable of wide dispersal and rapid growth in open sunlight. The progression runs from low, herbaceous cover (approximating the weeds of cultivated fields) to dense brush or thickets (often composed of a single species) to a slow ascension of forest trees if the site remains undisturbed.

Aridity induced by particular soil structures, often accentuated by slash-and-burn agriculture and forest fires, influences the distribution of the less tall and rich vegetation of the eastern portions of the Yucatan Peninsula.

Secondary vegetation is common, and in some places (particularly in northern Yucatan), it is difficult to distinguish between natural and dry evergreen formations and successional growth. The vegetation of Yucatan has been so greatly altered that Lundell (1934) is of the opinion that its original structure cannot be positively known. (It may, however, be approximated.) The consequences of human interference, including burning and grazing, may well result in a reduction of differences in vegetation in varying climatic and soil regions. When man's control becomes predominant, the natural boundaries fade, and the distribution of various flora clearly reflects human utilization of the land (Wagner 1964:260).

Maya Utilization of Forest Products

The tropical forests of Coba and the Peten, as described by Lundell (1937), reveal the continuous influence of prehistoric and, particularly, the intensive agricultural use of the land now covered by the upland forest. Some trees, particularly the useful breadnut (*Brosimum*), cluster on ancient Maya sites perhaps due to recent conditions ideal for its development (Lambert and Arnason 1982; Puleston 1973). The sapodilla (*Achras zapota*) was apparently dispersed with the help of man. Other useful trees whose present distribution was probably a result of Maya influence are the edible fruit-bearing guayo (*Talisia olivaeformis*), avocado (*Persea americana*), mamey (*Calocarpum mammosum*), the moraceous (mulberry family) *Pseudolmedia spuria,* perhaps the palm *Orbignia cohune,* tropical cedar (*Cedrela mexicana*), mahogany

(*Swietenia macrophylla*), and two resin-bearing trees—*Protium copal* and *Bursera simaruba.* The relative scarcity of *Achras,* exploited for chicle, and *Cedrela,* for building material, also may be attributed to man's intervention.

The Maya had a great selection of fruit, fiber, bark, and resin-bearing trees at their disposal for a considerable period of time, many of which proved domesticable. But recent research has indicated that not all trees were domesticated by the same class of people living in Coba, or in the same quantities, or in the same zone of the core area (Folan 1976, 1981c; Folan *et al.* 1979). Thus, nobles and priests living in the core area of Coba raised the greatest quantities of fruit, fiber, bark, and resin trees. Among the trees possibly raised in great numbers in their household orchards were the nut-producing ramon tree (*Brosium alicastrum*) that also provided a great deal of shade, the fiber-producing *pi'im* tree (*Ceiba aesculifolia*), the resin-producing *pom* tree (*Protium copal*), the bark-producing *balche* tree (*Lonchocarpus longistylus*) so essential to the production of ceremonial alcoholic beverages, plus several fruit-bearing trees.

The middle-class people living in the inner suburban zone around the ceremonial–civic core area of Coba also planted and harvested various trees but in lesser quantities than the elitist priests and nobles. For example, they had practically no direct access to the ceremonially associated *balche* and *pom* trees growing near the residences of the nobles (Folan *et al.* 1979).

Beyond and surrounding the middle-class segment of Coba is an outer suburban zone. Here only a few fruit, fiber, and bark trees grew in the yards of the lower-status people living there. Virtually all ceremonially associated and most fruit- and fiber-bearing trees were the property of the elite inhabitants of Coba. All that the lower-status people possessed were resin-bearing trees such as the *zapote* that provides the basic substance for producing chicle and has a delicious fruit that ripens once a year.

FAUNA

Any treatment of the extremely diverse fauna of tropical Mesoamerica is inadequate at best. The following discussion covers those animals sighted in Coba during the mapping project as well as those characteristic of the ecological niche occupied by the ancient and modern Maya in the Lowlands.

Mammals

Mouse opossums (*Marmosa*), the philander (*Philander*), and the woolly opossum (*Caluromys*) are found in southern Mexico. The majority of the bats (Chiroptera), like the opossums, are essentially southerners, either neotropical or pantropical. Eight families of bats occur within the limits of Middle America. Of the southerners, the American leaf-nosed bats (Phyllostomidae) and the funnel-eared bats (Natalidae) are found throughout Central America and in the Mexican lowlands. In general, these groups are not found in the Mexican plateau. The vampire bats (Desmodontidae) in Coba are represented in Middle America by two species, generally distributed in tropical areas. As carriers of rabies, they are of special concern to man (Stuart 1964:317).

Primates are represented in the tropical lowlands by monkeys (Cebidae). The howler (*Alouatta*) and a spider monkey (*Ateles*) are found in the Mexican lowlands. But none of these were seen in Coba proper although they are sighted along the road between Coba and the coast. Anteaters (Myrmecophagidae) are found in the lowlands (Stuart 1964:317). In Coba, many of the rodents (Rodentia) such as the pacas and the agoutis are utilized extensively as food. From a medical standpoint, the exotic *Rattus* and *Mus* (Myomorpha—diverse rats and mice) are of interest because they serve as intermediate hosts for *Trichinella,* which usually is communicated to man through the meat of the domesticated hog. These two rodents also harbor fleas, which occasionally transmit typhus to man (Stuart 1964:318–319).

Current legend states there were once many jaguars in Coba about 45 years ago, but most were killed off by an early village founder and partiarch to make it safe for cattle in the area. The cats (Felidae), including the ocelot, jaguar, jaguarundi, and margay, essentially are found in the southern lowlands. The skins of the lowland cats made up an important part of ancient trade and tribute in central Mexico and northern Central America where they were used to ornament costumes of priests, warriors, and nobles. Graphic representations of cats, especially the jaguar (*Felis onca*), held a significant place in religious symbolism and art in almost all pre-Columbian, Middle American cultures (Stuart 1964:319).

The tapir (*Tapirus*) is not currently native to Coba. This large, tasty mammal is the only perissodactyl (Perissodactyla) in the region other than the exotic horse. It is distributed over the lowlands from southern Mexico to South America. The indigenous, cloven-hoofed mammals (Artiodactyla) sighted in Coba essentially are represented in Middle America by the deer and the peccaries. Of the latter, the white-lipped peccary is found only in extreme southeastern Mexico and Central America; the former (Cervidae, Odocoileus), the white-tailed deer, is generally distributed throughout the region and into South America. The little brockets (small deer) are southerners and occur northward only to the tropical lowlands of eastern Mexico. In Coba, the peccaries, the deer, and the brockets were, and are, important food items.

Only a single siren (Sirenia) occurs in the region. It is the manatee (*Trichechus*), which today is found along the east coast in shallow waters southward from Veracruz. Its former range may have been continuous throughout the Gulf of Mexico (Stuart 1964:320) but only one or two were sighted in 1974 along the Caribbean coast (Arthur G. Miller: personal communication 1974).

Birds

Eisenmann (1955) lists some 1424 species divided among 94 families in his checklist of the birds of Mexico and Central America. In preconquest times, the Middle American Indians associated the eagle with the warrior class, and representations of the bird are predominant in pre-Columbian art. The green feathers of the quetzal were prized for ceremonial headdress by the ancient Maya as well as the Aztec. Aside from their use as food, the showy feathers of various tropical birds were important trade items in ancient Indian commerce. The quetzal tail feathers; the blue, green, red, and yellow feathers of macaws and other parrots; the turquoise and purple of the cotinga; the pink of the roseate spoonbill; the iridescent colors of hummingbirds; and the plumage of many other species, were prized items in the tropical lowlands (Stuart 1964:320–326). Wild turkeys were once common in Coba.

Reptiles

Reptiles are well represented in Middle America (Stuart 1964:326–332). Over 900 species have been recorded in Mexico by Smith and Taylor (1945, 1950). Sea and land turtles are of considerable economic importance for their shells and as food. Lizards are also well represented, including about 275 species in Mexico (Smith and Taylor 1950). The large iguana and its relatives, the ctenosaurs, are generally distributed throughout the lowlands, both food items prized in many places but not by contemporary Cobaeños.

Coba and Middle America have more than their share of snakes (Ophidia). Coral snakes (Micruridae) are relatively common in Coba and throughout Middle America in the lowlands and lower mountain slopes. Although generally docile by nature and reluctant to bite, the coral snake is poisonous. Pit vipers, including the fer-de-lance (*Bothrops*) and the bushmaster (*Lachesis*), are both found in Coba and the tropical lowlands. The bushmaster is common in the Yucatan and is the largest of poisonous snakes in the New World, growing 4–5 m in length. No rattlesnakes were sighted by us in Coba.

Amphibians

Frogs and toads (Anura) comprise the bulk of Middle American amphibian fauna. The family Phinophrynidae (primitive frogs and termite eaters) appears only in the Mexican lowlands, the Yucatan, and northern Guatemala. Toads (Bufonidae) are abundant throughout the region from sea level to timberline. In Coba, one species, the marine toad (*Bufo marinus*), is one of the most common animals found there and in the lowlands of Mexico and Central America (Stuart 1964.326–332).

Invertebrates

The invertebrate groups have had, and continue to have, a broad impact on man (Stuart 1964:337). This is particularly true of present non-European and precolonial cultural groups. As a source of food, as vectors of disease, and as contributors to certain artistic accomplishments, the invertebrates were, and continue to be, of major importance in the Middle American's way of life.

Two types of scorpions are found in Coba, one large and black, and the other small and red or tan. Crustaceans and mollusks were an important part of the diet of precolonial man. This was probably true of freshwater as well as the marine crustaceans and mollusks. Even today, the freshwater *langosta* is prized as a food item, and little river snails are edible. The abdomen of the carpenter ant, when swarming, is part of man's diet. The wild bees for which Coba is noted and a few honey-making wasps were major sources of sweet foods in Yucatan.

The arthropods have played an important role as vectors of disease. Among the endemic diseases they spread are mosquito-borne malaria, the fly-borne *leishmaniasis,* and *trypanosomiasis* (Chagas's disease), transmitted by species of assassin bugs (Reduviidae), which are a constant menace in certain areas of rural Coba. Both insect-borne yellow fever and *onchocerciasis* were introduced into the New World by the European slave trade. The beef worm, ticks, and a variety of body insects undoubtedly affected the life of the Maya in the past as they do today.

Maya Utilization of Fauna

The Maya possessed few domestic animals of considerable importance. The most common of these animals was the dog which, beside being consumed for food, assured the Maya of success in hunting deer, *jabalí* (peccary), and birds, including wild turkey. The turkey was domesticated from time to time and eaten as well as sacrificed. Beehives housed in tree trunks are still cut and set up in sheds where the industrious, stingless creatures produce prodigious quantities of wild honey and wax. The honey was used in the production of *balche,* the Maya ceremonial drink that included the bark of the *balche* tree and a toad skin mixed with ceremonially pure water. Wax was also used on ceremonial occasions.

CLIMATE

In the northern part of Yucatan a wet–dry climate (Köppen's classification Aw) is characteristic (Figures 3.11 and 3.12). Maximum rainfall occurs during July and August, and clear, almost cloudless skies are the rule during the long, dry season from late November to May. The prevailing dryness results in the desiccation of grass and a seasonal leaf fall from most trees and shrubs, giving

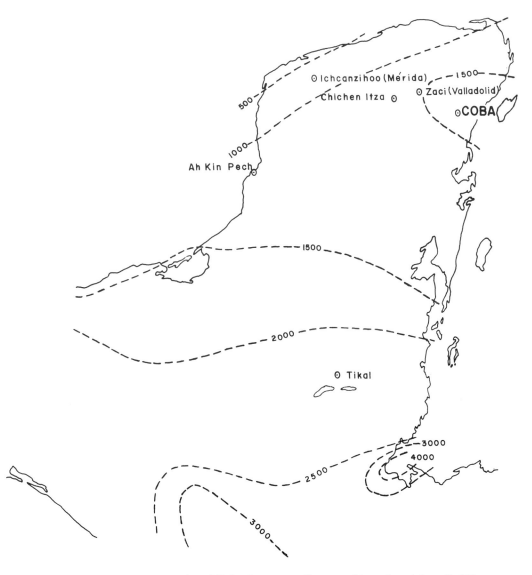

FIGURE 3.11 Mean annual rainfall distribution in millimeters. (Map adapted from E. Wilson 1980:24.)

a drab, gray-brown color to the landscape. The hottest and dustiest part of the year comes in March and April, just before the break of the rainy season. With the coming of the rains, the air becomes cooler, and vegetation turns a brilliant green.

In the southeastern part of the Yucatan a tropical, rainy climate (Köppen's classification Amw′) is characterized by dampness pervading the entire land-

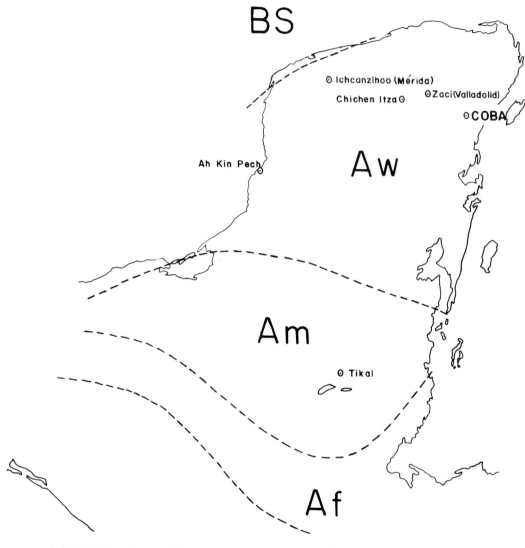

FIGURE 3.12 Climates of the Yucatan Peninsula, using the Köppen system: tropical rainy (Af), tropical monsoon (Am), tropical savanna (Aw), and semiarid (BS). (Map adapted from E. Wilson 1980:26.)

scape, and relative humidity is high for most of the year. Most of the rain comes in the form of afternoon thunderstorms. But during September through November (the wetter part of the year), tropical disturbances may cause prolonged downpours that continue for days with few interruptions. The temperatures in the rainy tropics are not excessive, ranging from lows of 25 to 30° C during the rainy season to a high rarely above 35° C on cloudless days (coupled with high humidity). Nighttime temperatures are cool (19–22° C).

During the winter, early morning temperatures may fall as low as 10° C (Vivó Escoto 1964:199).

Coba is situated in a region typed Aww', a subtype of the tropical rainy climates characterized by rain in virtually all months (approximately 1500–2000 mm), with a short, dry period of a few weeks' or more duration in February or March and a concentration of rain in September, October, and November (Vivó Escoto 1964:213). These humid tropical regions provided a rich environment for human habitation. The zone was a naturally attractive dwelling place then as it is today.

Climatic Change

Rainfall Distribution Lundell (1934) notes that rainfall distribution is an interesting part of the climatology of the Yucatan Peninsula despite the slight variation in relief (which accounts for a considerable amount of fluctuation in the rainfall patterns) (Wilson 1980:24). For example, stations in the interior recorded a higher annual rainfall than those on the coast. Aside from differences due to location, there is also considerable annual fluctuation of the total rainfall. Records examined by Lundell showed that during some years there was as much as three to four times more rain than others (Lundell 1934:261–262). This unstable rainfall regime, if characteristic of prehistoric as well as modern times, would have affected annual yields. Under such ecological conditions, a suprahousehold organizational system, including the distribution of emergency foodstuffs in lean years, would have presented an attractive adaptive mechanism.

Evidence of Fluctuating Water Table at Coba A possible clue to climatic change affecting the Maya over still longer periods of time is found in Coba in association with several small lakes within and around the civic–religious core of the city and several of the numerous *sacbeob* running out from this nucleus to the fringes (Thompson *et al.* 1932; Folan and Stuart 1974; Folan 1975, 1976, 1977a, 1978b; Benavides 1976a; Folan *et al.* 1980; Folan and Hyde 1980; Folan 1981a). Recent investigations indicate that these lakes are at least in part formed by ancient *sascaberas* (quarries) that ostensibly had been excavated down to the phreatic water table sometime during the Early Classic or earlier. To facilitate communication between the core area of the city and its fringes, two *sacbeob* were built across at least one *sascabera* (now known as Lake Macanxoc) when its bottom was dry or nearly dry. But this *sascabera,* in addition to others, became water-filled, ostensibly due to a rise in the phreatic water table. This could have been the direct result of increased rainfall after the construction of the *sacbeob* and a resultant rise in the water table. Thus, not only was the bottom of the *sascabera* covered by water but the *sacbeob* as well (Dahlin 1981; Folan 1981a; Folan *et al.* 1980; Thompson *et al.* 1932:22, 25). An additional indication of fluctuating water levels in Coba is the pres-

ence of a *sacbe*-associated ramp rising out of another relic *sascabera* underwater in 1975 (Folan 1975). Several walkways leading out into Lake Coba are
also currently underwater (Benavides 1976a), probably having been built when
the water table was lower (Folan 1975). Further clues to this type of water-
table fluctuation are found around the rims of virtually all other major bodies
of water in Coba. During the rainy season the water level rises above the tops
of what are thought to be the bases of ancient dikes (Folan 1975) (Figures
3.13, 3.14 and 3.15) and spreads into the surrounding area where, at times,
other dikes exist.

Additional data for climatic fluctuation in Yucatan are available from John
L. Stephens's description of the *aguada* at Rancho Jalal in Yucatan associated
with several *chultunob* or cisterns and wells, and a drawing by Frederick Catherwood (Figure 3.16). According to Stephens (1963, Vol. 2:149–150) and
Matheny (1976:188–191), this *aguada* was dry around 1830 and its bottom

FIGURE 3.13 Aerial view of core area with Lake Coba in background, Lake Macanxoc in middle, and Lake Sacalpuc in the foreground. (Aerial photograph courtesy of E. Wilson.)

FIGURE 3.14 Aerial view of Lake Coba showing dikes on west and partially underwater during the summer months, 1975–1976. The excavated and consolidated Ixmoja Temple is in background. (Aerial photograph courtesy of E. Wilson.)

FIGURE 3.15 Aerial view of Lake Coba showing close-up of flooded dikes on the western end. (Aerial photograph courtesy of E. Wilson.)

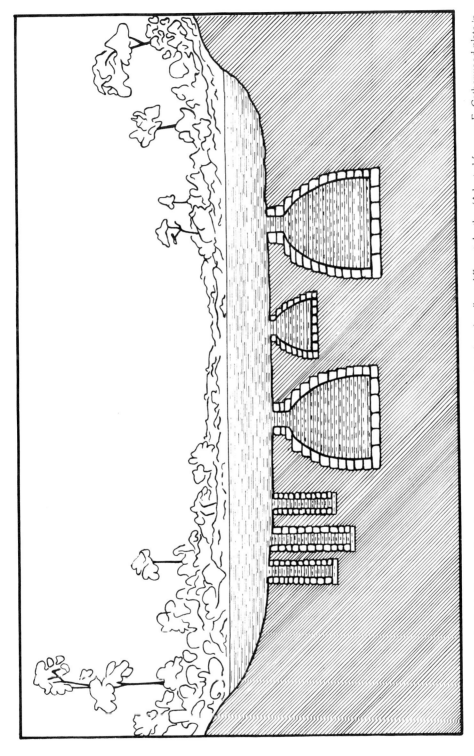

FIGURE 3.16 Rancho Jalal. Cross section of an *aguada* showing various *chultunob* and wells at different depths. (Adapted from an F. Catherwood plate in Stephens 1963:150, vol. 2)

covered with several feet of mud. While local people were digging into the bottom in search of water during a dry period, they located the openings to several *chultunob* and wells. If Stephens' description and Catherwood's section drawing of this *aguada* at least in part reflect past reality, it may be suggested that the ancient Maya excavated *chultunob* in its bottom down to two levels and wells down to three different levels. The depths of these *chultunob* and wells could indicate that the phreatic water table of the peninsula was at three or more levels through time, and that these water-collecting devices were excavated to varying depths at different times to take advantage of fluctuating water sources conceivably brought about by varying climatic conditions (Folan *et al.* 1980). A similar situation may exist in Dzibilchaltun and Chan Kom as well (Folan 1981b).

Evidence of variable rainfall was also found at Chac cave near Kabah. The cave is 65 m deep, which makes access more difficult. Despite this, approximately 75% more Early Classic ceramic fragments than Late Classic jars were found at this site. This suggests more frequent use of this cave for water procurement activities (Andrews IV 1965) during a period of time when the Yucatan Peninsula and the area around the cave were much more sparsely populated than during the populous Late and Terminal Classic periods. This, in turn, strongly suggests a lack of more accessible groundwater during the earlier in contrast to its later period of use.

Chichen Itza probably functioned during a period of relative dryness during the Early Postclassic (Gunn and Adams 1981). This is supported by the discovery of several Toltec–Maya-period charcoal-filled incense burners found under approximately 1.0 m of water in one of the inner passages of the Cave of Balancanche (Andrews IV 1961, 1970; Folan: personal observation; Folan *et al.* 1980). It can be inferred that these incense burners had been left by the ancient Maya on the floor of these passageways during a period of time drier than that of the 1959 rainy season in Yucatan. But following a climatic shift to a cooler and wetter period during the subsequent Mayapan period, the water level probably rose sufficiently to cover these ceremonial vessels (Folan *et al.* 1980).

Chapter 4

Urban Organization
and Social Structure
of Coba

William J. Folan

COMMUNITY PATTERNS OF MAYA SETTLEMENTS

Many scholars have described the ideal form of the Lowland Maya community (Adams 1981; Andrews 1969; Bullard 1954, 1960; Coe 1965; Folan 1975, 1976; Hammond 1972; Haviland 1965; Kurjack 1974: Landa 1941; Puleston 1973; Roys 1962; Sanders 1962, 1963; Willey 1956a,b). Landa (1941) wrote that Maya towns of the sixteenth century were centered about the temples. In these central or core areas priests, nobles, and the wealthy resided. Lower-class inhabitants lived farther away from the core. This model of concentric zonation appears to fit the general settlement pattern of Classic Maya cities such as Dzibilchaltun, Lubaantun, and Tikal. Although Landa's model of Postclassic Maya settlement patterns describes a preindustrial urban area, there have always been more than a few doubters as to whether the Maya actually developed true cities, especially during the Classic period. Andrews IV (1962:149) and most of his early collaborators, however, looked upon Dzibilchaltun as representing a very large urban area. Kurjack (1974:89-94) in his later attempts to delineate the boundaries of Dzibilchaltun discovered not only that Andrews IV and others were correct but that Dzibilchaltun was "divided into numerous precincts, neighborhoods, sectors and special areas" (Kurjack 1974:89). Whereas some authors suggest that clusters of ruins should be viewed as a number of closely interacting but separate communities, Andrews IV

(1959:personal communication), Kurjack (1974:89), and others believed that groups of structures in the peripheral areas of Dzibilchaltun formed an integral part of a single, integrated community.

Hammond (1975:80) presents an ideal concentric zone model for the Classic Maya center of Lubaantun, Belize, and describes distortions and deviations from this model that derive from topographic considerations. He suggests that other factors that might modify the annular model would be the distribution of soils suitable for cultivation and the location of other settlements in competition for them (Hammond 1973b:778).

Puleston delineated the boundaries of Tikal, which he viewed more as amoeba-like than as a geometrically shaped unit. He defined an Epicentral Tikal that measures approximately 1.40 km north–south by 1.25 km east–west and states that "these boundaries correspond to the area enclosed by the buildings illustrated by Guillemin (1968:2) as the 'main buildings' for the religious cult at Tikal" (Puleston 1973:21–22). Puleston then divides the elite residential sector of Epicentral Tikal into two groups: those at the core of the epicenter in the Central Acropolis and those with comparatively peripheral locations with respect to the Great Plaza (Puleston 1973:22). Central Tikal is defined as a 63-km^2 zone; Peripheral Tikal corresponds to the area between Central Tikal and the city limits and Residential Tikal is the combined areas of Central and Peripheral Tikal, encompassing 120.5 km^2. The sites of Jimbal and Navajuelal, at 10.0 km on the south *brecha* strip, are considered to represent smaller residential units of Tikal. The following relates what is now known of the urban organization of Coba.

URBAN ORGANIZATION OF COBA

Based on the combined efforts of the Coba Archaeological Mapping Project and work carried out by INAH, we know that the ancient city of Coba encompassed not only the building complexes mentioned by Thompson *et al.* (1932), but a continuously occupied area of approximately 63–70 km^2 (Benavides 1976b; Fletcher 1978; Fletcher and Kintz 1976; Folan 1975, 1976, 1978b; Folan and Stuart 1974; Kintz 1978). Greater Coba extends considerably beyond these limits (Folan 1975, 1976) and thus covers an area at least as extensive as "Peripheral Tikal," the termed coined by Puleston (1973) for an area extending 120 km^2 around this important regional center. The follow-up mapping in Coba by Gallareta Negron (1981) and Cortes de Brasdefer (1981a,b) under the direction of Norberto González Crespo approximates and reaffirms our earlier findings concerning the size and organization of Coba.

The early work of Thompson *et al.* (1932) indicates that Coba is characterized by several major administrative–ceremonial–residential zones formed around and among a constellation of five small lakes, presenting a residence and a hydrographic pattern peculiar to Coba alone among Classic Maya cities.

Research indicates that the ancient Maya modified virtually the entire urban area at Coba by a series of earth-moving activities. The landscape modifications undertaken by the Classic period residents included such activities as (1) intensive mining and quarrying, (2) road and structure building, (3) construction of walkways, linear boundary markers, house-lot walls and soil-retention walls, (4) construction of large patios and platforms, (5) kitchen gardens, (6) raised fields, and (7) the modification of areas large and small for the purpose of hydraulic control and development (Folan *et al.* 1979).

Analysis of the settlement pattern data from Coba has revealed the complex organization and use of space in the city and its surrounding areas. The residence pattern reflects the division of the overall socioeconomic organization into social classes, while the *sacbe* network that crisscrosses the city divides it into political and social sections of varying shapes and sizes. The residences and the administrative and religious structures located in and around the city core bespeak the differences of their inhabitants and their associated activities.

The Core Zone

The core or downtown zone of the city is characterized by palaces, plazas, and temples as well as less ostentatious residences. The principal units that make up this core area are the Coba, Nohoch Mul, and Chumuk Mul groups, forming a complex developed on a large man-made terrace about 1.5 km², known as the Great Platform. It was here that numerous stelae, dating from seventh to the early ninth centuries A.D. have been located. These and other large groups are also the origin of the complex system of the raised *sacbe* for which Coba is so well known.

At Coba, the elite households cluster near the core of the city. In the ideal concentric model of preindustrial cities presented by Park *et al.* (1925), Sjoberg (1960), and Wheatley (1971), the central zone preempts all other zones in terms of status. The majority of the important administrative and sacred structures are located in the core zone, as well as the residential dwellings of elite families. Servants, craftspeople, relatives, and workers allied or attached to the elite families also lived in this zone. Proximity to this high-status core zone or direct linkage to it by *sacbeob* symbolized status. Those closest to the core were at the very heart of the city and its vital exchanges, and hence in a more advantageous position vis-à-vis access to information, products, and services (Folan 1975).

The Market Area   The central market area in Coba probably was spread over the large area fronting the Ixmoja. Here goods would have arrived from near and far on inter- and intraurban *sacbeob* with their termini (or beginning) located here (Folan 1978b). Another reasonable choice for a major market area would have been the spacious plaza fronting Chumuk Mul, also a nexus for several *sacbeob* (Benavides 1976a). Local legend states that a prehistoric Coba market surfaces in Lake Macanxoc every New Year after dark, perhaps suggesting an ancient market on the shores of this ceremonially important lake (Folan 1978b, 1981a).

The Suburban Zone

Middle-class households were most numerous north of Sacbe 1 and south of the terminal site of San Pedro in Zone I, the northern survey zone. This inner suburban area is represented in other survey zones as well. Beyond San Pedro, the frequency of household units decreases, and the modest households in the peripheral zone are thought to represent lower-class housing on the boundary of the urban center. The settlement pattern, as a mark of social differences, can be used to elucidate the prehistoric social organization within the confines of a single settlement.

Several scholars have inferred that precolumbian towns were organized into neighborhood divisions. Michael Coe (1965), for example, suggested that the Maya ideally organized their communities into four divisions. But it appears that the extensive *sacbe* system divided Coba, like the spokes of a wheel, into more than the ideal number of divisions (see Figure 1.2) (Folan 1976). Preliminary analysis of the data collected at Coba suggests differential land use in the interstitial areas bounded by the spoke-like *sacbe*. Additionally, analysis of Zone I indicates that household units clustering in these areas formed social groups representing neighborhoods (Kintz 1978).

The survey and analysis of the 13 test zones surrounding the civic–ceremonial core at Coba has established that groups of structures vary considerably in form.

These units cluster in a combination of different shaped structures. These include rectangular-, apsidal-, and round-shaped buildings that were not roofed over by stone corbelled vaults. In addition to these units, there are rectangular vaulted structures as well as those laid out in the form of elegant C or L shapes.

Whereas some platforms served both civic–religious and domestic functions, the structures adjacent to platforms probably served as ancillary units. The complexity of organization in the residential precinct was initially demonstrated in Folan's (1975) analysis of Coba.

The variation in household structure has permitted an assessment of the family organization and has generated hypotheses concerning the utilization of various structures by the resident family as dormitories, kitchens, or storehouses.

The inner residential or suburban zone, occupied principally by the most important and middle-class members of Coba as well as craftsmen, encircles the core area. Here, large platforms support a few administrative and ceremonial structures in addition to many elite residences. The high, at times multizoned structures, designed for ceremonial purposes only, can best be described as akin to the churches and chapels found in most urban areas of the Christian world. Some of these ceremonial structures probably served a barrio-like community or neighborhood while others might have served an extended household (Folan 1975; Kintz 1978).

According to sixteenth-century ethnohistoric accounts, towns were divided by the *batabob* into wards resembling small districts of a larger division such as a parish. A rich and capable man was appointed by the *batab* to take charge of each ward, not necessarily based on lineage affiliations. In all probability, each ward had its local market as each modern Maya neighborhood within a town has its local store.

Many of the household and major social units in Coba were encircled by a complex system of stone walls that may have developed in response to increased urban population. In some cases, these walls represented property lines; in other cases, narrow walkways between households. Some walls served to check the erosion of raised kitchen gardens where the ancient Maya grew vegetables mainly for household consumption as well as the trees that provided shade and subsistence. A few walls probably served defensive purposes.

There existed a notable reduction of buildings and walls per square kilometer as well as a marked increase in the number of apsidal and round-shaped structures as distance from the core area increased. Many of the apsidal and round buildings were built directly on bedrock without benefit of platform as was typical of those usually constructed closer to the center of the city. These apsidal–round structures, often associated with kitchens and the shelter and storage areas of the farmers, blend into the rural zone surrounding Coba and its hinterland extending at least 14 km from the core area (Folan 1975, 1976).

The *Sacbeob*

The communication networks of more than 50 intrasite *sacbeob* that divide Coba and its environs into four or more major sections represent part of the infrastructure of the urban area and are a manifestation of its political control. They serve to join administrative or combined administrative–ceremonial and residential groups whereas longer *sacbeob* connect Coba and Yaxuna 100 km to the west and Coba and Ixil 20 km to the southwest; both sites probably represent outposts of Coba (Figure 1.2).

Local tradition also connects Coba and the Cenote Sagrado at Chichen Itza as well as the Cenote Sagrado and Mexico with an underground *sacbe* (Folan 1975). For those principal areas not connected to the city by a real or by a mythological stone *sacbe,* local beliefs supply an aerial *sacbe* in the form of a blood filled tube resembling an umbilical cord symbolizing consanguineal kinship links (Folan 1976; Miller 1974; Tozzer 1907).

The intrasite *sacbeob* primarily represent high status links between the central core of Coba and its peripheral zones. The intersite *sacbeob,* however, seem to represent both commercial and military right-of-ways (Folan 1975, 1977a).

Coba and its *sacbeob,* like Rome and its roads, were not the product of a single day, nor were they as essential to the survival of Coba during the early stages of its development as during the latter when it had reached a higher degree of social organization. Without doubt, some form of ground-level communication was indispensable for the inhabitants of Coba in the Classic and Postclassic as well as during earlier periods. In all stages of development, the people of Coba needed to communicate with other centers, whether it involved the exchange of goods or services or to enter into another social contract of a more complex nature. For members of the same family, the only requirement was a path between house and kitchen or, perhaps, both—with a separate storage facility. All that required was a trail of packed earth produced by the constant foot traffic of adults and children with an occasional addition of earth from time to time to raise the pathway above puddles during the rainy season. For longer trips, to exchange corn for squash for example, or to go to the nearest cenote to draw water, a trail partially formed by limestone slabs was in order. Frequent communication between two household groups was facilitated by a raised masonry walkway that also served as a visual indicator of the close relationship between two or more groups with common property lines or check dams used in conjunction with extensive horticultural plots (Folan 1975, 1978b).

In addition to the facets of the Coba transportation network, the intersite and intrasite *sacbeob* had as the most important function the joining or linking of distant noble lineage and ceremonial groups with those in the center of the city. As such, they represented high-status, on-the-ground links between these centers in the same way that dynastic marriage alliances provided bonds of kinship (Marcus 1976; Molloy and Rathje 1974; Proskouriakoff 1961; and Fletcher 1978: personal communication).

Communication between city and town and city and city were more complex than intracity links. Although the earth trails that cross the Yucatan were, and are, easily traveled during the daylight hours of the dry season or even during a moonlit night, this is not the case during the rainy season when the extremely slippery, mud-laden trails are difficult and dangerous to follow, day or night, especially if one is carrying a heavy load. The intersite *sacbeob* developed from these obvious needs, coupled with increased commercial and military activity, allowing travel anytime during any season of the year. This provided a 24-hour, 12-month-a-year communication system that fulfilled all the social and political needs of the city and state (Folan 1977c).

SOCIAL STRUCTURE

The earliest Spanish accounts have provided us with a fairly clear concept of the manner in which the Maya organized and ranked the members of their society. Although these records correspond to the sixteenth-century Maya, it is argued that they reflect a good part of the social organization of the earlier Classic Maya, as well as including later Toltec and other Mexican influence. Therefore, the following offers insights into the social organization of Coba during the seventh through tenth centuries and later. The data are drawn principally from the published works of Culbert (1974), Bishop Diego de Landa (1941), Ralph Roys (1943, 1962), Alfred M. Tozzer (1941), and an unpublished manuscript by Folan (1978b) (see also Chapter 11 in this volume).

According to these sources, the Yucatec Maya were divided into upper, middle, and lower classes. The members of these classes were usually referred to as nobles, commoners, and slaves.

The Noble Class

Nobles in general were *almehen*. From their ranks territorial rulers, heads of local towns, the higher officials who served under these local heads, and probably the priests were selected. The office of *almehen* was hereditary from father to son if the lords thought that the sons were acceptable candidates to the office.

Nobles were absolute in command, and territorial rulers obeyed the nobles in whose houses they held court. Nobles (who also served in temples), respected, visited, and entertained the most powerful of the territorial officials, consulting with them on important matters. Nobles also appointed territorial governors, often their own sons if they were capable to rule. The governors' functions were to treat the poor kindly and to maintain peace in town while maintaining the nobles and themselves through economic endeavors.

The townspeople planted, cultivated and harvested the nobles' fields, and shared the harvest with the noble and his household. The townspeople as a community also shared game, fish, and salt with a noble. People referred to as *principales* (who were inferior to nobles) were aided by their own families.

The most powerful individuals within the noble class were *ahau*. They were considered to represent the rulers of various territorial divisions located within a city or a regional or state territory.

Halach Uinicob   The *halach uinicob* was another title applied to rulers of a territorial province or city. They came from designated families, obtaining their positions through patrilineal descent. They were the local executives of their particular city or town which also at times represented the capitals of their province. Their duties included dividing the land, solving major problems (such as inheritance disputes), and keeping records of territorial boundaries. Occasionally, they served as priests, on public missions.

The income of a *halach uinic* was principally derived from his cacao groves and farms worked by his slaves. He received gifts as offerings and not as bribes from litigants and petitioners who came to be judged by him if they were not from his own town. He also received tribute from the towns in his province in the form of maize, beans, chile, poultry (mostly turkeys), honey, wax, cotton, cloth, game, fruit, salt, dried fish, shells, and slaves. Local officials probably acted as advisors of a *halach uinic.* For example, some of the local chiefs of other towns, especially if they were related to the *halach uinic,* were consulted on provincial affairs, whereas priests advised the *halach uinic* on political matters.

Batabob   The *batabob* were also members of the noble class and subject to the orders of the *halach uinic,* who appointed them for life. The *batabob* were the local chiefs who usually acted on local problems concerning administrative, judicial, and monetary matters. They were responsible for making sure houses in a village were maintained and that fields were cut, burned, and planted in cycles designated by the priest responsible for the calendrical calculations pertinent to these important yearly events. Deputies, called *ah kulelob,* served the *batabob,* who also commanded his own soldiers.

Batabob were treated with great respect. People bowed and spread mantles before them on ceremonial occasions while they were fanned by servants. The authority of a *batab,* however, was not absolute, but checked in some cases by the council members of a confederacy of independent towns.

The town of the *batab* apparently did not pay tribute to the *halach uinic,* but the *batab* was obligated to cultivate a field for the benefit of this ruler. The *batab* was responsible for building and repairing the house of the *halach uinic* and supplying him with domestic services.

Although a *batab* did not receive tribute from his people, he was maintained by them from their milpas and manufactured goods. Like a *halach uinic,* a *batab* received goods from petitioners and litigants when acting as a magistrate. If, however, there was no territorial ruler, a *batab* received a minimal tribute in the form of food and small cotton mantles. Some also received cacao, poultry, red shells, and jade beads.

A *batab* went to war, taking advantage of a situation to plunder the enemy and take slaves if he and his group were on the winning side. If his side lost, he and his men could end up slaves and, perhaps, sacrificial victims.

Additionally, there were special war chiefs, *nacom,* who were members of the town government and also performed human sacrifices. The *holcan* were mercenaries who lived in the villages during times of peace where they are said to have caused considerable trouble during periods of idleness.

Ah Cuch Cabob   Next in rank of status following the *batabob* were the *ah cuch cabob,* also considered members of the noble class. They had a role in the municipal government as members of the town council as well as being in charge of certain subdivisions of a town. The *ah cuch cabob* assembled the people in their wards for banquets and festivals as well as for armed conflict. They were also responsible for collecting tribute and organizing corvée labor.

Caluacob The *caluac* was a steward who lived in the house of the noble or *batab* for whom he worked and was readily recognized by the baton he carried as his badge of office. The *caluac* kept account with the rulers of the towns under a noble's domain and informed him of what was needed in the noble's house—such as fowl, maize, fish, game, honey, salt, or other things essential to maintain the household.

Ah Hol Pop The *ah hol pop* was the governor of a small town and overseer of the population, subject to the lords. The *batab* as well as the *halach uinic* governed through these individuals. The *ah hol pop* was in charge of the municipal building called the *popolna,* or rolled mat, where men came together to discuss public business. It was here where they learned and practiced dances for the town festival. The *ah hol pop* was considered "head of the mat," an authority symbol among the ancient Maya. People negotiated through the *ah hol pop,* who consulted with the nobles on visiting embassies and traveled with them. The *ah hol pop* became the chief singer–chorister in charge of drums and other musical instruments, presiding at weddings and assemblies in colonial times.

Other individuals included the *chun than,* described as one of the principal officials of a town with a Spanish title equated to that of *regidor* or alderman. The *ah dzib huun* was a town clerk, who, with several other minor officials, kept documents and maps up to date. There was a surveyor, who settled minor land disputes, and the town innkeeper. There were the *topiles,* minor peace officers who took care of the town stores and acted as the carriers of the litters of the *halach uinicob.* In addition, a group of men referred to as *nucteil uinicob* were the elders or principal men of a town.

Beside these political titles, people involved in different types of commoner civil activities were recorded in sixteenth-century Yucatec dictionaries. There were bearers, charcoal producers, dyers, farmers, fishermen, chert workers, masons, potters, salt gatherers, stone cutters, tanners, weavers, and wood-carvers (Adams 1970). There were hunters, foresters, miners, and people involved in other full- and part-time activities, as well as captives and slaves.

Sacred Authorities

Although there was certainly an overlap between church and state in the Maya culture, there existed sufficient division to consider each separately. We have already seen that a *halach uinic* could act as a priest in a capacity of sufficient importance to lead some sixteenth-century Spaniards to equate him with a Roman Catholic bishop. But beside a *halach uinic,* there was an organized priesthood in cities such as Coba to which he probably did not belong.

Priests, in general, were referred to as *ah kin mai* (literally "he of the sun") and the office was hereditary. The *ahau can mai* was the chief priest and chief teacher. His name refers to the rattlesnake, a sacred, mythologically endowed creature closely associated with the Quetzalcoatl–Kukulcan cult in Mesoamerica. The high priests examined candidates for the priesthood and appointed and invested the priests of the various towns throughout Yucatan. They provided them with codices. Although priests had political power as the advisers of the nobles, they were not supported by lower-status people as were the *halach uinicob* and the *batabob*. Priests were supported by nobles whose sons they educated in sciences and letters. They received red shell and green stone beads, cotton cloth, cacao, poultry, maize, and other necessities for their services. Among the skills they taught were calendric arts, methods of divination and prophecies, cures for diseases, and how to read, write, and draw, including hieroglyphics.

Priests were tattooed and, at times, readily identifiable by their unkempt hair smeared with sacrificial blood. They wore long, white, sleeveless robes of bark cloth and snail-shell-ornamented shirts; sometimes feather cloaks were added. They wore feathered headdresses and carried a hyssop on ceremonial occasions. Priests participated in all ceremonial events, including those associated with puberty ceremonies (sometimes assisted by *chacs*), weddings, confessions, sacrifices, and burials. They took part in all religious festivals, horticultural and hunting rituals, and rites associated with warfare. They also practiced firewalking rituals in special year-end ceremonies. All in all, it may be said that Maya priests were very powerful and conservative members of their society in the past as contemporary Maya *h'men* (or priests) are today.

In addition to the priests, there was another group of individuals involved in the religious aspects of Maya society. These were the *chilamob*, prophets or interpreters of the gods. They received and delivered prophecies from the inner room of a house in words and phrases not understood by the priests. The *chilam* would later interpret the prophecies for the priest. *Chilamob* were considered very important by the Maya as they alone held contact with the future. One famous *chilam*, Chilam Balam, seemingly predicted the conquest of Yucatan by the Spanish. Following the conquest, the *chilamob* were considered to be the chief agitators and rebels among the Maya.

The *chacs* were four old men appointed each year from members of the laity to assist in sacrifices often carried out by the *nacom*. The *chacs* also participated in other ceremonies such as puberty rituals.

CLASS AS RELATED TO STRUCTURES

Coba architecture more closely resembles that of the Peten than of the Yucatan. The structures at Coba are not akin to those of such Yucatecan Florescent period cities as Chichen Itza, Kabah, and Uxmal with richly carved, stone-decorated facades. Despite considerable modification, numerous examples of Peten-like Coba architecture are also to be found in such places as Acanceh, Aké, Dzibilchaltun, Izamal, and Oxkintok.

The architectural inventory of Coba includes a range of sacred structural complexes, from large temple structures to small oratories and shrines dedicated wholly to ceremonial activities involving priests and other high-status individuals (Thompson *et al.* 1932). Worshippers presumably approached sacred monuments, such as the Ixmoja and La Iglesia temple (Figure 4.1), to fulfill religious obligations and to make offerings and prayers amid great pomp and circumstance that involved ceremonial processions, singing, and burning incense at altars. In Coba, oratories and shrines generally are Postclassic and house reset stelae. There is a very large acropolis-like structure that appears to have been left unfinished. Although we are not certain, it is reasonable to assume it was dedicated to both sacred and secular activities. Palace structures, common to the Maya area, are represented by large multiroomed complexes such as (1) the building situated behind La Iglesia and fronting Lake Macanxoc, with Uitzil Mul on the south side of the lake and (2) the large palace to the north of the Coba Group B ball court. In these structures, members of the noble class resided and carred out their day-to-day activities. It is reasonable to assume that the *ahau* in charge of the multiple territories within the regional state of Coba (named in honor of the *ahau*'s lineage) lived in majestic buildings such as these. The *halach uinic* also lived in similar structures and structures of this type would, in some cases also have served as the *popolna* (meeting place) for conferences overseen by the *ah hol pop* (Folan 1978b).

Archaeologically, one would expect to find fewer ceremonial goods in these buildings in comparison to items that would be associated with a temple structure. Here would be indications of the numerous items linked with elite secular activities. One of the commonest interior features is the masonry benches on which the palace inhabitants rested and slept (Adams 1974a).

Early sixteenth-century documents inform us that members of the Maya priesthood lived in the core area of the cities (Landa 1941). Although there are several buildings that would seem to qualify for such a residence, it is most probable that the chief priest, or *ahaucan,* would have spent much of his time in an elaborate courtyard group such as the one on the south side of La Iglesia where four, multientranced, multiroomed, vaulted, roofcomb-decorated buildings surround a very deep patio that may have held water during the rainy season. Other high-status members of the priesthood, including the *ah kin mai,* probably lived in less prominent courtyard groups such as the one below and to the west of the residence of the *ahaucan.* Perhaps some priests also spent short periods of time in the vaulted buildings, such as those fronting and to the sides of La Iglesia, while attending to the needs of the gods and their supplicants (Folan 1978b).

Beside palaces, there are numerous elite residences that also bespeak el-

FIGURE 4.2   Main facade of El Cuartel. (Photograph by V. Fadziewicz.)

egance and power. These homes are situated mainly in the inner suburban area or at the termini of some *sacbeob*—rectangular, L, or quadrangular shaped, as were many nineteenth- and twentieth-century hacienda main houses in Yucatan. These prominent buildings were built on platforms that supported small temple structures and from 1 up to 15 or 20 less-elaborate buildings. The platforms and buildings housed members of an extended, elite family with their household retainers, craftsmen, and other lower-status families. At times, a daughter would marry and her family would add a small platform to the side of the platform of the main unit and build a modest-sized apsidal or round-based home for the budding family during the first 5 or 6 years of marriage.

Residences such as these may be represented by El Cuartel in Coba, a short distance to the south of Lake Coba (Valencia *in* Benavides 1976a) (Figure 4.2). This and many other similar-shaped residences near Chumuk Mul may have housed the *ah cuch cabob,* who were in charge of the subdivisions within a town. These types of houses could also have been the residences of the nobles outside the inner core of Coba as they were later on in Mayapan

FIGURE 4.1   Aerial view of the Coba core area. The Ixmoja Temple fronted by the Xaibe is shown in the right foreground facing Lake Macanxoc. La Iglesia is in the left background facing Lake Coba. Las Pinturas is situated between these two principal structures. The great white patch in the center background is a recent *sascab* extraction site. (Photograph by George Stuart.)

(Folan 1978b). It was here that the *caluac* acted as the noble's steward and attended to the people arriving from the noble's town. These people would stay in the noble's house during their official trips to Coba.

The residences of *batabob* stationed in tributary towns such as Ixil were much the same, thus identifying them as members of the noble class. Deputies of the *batab,* the *ah kulelob,* probably lived nearby in similar, but smaller, structures.

Differing somewhat from these elite residences were the large complexes at the termini of several intrasite *sacbeob* in Coba such as Xmakaba, Machu-kani, Pakchen, Kitamna, and Kukican. Although many of these structures served as residences of the noble class outside the core area, other magnificent buildings on the outskirts of Potonchan, Tabasco, served as country houses built for pleasure. They were said to be built like sixteenth-century Spanish dwellings with luxurious apartments and courtyards shaded from the sun (Toz-zer 1941).

In the nobles' residences, one finds domestic wares and many metates, sometimes in quantities large enough to suggest that, if not used for the preparation of large feasts, they were produced or at least distributed from this point. Here too are wells, catch basins, and numerous walled-in areas.

The temples, palaces, and other elite habitations described previously were usually constructed of stone masonry with stone-corbeled vaults. These vaults

FIGURE 4.3 A completed and partially assembled pole and thatch structure in Coba. (Photograph by V. Fadziewicz.)

provided the Maya with roomy, high-ceilinged interiors. Rooms were dimly lit due to the almost total absence of wall openings; light penetrated the interiors of these monolithic structures through single or multiple doorways, where it was reflected into dark corners by white-plastered walls.

The apsidal and round-based buildings—inhabited by such people as the *ah dzib huun* (scribes), *topiles* (constables), *nacom* (war captains), *holcan* (mercenaries), *macehuales* (commoners), and slaves—found in the suburban and rural areas usually were built of perishable materials. The roofs were thatched and the walls were sturdy poles, all set on a stone footing filled with pebble-free earth to form the floor (Figure 4.3). Sufficient sunlight filtered between the poled walls to produce a light interior and sufficient breeze to cool the already shaded interior. During the colder months, however, these houses provided little protection against the bitterly cold night. Another disadvantage was the copious quantities of dust that filtered between the pole walls during the windy dry season. During this time of the year, these residences were extremely flammable. The smallest fire started from wind-blown interior hearths or exterior fires from milpas could have consumed an entire building in a matter of moments (Folan 1978b).

Chapter 5

The Ruins of Coba

William J. Folan

THE BUILDINGS

What follows is a description and partial interpretation of some major buildings forming the core area of Coba to provide a better understanding of the city center. Unfortunately, virtually all buildings excavated, consolidated and restored by INAH in Coba as of this date are of a ceremonial nature. Thus, this section is mainly concerned with these aspects of life there some 1000 or more years ago as well as the deities to whom they may have been dedicated at one time in their history. Additional material on the residences of various classes of Cobaeños is presented in subsequent chapters.

La Iglesia Group

William J. Folan and George E. Stuart spent a few weeks during the early summer of 1974 gathering data on La Iglesia and its associated buildings (Figures 5.1, 5.2). Following Pollock and Thompson's earlier map (1932), the large (10,000 m²) plaza bordering Lake Coba and fronting the plaza of La Iglesia seems large enough to assemble as many as 10,000 or more people for special occasions. The plaza is formed on the west by a medium-sized, colonnaded temple structure and stela shrine facing Lake Coba, in addition to three other structures.

On the north and south sides of the plaza are two large multiroomed structures featuring numerous entryways. These are approached by a broad staircase that could have seated some 3000 additional people for any event.

FIGURE 5.2   La Iglesia. (Photograph by V. Fadziewicz.)

The structure to the south is divided near the center by a vaulted arch leading to Lake Macanxoc.

To the east of the plaza, there is another stela and a series of wide stairways leading to different structures in addition to another vaulted archway that leads to an interior patio. The major staircase (with a vaulted passageway underneath) is near the center of the plaza and leads to a large, colonnaded building facing west. A staircase to the north of the plaza leads to a small patio flanked on the north and south by a multiroomed, multiple-entrance structure with a roofcomb. A small altar is situated in the center of the patio and another, farther to the east, is associated with a stela fragment fronting the stairway that leads toward the top of La Iglesia.

The facade of La Iglesia was excavated by Antonio Benavides (1976b) and Jaime Garduño (1976) (Figure 5.3). It is a large, nine-zoned, 24-m-high temple originally faced with a thick layer of carved, polychrome stucco motifs. A broad staircase leads to a large block of masonry with a huge inset panel on its western face near the top of the building. Another staircase, divided like those in the Ixmoja and the Templo de las Pinturas, continues to a small Post-classic temple shrine that houses a stela fragment discovered earlier by Thompson *et al.* (1932:35). A small shrine with a long bench was built on both sides of the primary staircase near its base.

FIGURE 5.1   Aerial view of the south side of La Iglesia showing a patio between it and Lake Macanxoc. Note the numerous mounds to the rear of this complex. (Photograph by G. Stuart.)

FIGURE 5.3 La Iglesia after excavation and consolidation by INAH. Note stela fragment in center foreground. (Photograph by George Stuart.)

Recent excavations indicate that the temple crowning this building was modified on two different occasions (Benavides 1976b). After its primary construction, secondary additions were made to the inner face of its walls (thereby reducing its interior dimensions) and an antechamber was added to the temple facade. This architectural innovation was composed of two lateral walls and a wide entrance divided by two pilasters. The roof was probably thatched with *guano* (*Sabal mayarum* Bartlett), a locally available palm.

At the time that the La Iglesia stela was reset in the temple interior, an offering was buried beneath it, which consisted of a mother-of-pearl pendant, an orange-colored shell pendant filled with powdered cinnabar, and a jade kneeling figure representing a long-nosed merchant god (perhaps God M, also known as Ek Chuah). This figure had an orange shell bead on his head, a pearl at his feet, and was ringed by numerous jade beads (Benavides 1976b). This indicates the importance placed on jade, pearls, and shells by the Coba Maya who imported them into the city in large quantities through local and more distant merchants.

Fronting the above described offering was another, which was placed within a plate covered by another plate of similar shape and size inverted over the first.[1] This offering consisted of two large sea shells, two shell plaques, jade and shell beads, and unworked hematite, once again emphasizing the importance of these imported items.

Another offering was recorded during the excavation of this small temple (Benavides 1976b). It was an hourglass censer, a monochrome plate, and a miniature mano and metate similar to many discovered in the cave of Balancanche near Chichen Itza. This offering, found at floor level in front of the temple entrance, not only suggests rituals involving the fertility of the land for the production of corn for grinding, but also strongly suggests that people from the Mexican highlands were indeed associated with Coba as they were with Balancanche and Chichen Itza. In Balancanche, small censers such as the one described were found in the same context as Toltec deities brought into Yucatan (Andrews IV 1970).

Secondary additions also were made to the base and top of this structure. A broad stairway and two lateral rooms were added at the level of the patio fronting La Iglesia. Both rooms contained wall-to-wall benches. Beneath these rooms were earlier divided chambers that had been filled with unworked stones. These chambers represent the easternmost extensions of the vaulted building rimming both sides of La Iglesia patio. The fill was removed from the northern chamber and a small crypt was found beneath floor level. This north-to-south-oriented crypt contained the remains of an adult with round, yellow incrustations embedded in some of the front teeth. (A drawing by José Elías Cobá Nah of the burial suggests that this individual was buried with a jade bead in each hand, thus resembling the burial of the ruler Pacal in Palenque. Another jade bead is shown between the Coba internee's knees [Benavides 1976b; Ruz 1973].)

The Maya frequently buried high-ranking individuals in temples or in their homes. Although it is difficult, from available data, to ascertain how the Maya utilized the room in which an individual was buried, it could well have been the quarters of priests in charge of a particular temple.

The stela fronting the secondary staircase to the temple, an upper fragment containing part of a figure and numerous glyph blocks, was reset in its present location (Figure 5.4). (A small, low, circular altar of masonry fronts this stela just as a small, circular, monolithic altar fronts the stela set into the bottom of the Las Pinturas staircase.) A larger, circular altar was built in front and to the west of what appears to be the masonry base of a shrine erected

---

[1]The hearts of dogs sacrificed for rain were often placed in such containers.

FIGURE 5.4 Stela fragment *cum* sacrificial stone fronting La Iglesia. (Photograph by G. Stuart.)

around the stela on the north, south, and east sides. This apparently was followed by the addition of an irregular platform covering the two circular altars and a part of the stela fragment. Further excavations may encounter the base of this stela under the center of the secondary staircase behind it and, possibly, reveal the burial of an important personage behind the primary staircase.

The stela fragment and the round altar fronting the La Iglesia staircase are reminiscent of sixteenth-century descriptions of slender sacrificial stones, four or five palms high, associated with altars (Landa 1941:115). It would, therefore, be reasonable to suggest that the stela fragment fronting La Iglesia (and most other stela fragments inside buildings and shrines) was, in fact, the sacrificial stone where Maya men, women, and children were held by four *chacs* while a priest removed their hearts to propitiate the gods, thereby ensuring the well-being of the group (Folan 1978a; Kampen 1978:Fig. 7). (In fact, what Hammond [1982:396–403] interprets to be a plain Late Formative stela at Cuello, Belize, may instead be an early sacrificial stone.) The stela fronting the temple is the object of considerable veneration by contemporary hunters who burn candles and incense in front of the stela–sacrificial stone before going into the forest.

Local mythology associates this temple with Chibirias (or Ix Chebel Yax in Maya), a goddess associated with regeneration. Chibirias plays an important role in Coba. She is, in effect, the contemporary patroness of this village and as such, needs to be consulted on important decisions—for example, whether to remain in or to leave the village. It is believed that if Chibirias is not informed, the person who moved out of the village could become ill or die if the goddess is not placated by a series of offerings and prayers (Folan 1975).

An exceptionally deep patio, rimmed by four vaulted, carved, stuccoed, two-room residences with roofcombs built atop a high platform, abuts the south side of La Iglesia. (A stucco turtle was associated with an early construction period of this high platform forming part of its upper southwest corner.)

Other La Iglesia-Related Structures

A small ball court with rings and two stela fragments are to the north of La Iglesia, as is a large, high palace structure that may have been the building from which the *hol pop* operated. Behind and to the north and south of La Iglesia are several additional patios, temples, palace structures, and *sacbeob,* most dating from the Late Classic period. Together they formed the power center of Coba.

A circular offering box was excavated near the center of the ball court. Its contents, dating from the eighth century, included principally jade and shell offerings. Two snails, a pearl, and objects of hematite, obsidian, and pyrite were also recorded (Benavides 1976b). All offerings were imported into Coba. The pearl, shells, and snails came from the nearby coast and, because there are no known deposits of hematite, jade, or obsidian in the Coba area, it is assumed that the other items came from more distant sources.

Las Pinturas Group

Las Pinturas group, a Postclassic assemblage of structures to the west of the Ixmoja, was excavated by Piedad Peniche Rivero (1975; see Peniche and Folan 1978) (Figures 5.5, 5.6). The group consists of several ceremonially oriented structures and features that include 13 altars and several stelae. The name of this group is derived from the polychrome murals gracing the upper facade of the Templo de las Pinturas, the principal structure in this group (Fettweis–Vienot 1980). The 8-m-high temple is a four-zoned platform base with a small, vaulted, Tulum-style temple–shrine structure, reached by a broad staircase that is partially divided toward its upper levels (similar to the staircase associated with the latest platform addition to Ixmoja). The vaulted building

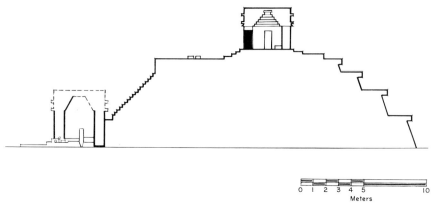

FIGURE 5.5 Pinturas complex. Section (from right to left) showing the vaulted temple with its small interior altar, two small altars fronting the temple, and the oratory at the base of the staircase with its interior bench, stela fragment, circular altar, phallus, and stone sphere. Section by Piedad Peniche R. (*in* Peniche and Folan 1978:Fig. 7).

had a single, rectangular room with a doorway divided by a single column with a capital on top. There is a single, narrow entryway on each side of the structure. The principal entrance abuts a broad stairway that had been added to and modified during the history of the building.

A small altar adjoined the rear wall of the building interior, and its walls were covered by four layers of differently colored stucco, including yellow, blue, red, and black. The outermost layer of stucco was red decorated with black lines, and a fragment of one small figure was visible near the southeast corner of the room. A pit in the center of the room showed signs of several floors and fragments of earlier masonry features. Because of the restricted area within the structure and the possibility of provoking a collapse, these features were not further excavated.

Two small altars and two offerings are on and in the platform fronting the vaulted building on top of the Templo de Las Pinturas. One of the altars contained a fragmented censer; one of the offerings that was concealed beneath floor level is an intact anthropomorphic, red censer (perhaps representing the Diving God associated with honey production in Coba) containing jade and shell beads, all dating from the east coast Postclassic period.

A stela fragment was found to be installed on a small platform in a slot in the center and at the base of the main staircase on the north side of the temple (see Figure 5.7). This stela may have served as a sacrificial stone. The badly calcinated stela fragment depicts one of the usual Coba patterns of a high-status individual standing on the back of a single captive figure. The captive, however, does not seem to represent an individual of Maya descent, but perhaps someone from outside the Maya area. The few glyphs beside the principal personage probably represent a date between the seventh and ninth centuries A.D.

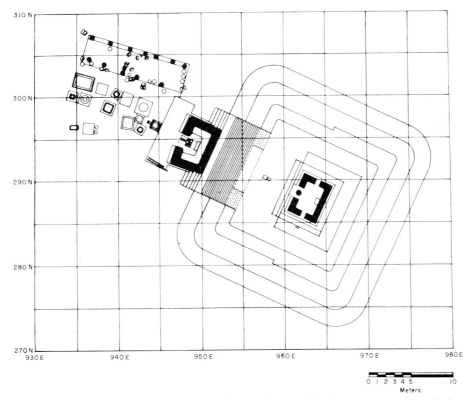

FIGURE 5.6 Las Pinturas complex. Plan showing (right to left) the temple structure with the small interior altar, column in front entrance, location of two offerings fronting entrance, and two small altars on platform. The *oratorio* at the foot of the staircase contains a bench, stela fragment, circular altar, phallus, and stone sphere. Thirteen altars and a single crypt front the *oratorio* with a colonnaded building completing the architectural inventory of the typical Postclassic complex. Plan by Peniche and Stuart. (From Peniche and Folan 1978:Fig. 6).

A small, circular stone altar similar to the one described by Landa (1941) fronts the stela. A stone phallus and sphere of stone are located to the north of the altar (see Figure 5.7). The sphere probably represented the gonads of the phallus thus demonstrating an association with fertility (this feature is often linked with the Itza (Fettweis-Vienot 1980; Peniche and Folan 1978).

A small, vaulted oratory was constructed over the stela–sacrificial stone on a separate platform; its rear wall rested on the fourth tread of a secondary staircase. The interior contained the stela fragment, and a wide bench rimmed its rear and two side walls. Subsequently, secondary jambs were added to its entrance and, at about the same time, the 13 altars fronting this structure were built in a line leading toward the north.

The interior and exterior walls of this smoke-darkened oratory were covered with numerous layers of stucco, each decorated with a series of complex

0   10
Meters

FIGURE 5.7 Pinturas *oratorio*. Plan showing the interior bench, stela fragment, circular altar, phallus, and stone sphere. The door jambs and the column drums are additions to the building with the columns serving a decorative rather than supportive function. Plan by Peniche and Stuart. (From Peniche and Folan 1978:Fig. 9).

murals; some resembled the style prominent on the east coast and in the Madrid Codex. Glyph elements representing the Maya merchant deity, Ek Chuah, were commonly drawn along the borders of a mural; another shows a ceramic vessel filled with *kan* (corn) glyphs similar to the mural on the upper facade of the temple. Another, an elaborate dragon, was painted on one of the jambs leading into the building. To ensure the preservation of these murals, they have been removed and transported to Mexico, D.F., where they will be separated and reproduced by INAH technicians before being put on display in a museum planned for Coba (Norberto González Crespo 1975: personal communication).

Both the fragment near the center of the building and the stone phallus were the principal objects of attention during pre-Columbian times. So many fiery offerings had been made to the stela that the stone was carbonized and cracked, causing many pieces to flake off. Fortunately, INAH technicians recovered numerous fragments and partially reconstructed the stela, providing a more complete vision of its composition and date.

The altars fronting the structure and its stela are 13 in number, as are the sky gods in Maya mythology. Most of the altars differ in shape and construction. The main altar depicts the remains of a stucco figure seated on a low stool, much like the figure found in nearby Tulum by Dr. Thomas Gann around the turn of the century. At Coba, however, only the feet of the individual remain; the upper part has been carried off, possibly by individuals who traveled from Sotuta to Coba in the sixteenth century with the objective of destroying elements associated with pre-Columbian religious practices (Tozzer 1941:110).

A Postclassic tripod cup, partially filled with jade beads, and a small copper bell were excavated outside the oratory shrine.

A small stone crypt on the west side of the altars contained the reburied skeleton of an adolescent. Although only the postcranial skeleton was located, two skulls were found outside the crypt.

Southeast of the Pinturas building is a colonnaded, Postclassic structure, built on a low platform, with secondary additions of masonry walls added to the rear of the building. This thatch-roofed, open-sided structure was probably used to house single, high-status young men during their indoctrination into the sacred and secular aspects of their society, including socialization with members of the opposite sex.

To the north of Las Pinturas are two additional stelae with Late Classic dates. These depict the same theme as other Coba stelae—a high-status personage with captives.

Cono, or Xaibe   What appears to be a cone-shaped temple structure fronts the Ixmoja in the Nohoch Mul group at the point where Sacbes 1, 5, 6, and 8 would meet to form a central point. It is this particular attribute to which this monument owes one of its latest names—the Crossroads Structure (Benavides 1976b) (Figure 5.8). This is a 15-m high building with several levels built on a rectangular base with sloping sides and rounded corners. On the building's east side, a staircase with balustrades provided access to a lower platform. A small *oratorio* seems to have been built at its highest point.

A badly weathered ninth-century stela (probably a sacrificial stone set into an altar) was discovered by Fernando Robles C. (1980) as he excavated the stairs of the first zone. The stela was accompanied by a stone serpent sculpture and a small offering of two long and two curved shell pendants, three seashells—perhaps pertaining to the genera *Classis, Murex*, and *Oliva*—two small, red, shell plaques, plus a fragment each of snail, conch, and jade.

What the use and function of this particular building may have been is problematical. Given its location in respect to the Ixmoja and the four *sacbeob* and its seemingly ceremonial–sacrificial nature, one could suggest that it was closely related to the rituals that would have been carried out by merchants before and after traveling to and from other destinations.

FIGURE 5.8 El Xaibe (or El Cono), a steep-sided monument that fronts the Ixmoja. (Photograph by V. Fadziewicz.)

Ixmoja

The huge (24-m high), seven-level Ixmoja temple structure is situated on the extreme northeastern corner of the enormous terrace on which is built a great part of the city core. The structure was built during two principal construction periods. The first, during the Late Classic, involved the construction of the multizoned base of the temple (Peniche 1975; Garduño 1976) (Figure 5.9); during the second period, the present temple topping it was built.

A small, vaulted structure with a single room, the entrance supported by two pilasters, was added to the base of the structure to the east of the main staircase (Garduño 1976). A long bench runs along its rear wall. Two of the ceramic offerings located in this structure pertain to the Puuc, Late Terminal Classic period of Yucatan, represented at such sites as Uxmal, Kabah, and Chichen Itza. The ceramic containers are small, flat-sided flasks; one is elaborately carved, perhaps to represent God L, the jaguar god of the underworld, about which little more is known.

FIGURE 5.9 Ixmoja after excavation and consolidation by INAH technicians. (Photograph by V. Fadziewicz.)

A Late Terminal Classic slateware plate fragment from this structure may record one of the latest dates so far found in Coba. A nine *ahau* glyph, clearly marked on the inside lip of the vessel, may record a date of A.D. 810, according to the Goodman–Martinez–Thompson correlation (if it represents a period-ending date) (Peniche and Folan 1978; Stuart 1978: personal communication).

Although a similar vaulted structure someday may be found on the west side of the staircase leading to the top of the main structure, it would, if it exists, have been covered by the staircase leading to a small, vaulted building on the fourth zone of the platform base. The entrance to the single room of this building is divided by two pilasters. Here, the lower fragment of a stela is set into the floor and against the rear wall of the temple. The lower part of the human figure that had been depicted on the stela faced the entryway, but the surviving glyphs faced the rear wall. Metates and charred fragments of deer and *jabalí* bone demonstrate the use of this temple as a center of ceremonial activity associated with fertility (as depicted in the Maya codices, where haunches of venison on metates are often shown as offerings) (Peniche and Folan 1978; Montoliú 1976/1977; Pohl 1981).

Several jade beads were located below floor level near the base of the stela as were shell pectorals and coral beads, all gathered in a small, rounded receptacle formed of mortar. Many of the ceramic fragments recorded in the room were of the type often located in the Puuc area.

Another room, added to the fourth zone of the temple platform base but to the east of the main entrance, was later excavated by INAH crews during the 1975 season (Benavides 1976b). This structure is similar to the building just described but has one rather than two pilasters dividing its entrance. It lacks a stela fragment in its interior and has no staircase leading up to it. This would suggest that this building was approached by means of ladders, as shown for a structure illustrated in the Dresden Codex.

Other additions were made to the Ixmoja during Postclassic times. These include the east-coast-style temple and its platform built on top of the earlier multizoned platform, and the addition of a balustrade with a carved serpent head to the original stairway. The single-roomed temple originally was decorated with figures of three polychrome Diving Gods formed into its upper facade. They represent a Maya deity linked with Ah Muzen Cab, the tutelary deity of Coba (Edmundson 1982:26). He is associated with bees and the production of honey, an activity for which Coba was well known. The interior of the shrine was occupied by a bench that almost covered the entire floor area of the structure. Unfortunately, the temple interior had been altered by pot hunters, leaving behind only fragments of Postclassic ceramics and the mammal bone remains of Maya sacrifices and offerings (Figure 5.10).

A small altar fronting the temple of the Diving God was associated with

FIGURE 5.10   The vaulted temple structure with interior bench topping the Ixmoja complex. Three Diving Gods originally formed part of the upper facade of this building. (Photograph by L. Florey Folan.)

numerous censer fragments, including some Mayapan-type anthropomorphic censers, further demonstrating a probable alliance between Coba and this Postclassic walled city some 150 km to the west.

The additional platform base on which the Diving God Temple is built is directly on the top of the earlier multizoned platform. It is a typical east-coast, Tulum-style structure with a divided staircase.

It was probably at this time that several stelae were installed, perhaps as sacrificial stones, at the base of the Ixmoja; some are fragments of monuments that may have been dedicated elsewhere in and around Coba and later were moved to their present location.

Structure X

This colonnaded, two-room, Late Classic building (reached by a wide, divided staircase) is southwest of the Ixmoja (Figure 5.11). This structure probably served as the residence of a high-status individual associated directly with ceremonials carried out in and around the Ixmoja and other nearby structures. One of the important aspects of Structure X is the large, well-preserved stela set into its western staircase in 1975, near where Pollock and Thompson (1932) found its lower half in 1930. The top part of the stela was not found

FIGURE 5.11 Structure X following excavation and consolidation by INAH technicians. The *guano*-topped stela fronting this structure was placed in its present position recently. (Photograph by V. Fadziewicz.)

until 1974 when the late Domingo Falcón Kinil, former chief guardian of Coba, found it mixed in with fallen masonry along the south side of the building. The complete stela, dated November 30, A.D. 780 (Stuart 1975), depicts a central, elaborately costumed official who holds a ceremonial bar while standing on the backs of two kneeling captive figures. Two small-scale captive or slave figures kneeling on each side of the principal personage are in the act of supplication. Unfortunately, no one can provide an event to go along with this date, but it may record the birth of the individual carved to cover most of the stela surface.

In addition to finding the stela fragment that included the introductory glyph to the calendric text, Falcón (1974) also discovered a cornice stone earlier used as the surface on which a series of incised Maya glyphs, arranged in a circular fashion, represent a hieroglyphic text perhaps stating that "Death . . . Smoking Mirror . . . [who was the child of] Lady MaCuc [and] the child of Lord . . . of [Coba]." One of the remarkable things about this text is that the mother of Smoking Mirror shares the name Cuc, or Squirrel, with the Lord Zic Cuc, known as Smoking Squirrel of Naranjo (Stuart and Stuart 1977:195).

Beside this structure, a huge platform west of the Ixmoja appears to be an unfinished acropolis. Numerous vaulted structures surround a patio on the east side of this complex and indicate that they were used by high-status individuals involved in sacred and secular activities of Coba.

Macanxoc

This group of ceremonial–civic buildings is southeast of the Coba group. It is reached by a wide *sacbe* leading off the east side of Sacbe 8 that links the Nohoch Mul group with Kukican at its terminus.

Although very limited archaeological work has been done on the multiple buildings forming the group, it is well known for its multiple stelae. Included among these dated monuments is the only stela that was standing in Coba at the time that the site was explored by Pollock and Thompson (Thompson *et al.* 1932). This large and important stone document includes the full-figure portraits of two Coba personages accompanied by many hieroglyphs. Among these glyphs are a set that read August 28, A.D. 682, exactly like the stela in Naranjo, Guatemala, that commemorates the marriage of a Naranjo ruler with a woman from nearby Tikal. Unfortunately, there are no emblem glyphs on this stela identifying Coba, Naranjo, or Tikal.

STELAE AND OTHER HIEROGLYPHIC MONUMENTS

Coba is well known for its Classic period stelae. Approximately 31 of these monuments have been located in varying stages of completion, and it is fairly certain that many more are covered by the fallen masonry of the numerous collapsed structures within the city core.

Stelae are also associated with at least one *sacbe* terminus. In addition to these stelae, at least one located at coastal Tancah and another at Tulum may also be from Coba (Proskouriakoff 1950). Most stelae already recorded had been removed from their original site during Postclassic times to be set up in new shrines, perhaps to form part of an ancestor cult (Peniche and Folan 1978). Others were probably used as sacrificial stones (Folan 1978a,b).

Many of these stelae depict a single principal personage standing on the back of one or two men with one or two others in positions subservient to the central figure, who probably represents a ruler or a high-status member of a ruling family. All the datable stelae from Coba were dedicated during the seventh through the ninth centuries when ongoing activity in Coba was oriented toward the development of the city and the state. Many of these events may be commemorated by both the dates and the yet-to-be deciphered, noncalendrical hieroglyphs inscribed on these and other carved monuments.

Although only limited work has been done on the hieroglyphic texts from Coba, it has long been thought that their style bears a close resemblance to that of some cities in the Peten area of Guatemala, thus suggesting alliances between Coba and other cities in this part of the Maya world, such as the Classic site of Naranjo (Stuart and Stuart 1977; Thompson *et al.* 1932).

Murals

Murals are common in Coba. The earliest depict Classic personages standing in file; the later murals closely resemble the style of the three surviving Maya codices. The similarity is so great that it may be suggested that at least the Madrid Codex, with its long text on apiculture, may have been produced in Coba or nearby (Folan 1975; Fettweis-Vienot 1980).

The Coba *Sacbeob*

The Coba roadways are noted for their quantity, length, complexity, and excellence of design. Aside from these general qualities, the *sacbeob* offer a great many structural facets that set them apart from the ground-level communication networks of other Maya cities (Figure 1.2).

Sacbeob were constructed by establishing first a line between two high architectural features or between provisional platforms, as done when the contemporary village of Chan Kom built its new road to Chichen Itza (Redfield and Villa Rojas 1934). In some cases it is possible that celestial sightings were used for particularly long roads. For example, very tentative observations made by Jonathan Reyman (1982:letter) from our map of Coba (Figure 1.2), without having visited the city, indicate that Sacbe 6 leading from the Ixmoja Temple to Chan Mul could have been set in alignment to the rise of Sirus, the brightest star in the sky between A.D. 500 and 1000, as it is now. Furthermore, Sacbe 5, leading from the rear of the Ixmoja Temple to Telcox, could have been set in alignment with Canopus, the second brightest star in the sky during the same period. Sacbe 19, leading from the Ixmoja to Manaachi, could have been set in alignment with Pleiades, a constellation of much importance in Mesoamerica. The same *sacbe* could also have been set in alignment with the summer solstice sunrise and winter solstice sunset. Sacbe 7, leading from Ixmoja to Kanakax, also may have been set in alignment with the Pleiades, moonrise (northern minimum) and moonset (southern minimum) among other possibilities including Sirius and Regulus, a first magnitude star in the constellation Leo. Sacbe 30 leading to Pakchen could also have been set in alignment with Pleiades and moonrise (southern minimum) and moonset (northern minimum). Sacbe 10, leading to Yax Laguna, could have been set to align with Deneb, a first-magnitude star in the constellation Cygnus, especially if this particular *sacbe* was built around A.D. 500.

After these types of alignments were made, several poles were lined up to ensure a straight trajectory. The Maya then opened a wide swath down the line with the aid of corvée and slaves, thus clearing the way for the construction of the road. Groups of workers were made responsible for the construction of a section of road and perhaps for its upkeep later. An incomplete *sacbe* recorded in Coba provides us with the valuable information that *sacbeob* were built in sections, as are many modern roads in Yucatan. A group of men were assigned a stretch of road to build, with the sections not necessarily contiguous. Thus, an isolated section of *sacbe* was at times completed with nothing but many meters of empty space between it and other finished sections. After raising retaining walls, the workers filled the area between them with large chunks of stone before building the exterior walls with large, shaped, and faced rectangular stones—apparently without the aid of mortar. A thin layer of *chich* (small stones) gathered in milpas was placed over the larger fill stones to produce a slightly convex surface (Figure 5.12). An additional thick layer of *sascab* (calcareous sand) was extended over the *chich,* pounded into shape, and wetted to produce a hard-packed, smooth, puddle-free surface. Multiple layers of *sascab* suggest that the *sacbeob* were frequently resurfaced. In some cases, a well-polished layer of stucco-like material was used to finish the surface of

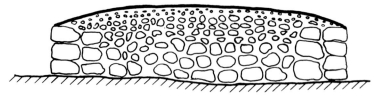

FIGURE 5.12   Cross section of a *sacbe* showing its outer and inner retaining walls, stone fill of varying sizes and *sascab* surface. (Drawing by José Francisco Prieto Pérez from sketches and notes. No scale).

FIGURE 5.13   Sacbe 3. (Photograph by V. Fadziewicz.)

a *sacbe* in Coba (Benavides 1976a; Folan 1975, 1976; 1977a; Navarrete *et al.,* in press; Villa Rojas 1934; Thompson *et al.* 1932) (Figure 5.13).

Most Coba *sacbeob* ranged from 3 to 19 m wide. The height varied according to the type of land features they crossed and, although there were sections of one *sacbe* that were at least 7 m or more above ground level, 75 cm to 1 m above ground level seems to have been the average height.

Several types of ramps are associated with the Coba *sacbe* system. One of the most exotic is at the junction of Sacbes 1 and 3. It was here that the Maya built a high platform with four ramps sloping up to its top. How this ramp was used during Classic times has not been established, but an associated, small Postclassic shrine and a stela fragment may contribute to our understanding of this unique feature (Figure 5.14).

An unusual feature is associated with Sacbe 3 between the ramp and the *sacbe* terminus in San Pedro. Here, the Maya built a large platform with a structure on top that served as a gateway. To follow the *sacbe* in a straight line, it can be suggested that one had to climb the stairs of this building and pass through an archway (with a room on each side) before walking down the other side and continuing the journey to or from central Coba (Figure 5.15).

Two ramps have been classified as administrative features. Both are near the limits of the urban area to the west of Coba. One is associated with the Coba–Ixil *sacbe* and is approximately 2½ km from the core of the city. The

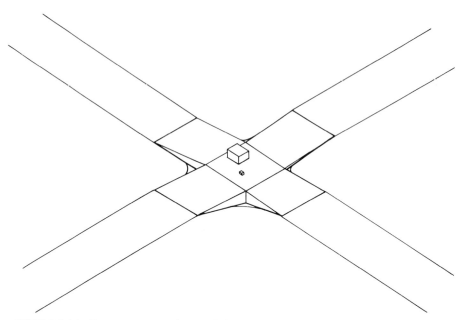

FIGURE 5.14 Four-way ramp with a small shrine at the junction of Sacbes 1 and 3. (Drawing by José Francisco Prieto Pérez from drawings and notes. No scale).

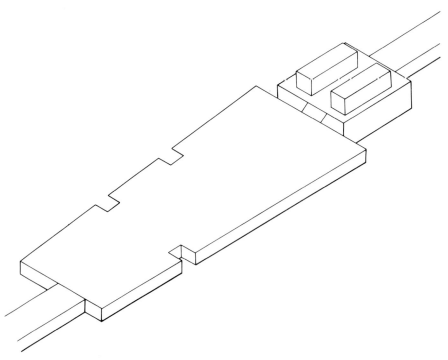

FIGURE 5.15 Large ramp on Sacbe 3 leading to San Pedro. (Sketch by José Francisco Prieto Pérez from drawings and notes. No scale).

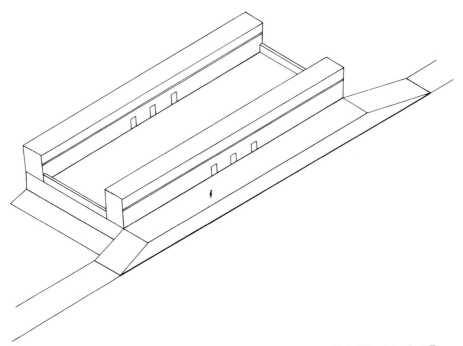

FIGURE 5.16 Ramp with added platform on *sacbe* between Coba and Ixil. (Sketch by José Francisco Prieto Pérez from sketch and notes. No scale).

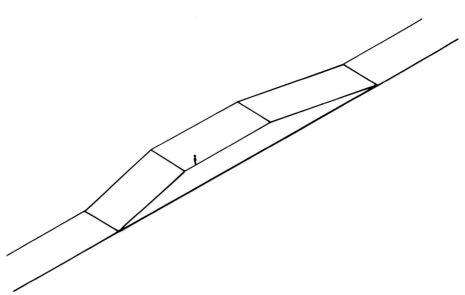

FIGURE 5.17 Ramp on *sacbe* between Coba and Ixll. (Sketch by José Francisco Prieto Pérez from sketch and notes. No scale).

ramp is about 4 m high, 7 m wide and 85 m long. A platform abutting its south side supports two vaulted buildings on two sides of a patio (Figure 5.16). A similar ramp exists on the Coba–Yaxuna *sacbe* about 4 km from the center of Coba. The principal difference between the two ramps is that the platform on the south side of the latter ramp is lower than the ramp surface and does not support any vaulted architecture. These ramps are referred to in Coba as "customs check points" (Folan 1975, 1977a,b; Villa Rojas 1934).

Another type of large ramp is more difficult to classify. These ramps are close to the termini of the Coba–Ixil *sacbe*. Beside being large, however, they reveal nothing further to help in their identification (Figure 5.17).

The most common type of ramp in Coba was developed to facilitate the construction of a particular *sacbe* over natural obstacles in the landscape, such as stone outcroppings. The shape and the size of such obstacles determined the characteristics and dimensions of the ramp. Although irregularities in the terrain could, at times, be eroded by shifting the path of a *sacbe,* the Maya did not usually choose this solution. They completely removed or adjusted the inclination of a *sacbe* to pass over an obstacle. But if an outcrop was too high or too long for either solution, the Maya usually built a ramp over it, which would allow a passenger to walk up one side to a platform and down the other side to continue his journey. On other occasions, a *sacbe* would dip into a deep depression and climb the sides of it at the other end. Or, a *sacbe* would even cross a body of water and could be used as a dike (Folan 1981a).

Only a few features are visible on the surfaces of most *sacbeob*. One of the commonest features is a line of flat, rectangular, 50-cm-wide stones that run down the center of a *sacbe*. Although it is uncertain how these linear features were used, it is very possible that they were walked on to preserve the surface. Culverts also cut across several *sacbeob* in and outside of Coba proper.

Sascaberas (quarries) are often visible along the sides of *sacbeob*. Stones and *sascab* supplied from the quarries were used to build the *sacbe* and to keep it in repair. Cenotes and water sources along the sides of *sacbeob* not only provided travelers with drinking water but with water for the maintenance of *sacbe* surfaces as the Maya today dampen the earthen floors of their homes to keep them compacted.

Features peculiar to the Coba–Yaxuna *sacbe* are defensive walls raised across the *sacbe* surface from place to place along its length, and the use of hieroglyphic-faced monuments that Villa Rojas (1934) thought to be distance markers. Another object of much discussion is a large, cigar-shaped stone Villa Rojas thought to be a road roller when, in fact, it probably represents a large stone phallus such as others described in the Yucatan area (Folan 1977a, 1978b).

Generally, it can be said that the Maya of Coba constructed many stone-surfaced roadways, pathways, elevated masonry walkways, and *sacbeob* linking administrative, commercial, ceremonial, and family units to provide a communications network essential for the maintenance of city and state (Folan 1975, 1977a, 1978b).

There are *sacbeob,* such as Sacbe 4, that permit communication between diverse social groups within the city core and others that permit easy communication between the core, the suburbs, and, in some cases, the rural area surrounding Coba. The longest *sacbeob* are those connecting Coba and its satellite cities, such as Ixil and Yaxuna. In this manner, the Maya of Coba managed a network of roads that facilitated the movement of its population for sacred or secular purposes, including the transportation of goods and services within the city and state. They also divided the city and state into recognizable sociopolitical units (Folan 1982).

Chapter 6

Linear Features in Zone I: Description and Classification

Laraine A. Fletcher

COMPARATIVE DATA ON LINEAR FEATURES IN THE MAYA AREA

Although linear features have been reported previously for the Maya area, no systematic investigation of these features had been undertaken until recently, with the exception of Bullard's (1952, 1954) study at Mayapan. Other investigations of linear features have been concerned with larger walls, such as the defensive earthworks at Tikal (Puleston and Callender 1967), the walls around Tulum (Lothrop 1924), fortifications at Becan (Webster 1976), and the defensive walls discovered in northern Yucatan sites such as Cuca, Aké, Muna, and Chunchucmil (Kurjack and Andrews 1976). The prominent long-distance *sacbeob* known to be associated with large centers such as Coba and El Mirador, as well as with smaller Maya sites, have been investigated with varying degrees of intensity. These studies indicate the multiple functions of the *sacbeob,* including their use as dikes (Benavides 1976a; Dahlin *et al.* 1980; Folan 1974, 1975, 1976, 1977a; Folan and Stuart 1974; Kurjack and Andrews 1976; Ruppert and Denison 1943; Sabloff and Rathje 1975b; Thompson *et al.* 1932; Villa Rojas 1934). These causeways span both Classic and Postclassic occupations with earlier time periods represented in Coba and elsewhere.

There has been a general lack of information on less obvious intrasite linear features in the Maya area, although Puleston (1973:12) pointed out that the importance of "roads, paths, gateways, boundary walls, stairways, passages and even doorways" should not be underestimated.

Aside from Landa (1941), Wauchope (1934) was one of the first contemporary investigators to mention linear features designated by him as "walls." During the excavation of house-mounds at Uaxactun, these walls were found to be

> associated with the house sites . . . the function of which was doubtful since they did not retain any core or fill. They were followed for some distance and, although they were never traced completely, [Wauchope] suggested that the walls leading from two neighboring mounds may have been connected. It seems likely that they were stone boundary walls [Wauchope 1934:9].

Andrews's survey (1943) of southwestern Campeche reported various linear features at the Late Classic and Late Postclassic site of Las Ruinas. The walls were classified by construction techniques and configuration. One group featured

> a number of very thick walls faced with heavy block masonry, with a rubble core. They averaged 1.5 m. in height and were usually over 2 m. thick. Segments of these walls, never forming enclosures, criss-crossed the zone in what seemed a thoroughly nonfunctional manner [Andrews IV 1943:36].

On their approach to Calakmul, Ruppert and Denison (1943:13, 50) discovered a number of linear features described as masonry walls or check dams crossing narrow, steep-sided valleys. Similar features were sighted near Oxpemul. Substantial new survey data report similar features in other Maya zones (Turner II 1978) that lend support to revised interpretations of the agricultural programs and soil-management practices of the Maya.

Sanders (1955), reporting on linear features on Cozumel, described house-lot walls as well as what might have been milpa boundary markers of the type later mentioned by Rathje and Sabloff (1975a:78) in the San Gervasio zone of the same island. Sanders wrote that

> for about 500 meters along a trail from the ranch house to the site are numerous remains of low dry stone walls enclosing large corral-like space. . . . The corral walls continue north for an undetermined distance. The extent of the walls to the west is not known [Sanders 1955:196].

Data on linear features are also available from the Postclassic site of Aguada Grande on Cozumel Island. The complexity and degree of nucleation of Aguada Grande is reflected in this description of linear features:

> The site evidently does not extend farther south than the south wall of the house yards, which runs on for 500 meters east of its junction with the east wall of the yards. Seven or eight side walls run off at right angles from it, all to the north, and probably delimit other yards [Sanders 1955:196].

This description of contiguous house-lot yards is similar to the settlement pattern at Coba, particularly as exemplified in the suburban zone north of Sacbe 1 and extending north for approximately 2 km. It approximates the configuration of house-lot boundary walls at Mayapan as well. Sanders (1960) also reported on linear features at Tancah, Quintana Roo, but suggested that although they resemble walls around the Main Plaza at Aguada Grande, they did not function as house-lot walls but possibly defined special-purpose areas within the larger ceremonial precinct.

Linear features mapped at Becan (Thomas 1975:139–146) were tentatively classified as either terraces or elevated walkways, some of which connected two or more house groups. Other ridges or linear features enclosed residential and ancillary structures forming clusters of from one to more than 15 structures (Thomas 1975:142–143). This settlement pattern, with the possible exception of terraces, again duplicates to a great degree the one at Coba and appears typical of the resident population of Classic as well as Postclassic Maya centers.

Hammond (1973a:57) proposes a substantial population at Colha, Belize, and a settlement pattern featuring single mounds interspersed with larger *plazuela* groups. Additional surveying located linear features connecting platform groups and "wall-like structures that seem to form semi-bounded areas which look like garden yards" (Wilk 1977:4).

Eaton's work (1975) in the Rio Bec region east of Xpuhil located and described households or farmsteads associated with (1) artificial field ridges, (2) hillside terraces, and (3) fenced enclosures adjacent to domestic structures. Eaton (1975:56) suggests the groups represent dwellings of nuclear and extended patrilocal and patrilineal families and that the linear features served both agricultural and nonagricultural functions.

Data from northwestern Yucatan sites, particularly from Chunchucmil (Vlcek *et al.* 1978:212–217) clearly document the existence of linear features, including one group designated as house-lot boundary walls. Additional information on the distribution and type of linear features associated with a Postclassic site is provided by Andrews and Andrews's (1975) study of the ruins of the Xcaret, Quintana Roo. This site comprises an area of approximately 10 km² with groups located as far as 20 km inland. It is further characterized as being "a steady scattering of platforms, housemounds, field wall systems, and other occupational debris." They note that "despite the scattered distribution of these outer groups, the intervening areas show remains of many house mounds, low walls, small sacbeob, chultuns, and heavy occupational debris" (Andrews and Andrews 1975:12). This parallels descriptions for Classic as well as Postclassic sites. It also points to the existence of well-populated hinterlands surrounding nucleated centers of all sizes as representative of Maya settlement patterns, as opposed to the model of dispersed settlements and lightly populated intersite zones. Andrews and Andrews (1975:13) postulate that the area around Xcaret is a combined suburban and sustaining area related to the core and claim the extensive system of field walls delineating small plots is comparable to field walls reported for Cozumel.

This brief review of the literature on linear features in the Maya regions has shown that a wide variety of these features formed part of the prehistoric Maya settlement pattern. They were variable in form, multipurpose, and have been found to exist in settlement types which range from the isolated farmstead of a full-time agricultural family group in the hinterlands to the complex urban settlement types of which Coba is only one example.

LINEAR FEATURES AT COBA: GENERAL DESCRIPTION

Mapping at Coba produced data on prehistoric linear features in association with a variety of archaeological remains. The linear features, excluding the major intersite *sacbeob,* have been classified into six major types. Their presence has made possible the delineation of the prehispanic Maya household compound and, as such, assists in a reconstruction of the demographic, economic, and political characteristics of Coba.

Due to the efforts of Folan, Jacinto May Hau, Nicolás Caamal Canche, and Lynda Florey Folan, the initial identification and plotting of the walls, walkways, retaining walls, and other linear features at Coba was accomplished in a preliminary form. Folan established three categories: (1) single-faced linear features (2) double-faced linear features with and without rubble fill, and (3) *sacbe*-like walkways.

Single-faced linear features consist mainly of unworked limestone slabs or boulders ranging in size from approximately 30 cm to 1.0 m in length, 20 to 60 cm in width, and 40 cm to 1.0 m in height. There was no evidence of mortar; it appears these features were dry laid and chinked. Almost all the single-faced linear features mapped in Zone I were at least partially collapsed, making it difficult to determine their original height, but it can be said that there existed some variability. Based on ethnographic data from Yucatan, it is suggested that a major portion of the single-faced linear features recorded in Coba functioned as house-lot walls as well as for soil erosion control (Figures 6.1 and 6.2).

The second category is double-faced linear features with and without rubble fill. Again, almost all the double-faced features had collapsed with limestone slabs and boulders scattered about, but in general alignment. Those with rubble fill averaged 50 cm to 1.0 m in height. They averaged less than 1.0 m in width and were never as wide as the *sacbe*-like walkways. The double-faced linear features without rubble fill can be subdivided into two groups. The first includes those features represented by two single-coursed rows of parallel stones or slabs. This subgroup appears to represent the stepping stones of an

FIGURE 6.1   House-lot boundary wall enclosing a modern *solar* in Coba. (Photograph by Laraine Fletcher.)

ancient pathway between household groups, leading to buildings or a water source (Figure 6.3). The second group are those more than one course high that probably served the same use as some single-faced walls: a few as household boundary walls, some as property markers not directly associated with household units, and others for soil and water control. Some of the wider double-faced linear features also are assumed to have functioned as walkways between platform groups, leading to water sources and *sascab* quarries or to other activity areas both inside and outside the domestic compound. Similar walkways were observed in use in modern Coba and other contemporary Yucatec villages. The construction techniques described for Coba by Folan are almost identical to those found at Mayapan. Bullard (1954:236) noted that the majority of the linear features at Mayapan were only single-coursed with the possibility of an additional course of small boulders applicable to only a few of the walls. It is also possible that at both sites perishable material was placed atop the stone base as is sometimes done with milpa boundary lines.

FIGURE 6.2 Barbed wire and low stone house-lot boundary wall extending around INAH compound in Coba. Garden wall to rear is formed of small poles. (Photograph by Laraine Fletcher.)

Typology of Linear Features at Coba

The presence of a variety of morphologically different linear features at Coba in association with different architectural types can greatly contribute toward an understanding of social organization at the site. We now turn to a more detailed description of the six major types of linear features encountered in Zone I.

Linear Feature Type I These are single- or double-faced and directly associated with household compounds. They functioned either as house-lot boundary or soil retention walls distributed around raised garden areas. They are variable in form (Figure 6.4) and include

1. Walls abutting the same platform at two points
2. Walls surrounding household compounds or platforms as well as ancillary structures and/or associated platforms and/or water sources
3. Walls connecting a platform to another but ancillary structure off the platform, in many cases forming a semienclosure

FIGURE 6.3 *Sacbe*-like walkway connecting two ancient household compounds at Coba. (Photograph by Laraine Fletcher.)

The majority of the double-faced walls in Zone I did not contain rubble fill. They were dry laid either of unworked or roughly shaped limestone; slabs and stones of all sizes were utilized within the wall. If a double-faced wall contained no fill, the stones were placed together in parallel rows, edges touching (in many cases with smaller stones used as spalls to form what appears to be an open-water conduit) (Folan 1976: personal communication). In the few instances when an interior space was filled with pebbles *(chich),* the space averaged 50–80 cm in width. No indication of a plastered surface was noted.

The larger walkways exhibited the most elaborate construction techniques. They were always rubble-filled with small and medium-size stones paralleling, in this way, the large intrasite and intersite *sacbeob.* The side walls were built of dry-laid worked and unworked rectangular and tenoned limestone blocks.

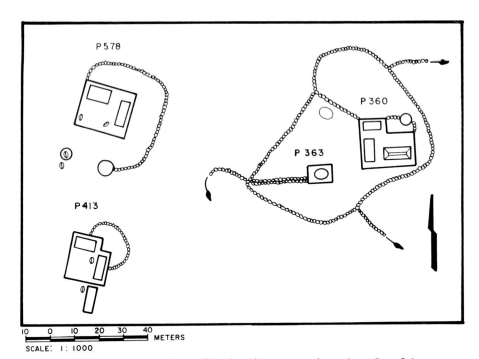

P 578

P 360

P 363

P 413

10   0   10   20   30   40
SCALE: 1 : 1000

METERS

FIGURE 6.4   Linear feature Type I: prehistoric stone house-lot walls at Coba.

The initial coursing is of large to medium size blocks ranging from approximately 30 cm to 1.0 m in length; 20 to 60 cm in width and 50 cm to 1.0 m in height followed by a layer of smaller stones and finally what was probably a *sascab* or plaster surface (Folan 1977a).

In Zone I, a total of 144 Type I walls were mapped. The enclosed areas range in size from 20 to 9077 m². The adjusted figure with land covered by architectural remains removed is 20 to 7160 m². The area enclosed by these features represents household activity space and is comparable to that area around modern household units in Yucatan, better known as the *solar,*

> the conventional dwelling compound of families in the community. The solar, which is physically contained by a mortarless stone wall in the typical case, spatially demarcates the functioning domestic group, which may consist of a nuclear family of a married couple and their minor children, or an extended family composed of three or four generations of patrilineally related kinsmen, who, with their spouses and children, form an economically interdependent household unit. . . . It is also the spatial locus of domestic group process [Thompson 1974:27; reprinted from *The Winds of Tomorrow* by Richard Thompson, by permission of the University of Chicago Press. © 1974 University of Chicago Press].

Linear Feature Type II   Type II linear features are single- or double-faced features that link platforms ($N = 45$). This type is further subdivided into two varieties.

Type IIA directly abuts two platforms ($N = 21$) spanning distances from 13 to 135 m with an average distance of 69 m (Figure 6.5). The distance spanned and height are important variables in determining function. Some of the more closely spaced linked-platforms are from 30 to 70 m apart. They probably reflect kin affiliation, whereas smaller platforms located only a few meters from a larger platform could have been ancillary to the main household unit and served as storage space, a kitchen, or possible locus for cottage industry activities. Linear features only one course high probably served as walkways between platforms; if higher, they may have enclosed a small work area. The walkway type has been noted at Becan where

> some of the larger ridges, especially those which do not twist about but run straight, look more like elevated walkways. Some of these were found to connect two or more sizeable house groups, which makes a walkway function quite reasonable [Thomas 1975:143].

Type IIB ($N = 17$) linear features connect household platforms (Figure 6.6). These features were probably multifunctional in that they could have served as boundary maintainers and/or acted as barriers to impede passage into different *solares*. The low walkway-type connections would have, on the other hand, facilitated communication between related households engaged in communal activities. Distance and height are again the important variables. The distance spanned is 28–230 m with a mean of 102 m.

With the exception of one single-faced wall associated with Platform No. 1323 in the more peripheral area of Zone I, the linear features in this category cluster in the inner suburban zone south of the San Pedro complex and appear to define space in areas adjacent to household compounds.

Linear Feature Type III   The linear features are single- and double-faced *sacbe*-like walkways associated with natural resources (Figure 6.7). At Coba, two important resources were water and the *sascab* mined from the numerous

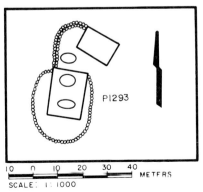

FIGURE 6.5   Linear feature Type IIA: connection between two platforms.

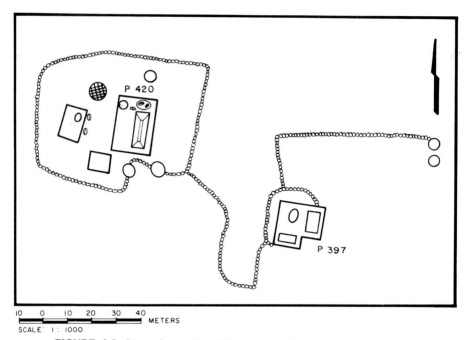

FIGURE 6.6 Linear feature Type IIB: connection between household groups.

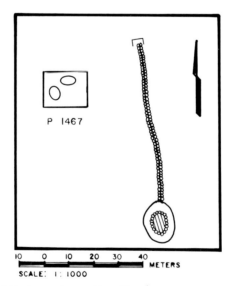

FIGURE 6.7 Linear feature Type III: connection to natural resources.

quarries recorded there. This group is divided into two types. The first is Type IIIA. This consists of linear features associated with natural resources and a visible architectural feature. The second type is Type IIIB linear features associated with resources without visible architectural features.

There are 16 cases of Type IIIA linear features. Three are single-faced, nine double-faced, and four *sacbe*-like. The three single-faced features were all recorded in the inner suburban zone where they served to connect platforms to stone-encircled depressions. Their lengths are 15, 25, and 38 m. They, as well as the double-faced features, probably served as walkways. Three of these features connected platforms and water-filled depressions. They spanned distances of 45, 55, and 60 m. The remaining four larger features in this category include one long *sacbe*-like feature which led 240 m to the large cenote known locally as Cola de Venado. A second prominent walkway spanned 163 m from Platform No. 531 to four apsidal structures and a pile of small building stones. The third and fourth cases occur in the outer suburban zone and span 60 and 70 m. They both lead to a large depression that becomes water-filled during the rainy season (Caamal and May 1976: personal communication) and are associated with household compounds.

There are three cases of Type IIIB linear features; all are double-faced. Two are in Zone I to the south of Sacbe 1 and the third is $\frac{1}{2}$ km north of this *sacbe* in the outer suburban area. Two lead to limestone quarries and the third extends approximately 300 m from Sacbe 27 to a water source while also serving as a public access route from a major causeway. Eight household compounds are situated within 50 m of this walkway.

Linear Feature Type IV Type IV linear features connect platforms to major *sacbeob* (Figure 6.8). Their function is variable as determined by their form

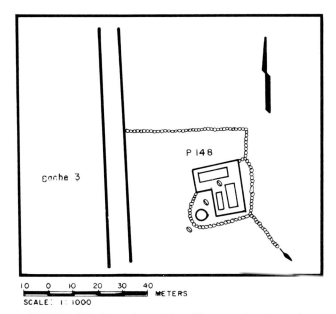

P 148

sacbe 3

```
I0    0    I0    20    30    40
                              METERS
SCALE:  I : I000
```

FIGURE 6.8 Linear feature Type IV: connection to a *sacbe*.

(single-faced, $N = 7$; double-faced, $N = 5$; or walkway, $N = 3$). In a few cases where the linear features connecting the household platform to a *sacbe* forms a semi-enclosure, it has been included in the analysis of the *solar* and placed in the category of linear feature Type I.

Single-faced linear features are visible in the more crowded inner suburban zone south of San Pedro. Their probable function was to delineate property lines along the *sacbeob* as well as to inhibit movement and access to household compounds. Platform-to-*sacbe* distances range from 62 to 93 m.

The three double-faced features of this type are located in a high-density zone of architectural remains adjacent to Sacbe 3. The distances spanned range from 46 to 108 m. It appears as if they too functioned to restrict access, provide passage and define household activity zones. Of the three remaining *sacbe*-like walkways, two are in the inner suburban zone near Sacbe 1 and one is in the outer suburban zone. This latter, 5-m-long feature joins a platform supporting a vaulted structure dedicated to the regulation of ingress and egress to the center. It is connected to Sacbe 27 which possibly functioned as a point of entry into Coba.

Linear Feature Type V   These features include single-faced, double-faced, and *sacbe*-like walkways connected to architectural features at one end and open-ended at the other (Figure 6.9), and linear features not associated with visible cultural remains. Their function is problematic. Some open-ended walls connected to architectural features at Mayapan were the result of stone robbing

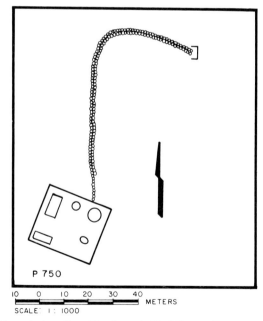

P 750

10   0   10   20   30   40
                                   METERS
SCALE: 1 : 1000

FIGURE 6.9   Linear feature Type V: a household platform with an open-ended stone wall.

(Bullard 1954:235) but this does not seem to be the case at Coba. Although modern milpa plots are located in the northern area, and they are generally marked by bush fences, with stone robbing minimal and, therefore, not a reasonable explanation for the freestanding, seemingly incomplete, linear features in Zone I. Some of the walls which run out from a household compound for 50 to 100 m could have functioned to impede passage and limit access to a family compound. An agricultural function is, however, the most feasible (soil and surface water control).

The second category includes linear features not associated with visible structural remains. It is possible that some of these might have been for defensive purposes as several walls west of Lake Coba are approximately 1.0–1.3 m high, 3.0 m long, dry-laid, and free-standing (Folan 1975). There were no similar walls in Zone I. Other walls are corral-like with 12 such enclosures in Zone I. The areas enclosed ranged from 20 to 1490 m². Wilkin (1971:433) reports "Lundell found numerous areas in the Campeche forest marked off by stones and concluded that these were plots assigned to intensive cultivation." Sanders (1955:196) also mentioned corral-like enclosures on Cozumel and made the same suggestion. Special zones might have been reserved for special attention and their produce designated for elite consumption as suggested by Puleston (1973:228–229) for areas on the outskirts of Tikal.

Linear Feature Type VI   Type VI linear features are on platforms (N = 19) (Figure 6.10). Five are double- and 14 single-faced. It has been shown by Eaton (1975) that walls occasionally were constructed on platforms to divide space into smaller work or storage units. In six cases, these features connected two superstructures on the same platform. Platforms associated with a Type VI linear feature cluster below the San Pedro complex.

CONCLUSIONS

The linear features present at Coba have been classified into six major categories. While these are found distributed throughout the entire city and have been recorded as such, they have been mapped only in Zone I. It has been pointed out that the recording of linear features had been sporadic for many years; only recently is a comprehensive data base being compiled of the intrasite and intersite linear features at archaeological sites in Mesoamerica.

The linear features at Coba, then, can be studied on three levels. The first level is the family and includes the individual structure or group of structures that functioned as the dwelling place. At this level, the demarcation of the *solar* in an archaeological context is of great assistance in determining the size of the prehistoric Maya family unit. Other linear features also associated with individual structures or clusters of structures can be analyzed in terms of their possible functions as either an impediment to interaction or to enhance communication, depending upon the context in which they are found.

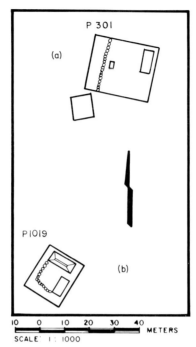

FIGURE 6.10   Linear Feature Type VI: stone walls on platforms.

The second level is the community and concerns the interrelationships between the individual household compounds as reflected in their spacing and in the presence or absence of physical buildings, community resources, and transportation routes. The third level is regional and interregional. *Sacbeob* such as the Coba–Yaxuna and Ixil causeways fall into this category.

As new settlement-pattern data are reported, a pattern emerges. There is one set of linear features associated with rural settlements such as those described by Eaton (1975), Baker (1976; 1977: personal communication), which include house-lot boundary walls, walkways, agricultural terraces, and milpa boundaries. The other set is associated with nucleated population centers of varying sizes and includes not only those mentioned but short-distance and long-distance *sacbeob,* defensive linear features, and city walls.

The first set of linear features, especially those that functioned as house-lot boundary walls, is the focus of Chapter 7. The importance of these features should be noted in that they circumscribed space probably utilized for subsistence-related activities: kitchen gardens, orchards, walls around milpa plots and agricultural terraces. Although these had been documented for the Late Postclassic, their presence during the Late Classic has implications for the type and intensity of food production during this earlier period. It can thus be suggested that the appearance of linear features, in all their variability, marks the transformation of the cultural landscape by the ancient Maya as new and more complex forms of social organization emerged.

Chapter 7

Solares, Kitchen Gardens, and Social Status at Coba

Laraine A. Fletcher and Ellen R. Kintz

INTRODUCTION

House-lot boundary walls recorded at Coba and the corpus of data amassed on these linear features allow for a quantitative analysis of *solares,* or yard areas, forming an integral part of Maya households. This material also makes possible an assessment of the space available to family units, the use of this area as kitchen gardens, and an evaluation of the relationship between *solares* and the social status of household residents (Figures 7.1 and 7.2).

The role of intensively cultivated kitchen gardens in prehispanic Maya cities of the Late Classic is also closely tied to demographic issues. The reconstruction of the resident population, in turn, is related to the question of the urban status of these centers (Adams 1974b; Eaton 1975; Fletcher and Kintz 1976; Folan 1975, 1976; Folan *et al.* 1979; Harrison and Turner 1978; Kurjack 1974; Matheny 1976; Puleston 1973; Vlcek *et al.* 1978).

The house-lot boundary walls at Coba and the enclosed *solares* delineate ancient familial compounds, providing data to reconstruct the size and composition of Maya households during the Late Classic, and to allow preliminary calculations of the amount of land available to the residents for possible kitchen gardening activities. It is argued that the *solar* was the locus of kitchen gardens

103

FIGURE 7.1   Modern *solar* in Coba. Small structure in background is probably a *nai nal* multi-purpose, storage facility. (Photo by V. Fadziewicz.)

at Coba, a suggestion already put forth by Folan (1976). The term *kitchen garden* or *dooryard garden* used here will mean

> a plot or space, surrounding or adjacent to a dwelling in which plants are cultivated. It should be noted that this definition is stricter than that supplied by Anderson [1952]. It is also important to note that this term should be applied to plots in which speciality or experimental crops are grown. Large-scale production of staples, regardless of their proximity to dwellings, is not considered to be kitchen garden cultivation, a form of agriculture that is usually highly intensive [Harrison 1978: 9–10].

In addition, the presence of house-lot boundary walls in Coba facilitates the testing of Bullard's (1954) hypothesis, based on his survey at Mayapan, that no relationship exists between the size of a house lot (*solar*) and the social status of the household group. Distance of the household compound from the core of the city—an additional variable possibly affecting *solar* size—is also evaluated in this chapter.

THE *SOLAR* AS KITCHEN GARDEN

The *solar* corresponds to the land immediately adjacent to, and surrounding, a household platform group. This space can be delineated by boundary markers, including both nonperishable and perishable walls. The data and its analysis presented here concern only the household complexes associated with

FIGURE 7.2   Modern *solar* in Coba. (Photo by V. Fadziewicz.)

stone house-lot boundary walls recorded in Zone I ($N = 144$), although similar walls were encountered in the other 12 zones at Coba. Thus, the numerous household compounds in Zone I that do not exhibit stone house-lot walls ($N = 204$) have been omitted from this study.

There is ample documentation from archaeological, ethnohistoric, and ethnographic sources (Anderson 1971:137–141; Folan 1975, 1976; Folan *et al.* 1979; Landa 1941:62, 193–200; Lundell 1938; Puleston 1973; Redfield and Villa Rojas 1934:46–47; Roys 1943:19–20, 39–40; Sanders 1962; Scholes and Roys 1968: 170; Steggerda 1941; Thompson 1939; Wilkin 1971) indicating that horticultural and arboricultural activities in Maya towns were commonplace and important supplements to the subsistence base. It is also evident that gardening activities were most often carried out in the immediate vicinity of the household compound. Wauchope (1938:132–133) documents the ancient practice of maintaining both flower and vegetable gardens as well as fruit trees around the home, citing a report to the King of Spain circa 1577 which states that a Spanish official "ordered them to set fire to all the fruit trees which they had behind their houses in said town." Scholes and Roys (1968:37) describe Pontonchan as covering a large area due to houses being separated by garden areas. Smith (1962:184), citing Clavigero, says "many of the houses [were] crowned with battlements and turrets, and their gardens had fish ponds, and the walks of them [were] symmetrically laid out." Roys (1943:39–40) suggests that "many vegetables now usually grown in the fields were formerly cultivated in town gardens adjoining the houses," and Steggerda (1941:18) reported the presence of small flower and vegetable gardens, a chicken coop, and some trees behind houses of the contemporary Maya. Thompson (1939:41) states that at San Antonio "in addition to the milpa, each family has a small patch of cleared land which is permanently under cultivation and in which perennials such as oranges and cacao mainly are cultivated." Sanders (1962:88) reports similar practices for contemporary northern Yucatan and Tabasco: "Each house has a relatively large house lot surrounded by a stone wall averaging some 5000 square meters, which is occupied by a fruit orchard with a great variety of crops." The present-day inhabitants of Coba likewise have large *solares* with stone walls and cultivate a great variety of plants and fruit trees within these household compounds.

There are many questions as to the nature of land tenure systems among the Classic Maya (Roys 1943:36, 1957:8–10; Villa Rojas 1961), including an assessment of private versus communally held lands. According to Villa Rojas (1961:22), lands were divided into six categories: (1) state or province, (2) town, (3) *calpulli* or *parcialidad,* (4) nobles, (5) lineage, and (6) special or private (*tierras particulares*). Using data from the petty chiefdoms set up by the Maya in Quintana Roo following abortive attempts at independence following the conquest, Villa Rojas outlines property relationships for the X-Cacal chiefdom in an effort to infer the land-holding arrangement of the ancient Maya from ethnohistoric and ethnographic data. According to Villas Rojas, agricultural lands were communally held, whereas land around each household was considered "private" in the sense that usufruct was granted to the family as long as it was in existence. This land could not be sold because it belonged to the lineage's estate and was managed as such. Villa Rojas (1961:25) writes

> El solar que rodeaba la casa habitación o las huertas plantadas de árboles frutales, se consideraban propios de la familia que los había cercado o plantado, retornando al dominio común en caso de acabarse los miembros de esa familia. En ningún case se podían vender, alquilar ni cambiar, ya que los usufructuarios eran considerados como simples depositarios de un bien común.

The land tenure arrangements of prehispanic Mesoamerican polities concerning public and "private" lands were undoubtedly complex, as indicated by Villa Rojas's work (1961) for the Maya regions as well as by the on-going debate as to the nature of Aztec land holding (Caso 1963; Carrasco 1981; Offner 1981a,b). At Coba during the Late Classic, "improved" or intensively cultivated kitchen gardens would probably have been considered as belonging to the kin group that resided in the adjoining household; their yields, most likely, were controlled by family heads. This arrangement would go hand in hand

with the demonstrated differential access to certain economically and ceremonially important trees such as the *balche* (*Lonchocarpus longistylus*), the
pom (*Protium copal*), and the *pi'im* (*Ceiba aesculifolia*) (Villa Rojas 1961:37–
42; Folan *et al.* 1979).

Garden–orchard space represents only one form of possible agricultural
intensification. Harris (1978:307) states that "we should expect to encounter
evidence for a multiplicity of food-getting activities across the spectrum from
gathering, hunting, and fishing to forms of long-fallow, short-fallow and continuous or 'permanent' cultivation." The potential for *chinampa*-type agricultural intensification at Coba, located in a favorable lakeside environment,
needs investigation as well. Folan (1975) has suggested, among other things,
that pot irrigation was practiced at Coba, using the ubiquitous catchment
ponds. Kintz (1981) has examined the water storage capacity of these numerous *charcos,* or ponds, located, in many instances, in close proximity to household compounds and, in some cases, within house-lot boundary walls. Kintz
(1981) discovered a correlation between the size of the ponds and their associated architecture. That kitchen gardens played an important role in the so-
phisticated and varied agricultural techniques undertaken by the Maya is no
longer questioned (Hammond 1978:31; Harris 1978:310–311; Harrison and
Turner 1978; Puleston 1978:239–240; Rice 1978:58).

We turn to a detailed analysis of gardening in the *solares* of Coba, based
on their size in relationship to the social status of their associated household compound as determined by dimensions of household platforms, presence or absence of vaulted architecture, and compound location vis-à-vis the
downtown area.

SOLARES IN ZONE I AT COBA: ANALYSIS

In Zone I, the northern test area, there exist 144 discrete family compounds with stone house-lot boundary walls. This sample represents less than
half of all households recorded in Zone I. It is assumed, however, that some
household compounds with no evidence of stone walls enclosing *solar* areas
may have been supplied with perishable boundary markers similar to those
seen surrounding households in modern Yucatec towns and villages (Figure
7.3).

The data presented in Table 7.1 include the ranking of *solares* by size,
including area enclosed by the boundary walls, their locations, the dimensions
of platforms associated with *solares,* and the presence or absence of vaulted
architecture as an element of the household compound. These data permit the
testing of Bullard's (1954:20) hypothesis that there exists no relationship between the size of the *solar* and the dimension and social status of household

FIGURE 7.3   Garden boundary marker formed of poles. (Photo by V. Fadziewicz.)

platforms and associated domestic structures. Bullard states

> A specific aim of the 1953 work was to look for correlations between the size of house-lots and the size of elaborateness of house groups, a correlation which would have important sociological implications since the most elaborate houses were probably the residences of the leaders of Mayapan. . . . No evidence was found that the elaborate groups have larger enclosures than the ordinary ones. Some had only small enclosures built along the side of the group, others, although they included dwelling-type structures, apparently lacked house-lot walls completely, a fact which might bear on the interpretation of their function [1954:240].

The questions posed in this analysis of Coba data are (1) Is there a relationship between *solar* and platform size? Does, for example, a large *solar* correlate with a large platform? (2) Is there a relationship between *solar* size and the presence or absence of vaulted architecture? Will, for example, a large *solar* be positively correlated with vaulted architecture? and (3) Is there a relationship between *solar* size and the location of the household compound? Will, for example, large *solares* be found in closest proximity to the downtown area and smaller ones be located further out from the core area?

Initially, to facilitate this analysis, Zone I was divided into geographical

TABLE 7.1 Rank Order of 144 *Solares* by Size: Zone I

Rank	Distance north of Lake Macanxoc (m)	*Solar* area (m^2)	Platform area (m^2)	Vaulted architecture (present/absent)
1	1705–1800	20	130	A
2	1500–1550	20	289	A
3	1050–1100	25	208	A
4	1000–1050	25	418	A
5	2250–2300	25	130	A
6	1000–1050	26	221	A
7	2350–2400	33	644	P
8	2300–2350	38	532	A
9	250– 300	40	572	A
10	1050–1100	40	297	P
11	1550–1600	52	90	A
12	950–1000	55	288	A
13	3850–3900	60	289	A
14	2550–2600	61	296	P
15	900– 950	65	804	A
16	2150–2200	66	151	A
17	2250–2300	70	391	A
18	750– 800	74	306	A
19	3650–3700	81	374	P
20	500– 550	81	130	A
21	1000–1050	84	320	A
22	2450–2500	85	225	A
23	1450–1500	90	221	A
24	1650–1700	90	263	A
25	1600–1650	90	221	A
26	2550–2600	90	289	A
27	2350–2400	91	391	A
28	2200–2250	92	63	A
29	2400–2450	93	70	A
30	3150–3200	96	221	A
31	2200–2250	99	356	A
32	1300–1350	100	872	A
33	1100–1150	105	144	A
34	2700–2750	106	63	A
35	1700–1750	120	359	P
36	2150–2200	120	206	A
37	3850–3900	125	598	A
38	600– 650	126	391	A
39	2200–2250	127	96	A
40	1600–1650	129	220	A
41	2800–2850	130	117	A
42	2750–2800	130	156	A
43	3700–3750	140	195	A
44	1550–1600	150	221	A
45	1600–1650	150	570	A
46	3300–3350	150	117	A
47	650– 700	154	403	A
48	1600–1650	158	368	P

(continued)

TABLE 7.1 (*continued*)

Rank	Distance north of Lake Macanxoc (m)	*Solar* area (m^2)	Platform area (m^2)	Vaulted architecture (present/absent)
49	1050-1100	160	220	A
50	3800-3850	170	391	A
51	3600-3650	171	130	A
52	1800-1850	175	391	A
53	650- 700	200	6020	P
54	2450-2500	258	3374	P
55	3250-3300	259	572	A
56	1900-1950	263	272	A
57	750- 800	271	594	P
58	2950-3000	272	116	A
59	2700-2750	288	566	A
60	2850-2900	300	81	A
61	1100-1150	306	750	P
62	2300-2350	308	221	A
63	1000-1050	309	288	A
64	2650-2700	312	391	P
65	1550-1600	315	598	P
66	3450-3500	319	184	A
67	3150-3200	348	221	A
68	1950-2000	349	242	A
69	1700-1750	355	1305	A
70	350- 400	360	272	A
71	1450-1500	405	1104	A
72	3150-3200	406	865	A
73	2100-2150	426	189	A
74	2500-2550	430	391	A
75	1500-1550	464	130	A
76	1150-1200	483	2000	A
77	1000-1050	493	88	A
78	3800-3850	518	318	A
79	3500-3550	525	120	A
80	3150-3200	531	1085	A
81	3350-3400	536	374	A
82	2000-2050	550	117	A
83	3250-3300	550	598	A
84	3550-3600	550	253	P
85	3800-3850	558	391	A
86	3300-3350	573	272	A
87	3600-3650	633	408	A
88	3200-3250	645	272	A
89	2000-2050	689	408	P
90	3450-3500	690	391	A
91	1900-1950	701	117	A
92	3000-3050	754	323	A
93	1950-2000	804	374	A
94	1850-1900	864	130	A
95	2900-2950	887	642	P
96	1750-1800	890	1136	A

TABLE 7.1 (*continued*)

Rank	Distance north of Lake Macanxoc (m)	*Solar* area (m^2)	Platform area (m^2)	Vaulted architecture (present/absent)
97	1200-1250	900	99	A
98	2900-2950	909	221	A
99	950-1000	914	131	A
100	2250-2300	915	537	A
101	1350-1400	938	552	P
102	2600-2650	952	274	A
103	2050-2100	954	90	A
104	1350-1400	1132	391	A
105	950-1000	1167	1833	P
106	2100-2150	1267	221	A
107	2450-2500	1267	221	A
108	2650-2700	1316	240	A
109	1850-1900	1322	272	A
110	3250-3300	1509	572	P
111	1900-1950	1594	1129	P
112	750- 800	1608	1143	P
113	1100-1150	1630	334	A
114	2550-2600	1702	801	A
115	2650-2700	1750	598	P
116	950-1000	1768	374	A
117	900- 950	1780	572	A
118	1950-2000	1820	636	P
119	1200-1250	1850	1610	P
120	1100-1150	1921	1652	A
121	1850-1900	2038	391	A
122	1300-1350	2142	316	A
123	1650-1700	2155	374	P
124	2050-2100	2286	474	P
125	1500-1550	2302	358	P
126	2900-2950	2410	120	A
127	3600-3650	2663	63	A
128	1000-1050	2666	286	A
129	2450-2500	2757	598	P
130	450- 500	2841	1682	P
131	1700-1750	2927	270	A
132	800- 850	3478	474	A
133	1200-1250	3536	552	A
134	2450-2500	3697	2000	A
135	2900-2950	3697	598	P
136	1100-1150	3786	182	A
137	1100-1150	3834	155	A
138	700- 750	4089	272	P
139	1450-1500	4102	776	P
140	2450-2500	4407	598	A
141	1950-2000	5106	598	P
142	2350 2400	6357	90	A
143	750- 800	7034	882	P
144	750- 800	7160	1810	P

TABLE 7.2 Location of Geographical Units A–G in Zone I

Geographical unit	Distance north of Lake Macanxoc (m)	Area (m²)
A	250–750	193,000
B	750–1250	257,000
C	1250–1750	315,250
D	1750–2250	380,500
E	2250–2800	493,900
F	2800–3350	580,250
G	3350–4100	668,690

units, A–G, composed of seven groups measuring approximately 500–550 m wide and extending north from the shore of Lake Macanxoc to Xmakaba (Table 7.2). A scattergram of *solares* based on distance from the core and their size showed that they fell into three clusters: *solares* smaller than 1000 m² ($N = 103$); *solares* from 1000 to 2999 m² ($N = 28$); and those *solares* larger than 3000 m² ($N = 13$). The most frequent *solar* size is less than 1000 m², and, as reflected in the histogram (Table 7.3), is continuously distributed from the center out to the suburban periphery of the city. Household compounds associated with *solares* larger than 1000 m² are also found in all geographical units from A–G with a decrease noted in units F and G located furthermost from the city center. Although it may be suggested that in less densely populated outer areas the household compounds would have been associated with larger *solares*, barring the possibility of large *solares* bounded by walls of perishable materials, this does not seem to be the case.

A scattergram on the size of the principal household platform associated with the *solares* indicated three clusters of platforms: those smaller than 600 m² ($N = 119$); those from 600 to 1500 m² ($N = 16$); and those larger than 1500 m² ($N = 9$) (Table 7.4). The majority of all household platforms in the sample were smaller than 600 m² and accounted for 82.6% of all household platforms

TABLE 7.3 Distribution of *Solar* Area by Geographical Units A–G, Zone I[a]

< 1000 m²	1000–2999 m²	> 3000 m²
A · · · · · · ·	A ·	A ·
B · · · · · · · · · · · · · · · · · · ·	B · · · · · · · ·	B · · · · · · ·
C · · · · · · · · · · · · · · · · ·	C · · · · ·	C ·
D · · · · · · · · · · · · · · · · · ·	D · · · · · · ·	D ·
E ·	E · · · · · ·	E · · ·
F · · · · · · · · · · · · · · · · ·	F · ·	F ·
G · · · · · · · · · · · · ·	G ·	G Absent

[a] Each asterisk indicates one *solar* area by grouped units. A through G designate geographical units.

TABLE 7.4   Distribution of Household Platforms: Areas Associated
with *Solares* by Geographical Units A-G[a]

	$<600 \text{ m}^2$	$600 \text{ m}^2\text{-}1500 \text{ m}^2$	$>1500 \text{ m}^2$
A	* * * * * *	A Absent	A * *
B	* *	B * * * *	B * * * * *
C	* * * * * * * * * * * * * * * * *	C * * * *	C Absent
D	* * * * * * * * * * * * * * * * * * * *	D * * *	D Absent
E	* *	E * *	E *
F	* * * * * * * * * * * * * *	F * * *	F *
G	* * * * * * * * * * * * *	G Absent	G Absent

[a]Each asterisk indicates one household platform by grouped units. A through G designate geographical units.

recorded in Zone I associated with *solares*. They were also found to be distributed continuously from the area closest to the city center to the outermost area with a slight decrease noted in the suburban periphery. Medium-sized household platforms (600–1500 m²) were located between the area closest to the core, and the outermost area. Those platforms larger than 1500 m² were located in areas closest to the downtown area in units A and B as well as in units E and F. None were recorded in unit G.

In order to retain the sensitivity of the data for additional statistical tests, *solares* smaller than 1000 m² were further subdivided as follows: 20–99 m²; 100–288 m²; 300–690 m²; and 701–954 m². An examination of the relationship between *solar* size and principal platform size (Table 7.5) demonstrated that platform dimension is not a good indicator of *solar* size. Pearson's *r* value of .1387 (significant at the .05 level) shows only a weak positive correlation between *solar* and platform size. The relationship between *solar* size and distance from the center of the city again presents a very weak negative correlation (Table 7.6 Pearson's $r = -.18$, significant at the .01 level). An examination of the relationship between *solar* size and the presence or absence of vaulted architecture (Table 7.7) does, however, demonstrate, contrary to Bullard's (1954) thesis, a statistically significant correlation ($\chi^2 = 13.4155$ with 6 df, significant at the .0369 level) between these two factors. In other words, the relationship between *solar* size and the presence or absence or vaulted architecture is not a random occurrence.

Although the sample consists solely of the 144 residential units with stone house lot walls and excludes the remaining 204 identified household compounds in Zone I, many of the household compounds without boundary walls do, in fact, exhibit vaulted architecture. But contrary to recent statements suggesting a random distribution of structures at Lowland Maya cities (Arnold and Ford 1980), with the total sample of mapped structures at Coba considered, it is clear that a differential ratio of high- to low-status architecture does exist between those residential units close to the downtown areas as compared to those farther out from the center (Folan 1975, 1976; Folan *et al.* 1979;

TABLE 7.5 Pearson's Correlation Coefficient: *Solar* Area and Platform Size in Zone I[a]

Solar area (m²)	Platform area (m²)	Solar area (m²)	Platform area (m²)
20	130	170	391
20	289	171	130
25	208	175	391
25	418	200	6020
25	130	258	3374
26	221	259	572
33	644	263	272
38	532	271	594
40	572	272	116
40	297	288	556
52	90	300	81
55	288	306	750
60	289	308	221
61	296	309	288
65	804	312	391
66	151	315	598
70	391	319	184
74	306	348	221
81	374	349	242
81	130	355	1305
84	320	360	272
85	225	405	1104
90	221	406	865
90	263	426	189
90	221	430	391
90	289	464	130
91	391	483	2000
92	63	493	88
93	70	518	318
96	221	525	120
99	356	531	1085
100	872	536	374
105	144	550	117
106	63	550	598
120	359	550	253
120	206	558	391
125	598	573	272
126	391	633	408
127	96	645	272
129	220	689	408
130	117	690	391
130	156	701	117
140	195	754	323
150	221	804	374
150	570	864	130
150	117	887	642
154	403	890	1136
158	368	900	99
160	220	909	221

TABLE 7.5 (*continued*)

Solar area (m²)	Platform area (m²)	Solar area (m²)	Platform area (m²)
914	131	2142	316
915	537	2155	374
938	552	2286	474
952	274	2302	358
954	90	2410	120
1132	391	2663	63
1167	1833	2666	286
1267	221	2757	598
1267	221	2841	1682
1316	240	2927	270
1322	272	3478	474
1509	572	3536	552
1594	1129	3697	2000
1608	1143	3697	598
1630	334	3786	182
1702	801	3834	155
1750	598	4089	272
1768	374	4102	776
1780	572	4407	598
1820	636	5106	598
1850	1610	6357	90
1921	1652	7034	882
2038	391	7160	1810

[a] r = .1387, significant at .05 level. Reference to Pearson's correlation coefficient taken from Blalock (1972: 376–383).

Folan *et al.* 1982). The number of household compounds, including vaults indicating elite dwellings, decreases as distance from the core increases.

In summary, household *solares* associated with stone house-lot boundary walls in Zone I were often significantly smaller than 1000 m². Those walled areas ranging between 20 and 100 m² most probably served as retaining walls to retard soil erosion from raised garden areas. These were probably formed by humus-rich soils transported by the ancient Maya from the surrounding forest to their household area for this purpose as is done by the contemporary residents of Coba (Folan 1976). These small gardens are sometimes located near catchment basins which would have facilitated irrigation during part of the year. *Solares* smaller than 1000 m² are also associated with household platforms usually smaller than 600 m² that are distributed throughout Zone I, albeit in fewer numbers closest to the core area. This section of Coba is characterized by numerous large, vaulted structures associated with the bureaucratic and religious activities involving Coba's elite, and is, therefore, distinct from residential areas further to the north of Sacbe 1.

There definitely exists a correlation between *solar* size and vaulted architecture. But platform dimensions and the location of a compound do not

TABLE 7.6 Pearson's Correlation Coefficient: *Solar* Area
and Distance North of Lake Macanxoc in Zone I[a]

Solar area (m^2)	Distance north of Lake Macanxoc (m)	*Solar* area (m^2)	Distance north of Lake Macanxoc (m)
20	1750-1800	158	1600-1650
20	1500-1550	160	1050-1100
25	1050-1100	170	3800-3850
25	1000-1050	171	3600-3650
25	2250-2300	175	1800-1850
26	1000-1050	200	650- 700
33	2350-2400	258	2450-2500
38	2300-2350	259	3250-3300
40	250- 300	263	1900-1950
40	1050-1100	271	750- 800
52	1550-1600	272	2950-3000
55	950-1000	288	2700-2750
60	3850-3900	300	2850-2900
61	2550-2600	306	1100-1150
65	900- 950	308	2300-2350
66	2150-2200	309	1000-1050
70	2250-2300	312	2650-2700
74	750- 800	315	1550-1600
81	3650-3700	319	3450-3500
81	500- 550	348	3150-3200
84	1000-1050	349	1950-2000
85	2450-2500	355	1700-1750
90	1450-1500	360	350- 400
90	1650-1700	405	1450-1500
90	1600-1650	406	3150-3200
90	2550-2600	426	2100-2150
91	2350-2400	430	2500-2550
92	2200-2250	464	1500-1550
93	2400-2450	483	1150-1200
96	3150-3200	493	1000-1050
99	2200-2250	518	3800-3850
100	1300-1350	525	3500-3550
105	1100-1150	531	3150-3200
106	2700-2750	536	3350-3400
120	1700-1750	550	2000-2050
120	2150-2200	550	3250-3300
125	3850-3900	550	3550-3600
126	600- 650	558	3800-3850
127	2200-2250	573	3300-3350
129	1600-1650	633	3600-3650
130	2800-2850	645	3200-3250
130	2750-2800	689	2000-2050
140	3700-3750	690	3450-3500
150	1550-1600	701	1900-1950
150	1600-1650	754	3000-3050
150	3300-3350	804	1950-2000
154	650- 700	864	1850-1900

TABLE 7.6 (*continued*)

Solar area (m^2)	Distance north of Lake Macanxoc (m)	*Solar* area (m^2)	Distance north of Lake Macanxoc (m)
887	2900-2950	1921	1100-1150
890	1750-1800	2038	1850-1900
900	1200-1250	2142	1300-1350
909	2900-2950	2155	1650-1700
914	950-1000	2286	2050-2100
915	2250-2300	2302	1500-1550
938	1350-1400	2410	2900-2950
952	2600-2650	2663	3600-3650
954	2050-2100	2666	1000-1050
1132	1350-1400	2757	2450-2500
1167	950-1000	2841	450- 500
1267	2100-2150	2927	1700-1750
1267	2450-2500	3478	800- 850
1316	2650-2700	3536	1200-1250
1322	1850-1900	3697	2450-2500
1509	3250-3300	3697	2900-2950
1594	1900-1950	3786	1100-1150
1608	750- 800	3834	1100-1150
1630	1100-1150	4089	700- 750
1702	2550-2600	4102	1450-1500
1750	2650-2700	4407	2450-2500
1768	950-1000	5106	1950-2000
1780	900- 950	6357	2350-2400
1820	1950-2000	7034	750- 800
1850	1200-1250	7160	750- 800

[a] $r = -0.18$, significant at .01 level. Reference to Pearson's correlation coefficient taken from Blalock (1972: 376-383).

seem to be as significant a factor for predicting the size of a *solar* area. With the exception of unit G, each geographical unit in Zone I included some elite household compounds with a *solar*. Each area also exhibited platforms in all three categories of platform size. Perhaps, as pointed out in Chapter 12, Kintz's analysis of neighborhoods, or wards, can best explain this distribution: elite households are located in all areas of the city serving as nodal points in the regulation of lineage groups or possibly in controlling the production of goods (Wilk 1977). Regulation and integration of the city's population by religious mechanisms was probably an added function of the elite leaders of each neighborhood (see also Folan 1975, 1976; Kintz 1978).

A key variable in determining the amount of land available to city residents for limited crop cultivation is the density, or packing, of the domestic compounds. Although the presence of a small- to medium-sized *solar* would not necessarily preclude swidden-type cultivation in nearby areas outside the house-lot wall, the number of platform groups at Coba that functioned coevally as residential units during the Late Classic are so closely spaced from the

TABLE 7.7   Contingency Coefficient:
Solar Area and Social Status in Zone I[a]

Solar areas (m²)	Vaulted architecture					
	Present		Absent		Totals	
	No.	%	No.	%	No.	%
20- 99	4	2.77	27	18.75	31	21.52
100- 288	5	3.47	23	15.97	28	19.44
300- 690	5	3.47	26	18.05	31	21.52
701- 954	2	1.38	11	7.63	13	9.02
1132-1921	7	4.86	10	6.94	17	11.80
2038-2927	5	3.47	6	4.16	11	7.63
3478-7160	6	4.16	7	4.86	13	9.02
Totals	34	23.61	110	76.38	144	99.99

[a] $x^2 = 13.4155$ with 6 df, significant at the .04 level.

northern edge of the Great Platform out to approximately 2500 m, that an average of only 50 m separates these groups. Construction density was such in this suburban zone encircling the downtown area of the city that insufficient space would have been available for maize cultivation, at least by swidden-type farming techniques.

When comparing these figures on packing from Coba with data from other Classic Maya cities, it is apparent that Coba was at least as tightly nucleated, if not more so, than other major sites from which we have comparable mapped information. Puleston (1973:330), for example, cites spacing of ancient Maya plaza groups at Tikal on plots of land ranging between 0.6 and 1.5 ha. He argues that this land, if intensively cultivated, was enough to support a single family. But, as suggested by Folan (1976: personal communication), it would not have been sufficient to support a regional capital and all its inhabitants without some form of food importation. Puleston (1973:305) also states that intensive dooryard horticulture, or arboriculture, has left unrecognizable traces on the land in the form of the "scattered appearance of structure plaza units even in the immediate vicinity of the site epicenter." A similar pattern is present at Coba for the same reason as that cited by Puleston: the terrain around most household units served as the immediate activity area for domestic-related tasks, including garden and orchard plots and, perhaps, in some cases, cottage industry areas. Other special activity zones which leave almost imperceptible remains also may have been located between these platform groups (both residential and nonresidential). But the use of these areas can only be determined by an examination of the microenvironments within the city by means of spatial analysis coupled with excavation as well as ethnographic analogy. These are the areas Puleston (1973) points out as possible zones of apiculture, quarrying, forest reserves of special-purpose trees, and hunting areas. Folan's (1976) work on prehispanic mining techniques and numerous quarries (*sascaberas*) in the western Zone II at Coba document how quarrying activities, for one, affected the settlement pattern as suggested by Puleston (1973).

CONCLUSIONS

The presence of prehispanic *solares* is evidence that certain postconquest patterns demonstrate considerable time depth. The suggestion that these *solares* were used for the elaboration of gardens and orchards is also supported by ethnohistoric and ethnographic information. It has been argued that with higher population densities now reported for the Late Classic, these gardens and orchards were probably intensively cultivated (Puleston 1973), thereby representing a variant of an infield–outfield system.

This analysis has been an effort to specify some factors affecting the ancient Coba residents' spatial arrangements vis-à-vis subsistence resources. The importance of linear features, especially those which functioned as house-lot walls, lies in their delineation of space available to individual households and the correlation of the archaeological *solar* with ancient food production practices.

At Coba, there exists a nonrandom distribution of *solares* by size and vaulted and unvaulted architecture—contrary to Bullard's (1954) statement on the lack of a relationship between social status and yard size for Mayapan. Thus, while the dimensions of main platforms and compound locations were not strongly correlated with large *solares,* the presence of high-status architecture allows for the prediction of *solar* size.

Additional factors for future analysis include a refinement of the term *elaborateness* to encompass platform volume and the number of structures and ancillary platforms associated with each household compound as well as the area of the main platform (Turner *et al.* 1981). Thus far, however, all evidence suggests that the elite at Coba lived in vaulted structures closer to the heart of the city center and had larger walled compounds than nonelite residents. Following Landa's description (1941:62–63), and assuming that in a society manifesting economic stratification, rich people will live like rich people, we conclude that residential compounds with the largest *solares* are associated with vaulted architecture.

Chapter 8

Coba and Mayapan: A Comparison of *Solares*, Household Variation, Sociopolitical Organization, and Land Tenure

Laraine A. Fletcher

INTRODUCTION

The Coba and the Mayapan mapping projects were undertaken to provide a graphic record toward a better understanding of Maya social organization based, in part, on a comparative analysis of their surface features.

Among the questions we (Fletcher 1978; Folan 1975, 1976) and Bullard (1952, 1954) wished to answer in Coba and in Mayapan concerned the relationship between house-lot boundary walls, the area of the property enclosed by these linear features, and the size and status of their associated household. We also hoped that linear features would provide information on land tenure and urban planning.

Linear features designated as house-lot boundary walls have been mapped at Maya sites prior to (Thomas 1975) and following (Vlcek *et al.* 1978) the extensive mapping project at Coba. However, Mayapan was the first example of an extensively mapped Maya city that exhibited household compounds surrounded by stone walls. Following two field seasons, Bullard (1952, 1954) concluded that the emphasis on the delineation of property boundaries was a relatively late phenomenon among the Maya and that the "reason for this will not be clear until we have more knowledge of Maya settlements and their changes" (Bullard 1954:247). Smith (1962:209) also noted the seemingly unique character of the Mayapan settlement pattern. Since then, however, knowledge of Maya settlement patterns has expanded considerably both on macro- and micro-levels (Harrison and Turner 1978; Ashmore 1981b). Configurations of linear features, their form, functions, and temporal dimensions can now be evaluated more precisely during both the Classic and Postclassic periods of Maya development.

The general pattern formed by linear features over a large area at both Coba and Mayapan is handled by a comparison of a sample unit from Zone I at Coba with several quadrangles mapped by Bullard at Mayapan. The relationship between walls and ceremonial groups is also evaluated at both sites. In addition, the overall residential pattern in the two sample areas is examined to make possible a comparison of household-level organization during the time periods in which these urban centers existed.

In addition to the objectives already mentioned, one of the principal goals of this chapter is to evaluate areas of continuity and disjunction between Coba and Mayapan that are currently a central issue in the diachronic approach to Maya social development (Freidel 1981a:311–312). For example, we will define which cultural components of Maya social organization have persisted through time essentially unchanged and why; also, we will consider which cultural subsystems have been more dynamic than others in responding to various pressures, thereby changing substantially through time.

SAMPLE AREAS: COBA AND MAYAPAN

At Coba, all linear features encountered in Zone I were mapped in addition to other architectural remains. The major portion of linear features in this city represent house-lot walls.

Low boundary or property walls also surrounded most house compounds in Mayapan. These were recorded from an area within approximately 1 km² of the city core area in squares D and K in the northcentral area, and squares Z, AA, BB, DD, and EE in the southwestern sector. Subsequently, linear features in squares H, I, and Q of the Jones's 1952 map were also plotted to provide a larger sample for an in-depth study of these linear features (Smith 1962:Fig. 1). These additional squares were selected because they contained the most information on (1) the lane system, (2) the boundary or house-lot walls, and (3) the ceremonial group at Cenote Itzmal Ch'en. Square Q was specifically chosen because it includes the main ceremonial group at Mayapan and because the plotting of the occurrence of linear features would help determine the association of these features to civic–ceremonial architecture in contrast to the association between linear features and residential architecture.

Fortunately, at Coba, there exist very few modern walls to disrupt the overall prehistoric pattern of linear features. At Mayapan, however, a great number of modern walls (built historically to demarcate swidden-type fields or to serve as cattle enclosures) were found interspersed among prehistoric linear features (Bullard 1954:234). Although fragmentary sections of ancient walls could easily be related to house structures, the complete pattern of ancient walls over a large area was very often difficult to ascertain in this Postclassic center.

It is significant that ancient and modern walls are distinguishable, however. Whereas ancient walls are usually associated with platforms or structures, postcontact walls function as plot boundary markers of swidden-type fields. As such, they are laid out without regard for the configurations of prehistoric features; they cross over house platforms and cut across older wall lines in both Coba and Mayapan (Bullard 1954:237; Folan 1975). At Coba, contemporary field fences generally were constructed by piling up felled bushes and trees. In both areas, however, ancient walls are occasionally used as foundations by contemporary Maya for field fences but without altering their original association with ancient architectural features.

LINEAR FEATURES: CONFIGURATION AND DISTRIBUTION

The data base for linear features in Coba includes all information collected and recorded by Folan during 1974 and 1975 from the 13 zones analyzed by him, as well as the settlement pattern analysis of Zone I by Fletcher and Kintz during 1975 and 1976 to determine their configuration and distribution. For the analysis of linear features in Mayapan, Bullard used similar data available from Jones's map, the Mayapan report (Pollock *et al.* 1962), and the various surveys conducted by Ruppert and Smith (1957) on house types in the environs of Mayapan, Uxmal, Kabah, Sayil, Chichen Itza, and Chac Chob.

House-lot walls are not found with the same frequency everywhere within these two urban areas. In Coba, for example, there exists a paucity of boundary walls in the civic–ceremonial core area; some that do exist in the central plaza are assumed to postdate Late Classic times, according to Folan (1975: personal communication). In the Late Classic, civic–ceremonial complexes outside the core area also lacked boundary walls. This would seem to support Folan's observation regarding their presence in the central plaza.

For example, the complex adjacent to the Cola de Venado Cenote is composed of a total of eight structures, including four vaulted structures, three unvaulted rectangular, and one apsidal structure, but no house-lot wall. That this complex is not associated with a wall probably is due to the type and number of its susperstructures as well as the presence of a prominent *sacbe* leading to the group, plus a large cenote that signals its high status, which is synonymous with barrio-level organization and control.

The walls in Mayapan that are close to the main ceremonial center group as well as those more distant from the core were mapped to determine differences between wall configuration near the downtown area and further out from the center core area. Although the wall system near the core was quite disturbed by modern wall construction, thereby making any comparison to the outer zone inconclusive, the pattern did allow Bullard to state that

> All data clearly indicate that the temples, shrines, colonnaded halls and other ceremonial public buildings did not have associated boundary walls; these walls are almost exclusively associated with residential buildings [1954:242].

Smith noted

> Only near the ceremonial centers are boundary walls lacking around dwelling groups. It has been suggested that these residences may have had some special function in connection with religious centers, such as places for priests or officials to live [1962:208].

An understanding, then, of the relationship of linear features to sacred and secular precincts at both cities is now possible: structures around the main civic–ceremonial groups, as well as those which functioned as smaller, local level, parish-type sacred centers within the city proper, were characterized by a lack of stone house-lot walls.

HOUSE-LOT WALLS AND *SOLARES*

The distinctive features of house-lot compounds from Coba and Mayapan, including their walls and *solares,* are summarized in the following (from Bullard 1954 and Smith 1962:212, 218, 265–266).

1. Houses occur alone, but more frequently in groups.

2. A house group most frequently consists of two or three associated structures. The house groups sometimes are aligned in formal rectangular arrangements, but overall arrangement of structures in a house group varies considerably.

3. The units often include ancillary structures probably utilized as dormitories, kitchens, storage rooms, or shrines.

4. The structures are often found to share a common platform or terrace.

5. Ancillary platforms with no visible superstructures are sometimes found in association with house groups.

6. Considerable variation is present: the two major categories include probable dwellings of elite families and commoner families.

7. Property or house-lot stone boundary walls which enclose ancient house groups are similar to modern house-lot walls; they are dry-laid of large stones set on end with smaller stones set between them.

8. Smaller stone enclosures sometimes lie within an ancient house-lot in a layout similar to those associated with modern house compounds. By analogy, it is probable that they functioned as borders for raised gardens, to retard soil erosion, or as animal pens.

9. Discovery of entrances in the house-lot wall was infrequent. They may have been of the "step-up" kind used in modern Yucatec villages and not easily discerned in the archaeological remains.

10. Houses of the wealthier residents increased in size and number of structures and in degree of elaborateness (indicated at Coba by presence of masonry walls and vaults; at Mayapan by masonry walls, stone columns, beam-and-mortar roofs, and more "Puuc"-like stones).

At Coba, of 488 platforms recorded in Zone I, 271 are associated with some type of linear feature. Of these features, 144 were definable house-lot walls. Although many served as boundary markers between groups, at times some families residing on platforms near major *sacbeob* in Coba and Mayapan used causeways to delineate their *solar* unit.

The comparison of walled enclosures and their associated buildings consisted of a sample that includes unit D, Zone I. This sample area is located approximately 2000 m north of the downtown area. It measures 380,000 m² and is characteristic of the settlement pattern in other areas of Coba in that it displays a variety of household compounds, including walled and unwalled dwelling units as well as elite and nonelite family housing. The Coba sample from unit D contains 24 cases of walled *solares* ranging in size from 20 to 5844 m² with a mean of 1186 m² (943 m² with the area covered by architecture removed) and a median of 781 m² (Table 8.1). There was no modal category.

The sample of walled enclosures and their associated buildings from Mayapan includes squares H and I. It is here that these features were completely mapped and the least amount of postconquest disturbance was noted. Given Smith's (1962: 204–231) detailed description of Mayapan dwelling units, the sample chosen for Mayapan does not seem to deviate from the overall settlement pattern of this urban center. Squares H and I at Mayapan are located in the northeastern sector of the city, approximately 250 m north and 125 m east of the central point of the civic–ceremonial core. They measure approximately 375,000 m². While only a portion of square H is situated within the city wall, approximately 125,000 m² are located outside the wall. Square I, however, is contained completely within the wall.

The *solares* from squares H and I at Mayapan included those household compounds with house-lot walls completely encircling them that Bullard (1954) classified as being entirely of prehispanic construction. Two exceptions were structures 28 and 34 in square I where the closure of house-lot walls was incomplete but predictable. The 30 *solares* included in the Mayapan sample range in size from 104 to 2528 m² with a mean of 845 m² (725 m² with the area covered by architecture removed) and a mode of 708 m². In this manner, a sample of 30 household compounds (Table 8.2) was established for Mayapan that includes 2.7% of the 1100 household compounds recorded there.

In order to determine quantitatively the relationship between *solar* sizes from Coba and Mayapan, the two sample means and standard deviations were calculated initially to include all cases from Mayapan ($N = 30$) and Coba ($N = 24$):

	$\overline{X}$ (m²)	s (m²)
Coba	943	1106 m²
Mayapan	725	514 m²

Although the means between the two samples with all cases included vary by only 200 m², the standard deviations are significantly different (Cochran's C = 0.8227 [Winer 1971: 304–305] and Bartlett's Box F = 14.337 [Winer 1971: 208–209]). It was decided, therefore, to recalculate after removing the two units at the extreme ends of the range from unit D in Coba. The smallest of these samples measures 20 m² and the largest 5106 m².

The rationale for removing these units involves the function of *solares* in Yucatan. Of the 144 *solares* in Zone I, for example, those measuring less than 30 m² ($N = 6$) possibly did not function as *solares* but as restricted-access yard areas, small animal pens, sheltered work or storage areas, or possibly as small raised gardens. These smaller enclosures, therefore, are not comparable to the

TABLE 8.1   *Solar* Units in Unit D at Coba

Platform number	Platform area (m²)	Total *solar* area[a] (m²)	*Solar* area with architecture removed[b] (m²)
Pl. 463	1136	2026	890
Pl. 483	130	20	20
Pl. 490	391	2429	2028
Pl. 517	391	175	175
Pl. 531	272	1594	1322
Pl. 540	130	1042	864
Pl. 558	117	781	701
Pl. 562	1129	2423	1594
Pl. 567	272	263	263
Pl. 578	374	1226	804
Pl. 582	242	600	349
Pl. 585	598	5884	5106
Pl. 596	636	2271	1820
Pl. 607	117	550	550
Pl. 615	408	1174	689
Pl. 630	90	1019	954
Pl. 646	221	1267	1267
Pl. 654	189	426	426
Pl. 660	206	120	120
Pl. 673	151	66	66
Pl. 681	96	127	127
Pl. 687	63	92	92
Pl. 689	356	99	99

[a] $\overline{X}$ Total *solar* area = 1186.4 m².
[b] $\overline{X}$ *Solar* area with architecture removed = 943 m².

TABLE 8.2   *Solar* Units in Squares H and I at Mayapán[a]

Household number	Land occupied by structural features (m²)	Total *solar* area[b] (m²)	Solar area with architecture removed[c] (m²)
17	40	400	360
No number	28	104	76
No number	15	104	89
28	170	1084	914
84	82	492	410
95	351	2064	1713
31	200	708	508
32	102	644	542
83	223	1020	797
12	60	476	416
34	76	412	336
33	149	708	559
71	68	580	512
72	100	644	544
103	195	2528	2333
107	81	1884	1803
69/70	198	916	718
40	132	516	384
67	108	1380	1272
114	225	748	523
112	72	452	380
61	84	476	392
64	100	852	752
9	225	904	679
9a	195	824	629
27	82	1392	1310
5	35	464	429
33	80	1276	1196
37	70	608	538
38	70	708	638

[a] Taken from Smith 1962: Fig. 1.

[b] $\bar{X}$ Total *solar* area = 845 m².

[c] $\bar{X}$ *Solar* area with architecture removed = 725 m².

solar as we define it. The largest enclosed area was removed since its function as a *solar* was questionable for the following reasons. Of the 144 *solares* in Zone I of Coba, only 13 measured larger than 3000 m² with many of these including vaulted architecture recorded in proximity to the downtown zone. Although the household platform in association with the large *solar* in unit D supported vaulted architecture, it is not adjacent to the downtown area. These larger enclosures are limited in number, probably representing special activitity areas and, therefore, are not comparable to other *solares* included here.

The recalculated means and standard deviations with the removal of these two cases from Coba provides the following results.

	$\bar{X}$ (m²)	s (m²)
Coba	795	672
Mayapan	725	514

The means now differ only by 70 m², the standard deviations are less and the variance in the sampling distribution more homogeneous (Cochran's C = 0.6315 and Bartlett's Box F = 1.761).

Although a close correlation exists between *solar* sizes recorded in Coba and Mayapan, it does not follow that *solar* distribution is the same in both cities. For example, some of the smallest walled enclosures in Coba are associated with some of the smaller, commoner dwellings located farthest from the city center. This is the case even though it would seem that people living in this area of Coba would have had more land available to them for *solares* than those living in the more closely packed, inner area of the city. This situation would seem to suggest that low-status families in Coba tended to have smaller walled-in *solares* than high-status families regardless of their location. In contrast to Coba, however, Bullard (1954:240) found for Mayapan that

> the size of individual houselots varies, but usually there is only enough space for a small yard around the building. The amount of available land does not seem to be a factor. Lots are not appreciably larger in the lightly occupied parts of the city than where population was dense, nor in the most isolated groups on the fringes of settlement outside the city than those inside.

This suggests that social differentiation was manifested more through *solar* size in Classic Coba than Postclassic Mayapan.

At Coba, a nonrandom correlation exists between *solar* size and the presence of vaulted architecture in contrast to Bullard's (1954:240) conclusions concerning the lack of an association between *solar* size and elaborate household compounds at Mayapan (see Chapter 7).

It appears as though many urban residents in both ancient Coba and Mayapan possessed considerably smaller walled-in compounds in comparison to modern *solares* in Yucatan estimated by Sanders (1962:88) to average 5000 m². In contrast to Sanders' findings, however, *solares* associated with present-day Coba ($N = 11$) households range only from 375 to 2500 m² with a mean of 1392 m², although there exist few territorial pressures in this recently formed hamlet. The *solares* at Chan Kom (Redfield and Villa Rojas 1934), for example, are also generally smaller than 1000 m² and in both instances, fall more into line with Classic through Postclassic *solar* size than those recent enclosures observed by Sanders (1962).

Obviously, more comparative data are needed on house-lot size before more definitive statements can be made concerning the relationship between *solar* size and sociopolitical factors. It is thought, however, that house-lots would have been more closely spaced in urban centers where land was at a premium and that smaller *solares* would be expected to reflect this packing.

But there is much variation in *solar* size in all stages of Maya sociopolitical development, making a one-to-one correlation somewhat difficult.

HOUSEHOLD COMPOUNDS: COMPOSITION AND DISTRIBUTION

The type and number of superstructures recorded by us in Coba varied, as did the type and number of ancillary structures associated with walled household compounds. The most frequently recorded, however, were those that included two and three superstructures as well as ancillary structures or platforms. There were five cases of household platforms supporting vaulted superstructures among the 24 *solares* chosen for this analysis and three cases of platforms supporting vaulted superstructures but without house-lot walls.

Although at Mayapan there is considerable variation in residential complexes (Smith 1962:Fig. 8), the dwelling units in squares H and I were representative of modest housing arrangements. Although 30 household compounds included in these quadrangles were composed of one to three rectangular structures, most frequent were households formed of two rectangular structures. Moreover, while the number of dwellings in a household group usually varied from one to four, the majority (over 600) of all households mapped at Mayapan include only one structure (Smith 1962:205–206). This represents a typical dwelling for the lower class at Mayapan. Accordingly

> the majority of the people probably lived very simply in their two-room, thatch-roofed houses. Inside their property wall they undoubtedly had a kitchen and possibly another dwelling which housed relatives. Many of them may have had a small altar in the house for family worship, although this may not always have been true, as the poor probably paid less attention to family worship than the nobility [Smith 1962:267].

More than 300 groups consist of two structures; only 35 units include three structures, and approximately three groups, four structures. Thus, whereas larger units (composed of two to three structures as well as ancillary structures and/or platforms) characterized the Coba sample, walled compounds of one or two rectangular structures were most frequent at Mayapan. With some qualifications concerning the problems involved in stipulating how many structures one family would have utilized, I suggest that larger family units predominated at Coba in comparison to smaller units in Mayapan.

If more than one structure is associated with a group in both Coba and Mayapan, one of these is usually more elaborate than the others and, as such, was probably occupied by a family head. Less elaborate, smaller structures were, most likely, those of sons-in-law and their families, servants to the principal family groups, or kitchens and storehouses (Kintz 1978; Landa 1941:40; Smith 1962).

In addition, the presence of vaulted superstructures within walled domestic compounds is evidence of the complex social organization of the Coba neighborhoods described by Kintz (1978). It is not possible, for the sample taken from the Mayapan map, to discern differential status other than that exhibited by compounds composed of more structures than others; however, following descriptions of that city (Freidel 1981a; Smith 1962; Thompson and Thompson 1955), it is known that variation in residential compounds ranged from the plainer dwellings of the poorer, commoner families to the more elaborate dwellings of the wealthy elite (Smith 1962:217–219).

CONCLUSIONS

A comparison has been drawn between the Late Classic city of Coba and the Middle Postclassic city of Mayapan to investigate similarities or possible differences between the organization of the residential zones at the household level. For one, a complex configuration of household walls characterized both cities, although these house-lot walls had been previously considered a Postclassic phenomenon, representing, perhaps, a response to population nucleation with a concomitant demarcation of property on the household level.

The distinctive features of residential units in these cities exhibit parallel spatial organization on the household level. For example, house-lot walls are not found in association with sacred precincts in either city. At Coba, no house-lot walls are associated with the ceremonial complex at Cola de Venado, although house-lot walls surround residential units adjacent to the complex. Similarly, at Mayapan, house-lot walls are not associated with the Cenote Itzmal Ch'en, although residential complexes adjacent to the ceremonial complex do exhibit linear features.

At Coba there is a wider range in the number of structures associated with households (1–11) with the *solar* area of unit D, ranging from 66 to 2286 m^2 with a mean of 795 m^2. In contrast to Coba, the size of the household compound in squares H and I in Mayapan is relatively standard: one to three structures per enclosed unit. But when the area covered by structural remains is excluded from Mayapan, the *solar* area there ranges from 104 to 2333 m^2 with a mean of 725 m^2 as in Coba. Furthermore, the results of the comparisons of means, standard deviations, and the one-way analysis of variance that support the hypothesis of no significant difference between the means of the *solar* areas in the samples from Coba and Mayapan (F ratio = 0.182) lends credence to my suggestion of continuity in household organization from earlier Classic times to just before the conquest. The difference in the number of structures associated with their respective households in Coba and Mayapan suggests different family composition, *solar*-related activities, and perhaps different mechanisms for establishing status in the two cities.

Based on our findings, it has been demonstrated that the residential settlement patterns of Classic Coba and Postclassic Mayapan exhibit several similar features. Although the organization of leadership in the upper ranks of Maya bureaucracy may have differed at times (Freidel 1981a:330–332), it may also be said that, in all likelihood, a land-tenure pattern was operative in Coba during the Late Classic. Land was probably not individually owned but its use was granted by a higher authority to lineage groups as stated for Mayapan.

> The walls mark property boundaries around the house. Evidently each household or family group had its own fenced yard. This does not necessarily imply, however, that there was private ownership of land in the modern sense. Quite possibly, property was held only by permission from a higher authority [Bullard, 1952:38].

Mayapan housed a population consisting mainly of ruling nobles, their families and servants, retainers, merchants, and artisans. These urbanites would have supported the political, religious, and economic infrastructure of the city. In light of the present data documenting the links between kinship, land, and political office, and taking into account variability in the manifestation of these ties, it seems reasonable to assume that property at Mayapan was controlled by the political and religious elite. Usufruct of land was probably granted to individual family groups on a long-term basis (Roys 1957) as is also pointed out by Bullard (1952).

Despite the specified differences between Coba and Mayapan, in agreement with Friedel (1981a:331–332) this analysis lends support to the suggestion that the overall pattern in the organization of commoner domestic space manifested by stone house-lot walls bounding discrete household units seems to have remained fairly constant from Classic through Postclassic times on the Peninsula of Yucatan. Moreover, the characterization of garden cities (full of greenery in the form of kitchen gardens) and urban orchards, used for (1) the cultivation of economically and ceremonially significant items, (2) special preserves for parks, and (3) space for other open-air activities, applies to patterns characteristic of both Classic and Postclassic period centers as described by the Spanish. This leaves open the question of whether the regimentation exhibited by Mayapan dwellings in the tandem plan is actually indicative of a major discontinuity in urban organization, as suggested by Friedel (1981a:315–320). Perhaps one should look elsewhere to explain this architectural innovation developed from Classic through Postclassic to modern times.

Chapter 9

Household Composition: An Analysis of the Composition of Residential Compounds in Coba

Ellen R. Kintz

INTRODUCTION

The Coba Archaeological Mapping Project has recorded data sufficient for a preliminary investigation of household organization in the residential precincts of Coba. These data demonstrate that Late Classic households consisted variously of (1) nuclear families living under the same roof, (2) nuclear families utilizing multiple structures, (3) household units containing an extended family living under the same roof, or (4) multiple structures forming an extended family compound.

The clustering of structures and features recorded by us in Coba include single or multiple occurrences of vaulted and unvaulted structures constructed both on and off platforms. These configurations, as well as the linear features at times serving to delimit *solar* areas, have made possible a more precise construct of large, complex Classic Maya regional center household composition than offered previously (Fletcher 1978).

Elite and nonelite compounds together represent the household range of urban Coba. They exhibit clusters including vaulted and unvaulted buildings on and off platforms; ancillary structures adjacent to platformed structures, altars, shrines; and metates representing food preparation activities. Some areas served both domestic and religious functions (Folan 1975). Although a construct of household organization from settlement data is problematic, this analysis provides, at least, a preliminary evaluation of the residential organization pattern as interpreted in this large civic–religious center.

Haviland (1966), Kurjack (1974), and Stenholm (1973) have discussed problems in defining house-mounds in the Maya area. Willey *et al.* (1965:577) described ordinary house-mounds and *plazuela* groups, whereas Ashmore (1981b) later determined a more precise distinction between formal and informal *plazuela* groups. Drawing a distinction between domestic and/or ceremonial use of these structures also presents a problem. Without excavation, it is risky to assign a function to all of the architectural remains in a residential district. For example, it is difficult to distinguish those structures that may have served as dormitories from buildings that functioned as kitchens, storage units, or other nonresidential related activities (Figure 9.1). Estimating the number of occupants per household in ancient settlements is problematic as there is a general lack of adequate ethnohistoric and ethnographic data on the number of families or persons occupying a household compound (Folan 1975; Puleston 1973; Redfield and Villa Rojas 1934; Roys *et al.* 1940; Stenholm 1973; Thompson 1974; Villa Rojas 1945; Wauchope 1938). If the number of structures associated with a household is any indication of the family size, however, residential group size and composition varied considerably (Kurjack 1974).

Domestic cycle changes are also difficult to evaluate. Although associated structures in a discrete household compound can be interpreted as physical expressions of the domestic cycle, they represent the furthermost extension of

FIGURE 9.1   Kitchen area in present-day Coba. Note the three stones supporting the metal *comal.* (Photograph by V. Fadziewicz.)

this cycle for each unit. At one point, associated structures may have served as nuclear family residences while at other times these same structures and ancillary units may have served the needs of an extended family. This is a pattern still evident in modern-day Yucatec communities, where it is possible to identify ethnographically groups of related buildings and to reconstruct the development of a given household unit from its inception to the end of its growth cycle. This has been done in Chan Kom (Redfield and Villa Rojas 1934) and in Ticul, Yucatan (Thompson 1974).

Despite these difficulties, a distinction can be made between prehistoric compounds that housed small nuclear families and those that housed larger extended family groups in ancient Coba.

ARCHAEOLOGICAL EVIDENCE: THE FORM OF THE HOUSEHOLD

House-mounds in the Maya area are numerous, with the most significant information collected on them, to date, being their remarkable variety (Ashmore 1981b; Bullard 1952, 1954, 1960; Folan, 1975, 1976; Kurjack 1974; Puleston 1973; Stenholm 1973). Three factors mark the variability of household units at Coba: (1) the range in the number of structures associated with the unit, (2) the variation in the size of structures within the units, and (3) the distinction between vaulted and unvaulted architecture.

In general, architectural remains at Coba are similar to those recorded by Bullard (1960) during his northeastern Peten survey. It was here that he located structures built on platforms as well as on terraces. The platforms were, in most cases, rectangular mounds with one axis longer than the other, which supported from one to four structures. More than four structures in a cluster was rare, however.

Large groups similar to these recorded by us in Coba were defined by Bullard (1960) as large household clusters, including small pyramidal type structures utilized as shrines. The Cola de Venado group in Zone I of Coba is such a cluster. It is not readily apparent, however, whether units such as these were dedicated to civic–ceremonial or residential activities, or a combination of both.

Isolated room foundations that supported pole-and-thatch structures are the most numerous architectural features recorded in Coba, whereas vaulted architecture (in association with unvaulted rectangular and apsidal structures) are the least numerous types of dwellings recorded. Although substructural platforms support from 1 to 14 structures, 3 structures are most commonly associated with any given household. It is assumed that the number of structures associated with a domestic unit corresponds to the size of the group that inhabited that household (Tourtellot 1976). It also is probable that the area of the platform involved was directly associated with the potential wealth of the household (Kurjack 1974).

There are platforms in Coba similar to those recorded at Uaxactun that support both vaulted and unvaulted buildings. Wauchope (1934) designated these clusters as representing either minor temple or residential units. Our survey of Coba also defined architectural aggregates that include patterns identified by Tourtellot (1970, 1976) at Seibal. He classified some of the single-structure units at Seibal as barrio shrines associated with burials in the more complex units. These are similar to our findings in Coba and those made by Wauchope (1934) at Uaxactun.

Household complexes in the residential district of Coba that consist of more than one structure are similar also to those at Seibal where Tourtellot (1976) suggests that these multistructural compounds housed extended families. Household units at Coba and Seibal follow the same pattern in that these compounds range from small pole-and-thatch structures to larger, more elaborate units. Small, low platforms exhibiting room foundations in association with larger units at both Coba and Seibal, thought to have been kitchens (Folan 1975; Tourtellot 1976), suggest that a preliminary distinction can be made between multipurpose specialized ancillary structures such as the small temples, domestic shrines, and kitchens recorded in virtually all Maya sites.

Investigations in Coba and in the Rio Bec region (Eaton 1975) provide additional data on household units. The composition of domestic compounds described by Eaton lends support to the contention that household units in Coba (and elsewhere) contained more than one structure, were variable in form, and housed either nuclear or extended family groups.

Walled household compounds and associated structures at Coba are similar to those mapped at Mayapan (Fletcher 1978). The urban character of Mayapan, with its population concentrated around a civic–ceremonial core coupled with the relatively good preservation of its architectural remains, make this city particularly suitable for investigation of Maya household level organization (Bullard 1952, 1954; Pollock 1953:249; Ruppert and Smith 1954; Thompson 1954a; Thompson and Thompson 1955). Ruppert and Smith, for example, excavated an elite household complex bounded by a house-lot wall enclosing an approximately 900-m^2 *solar* area. Five structures were situated within the wall, whereas a single structure was located outside of it.

Another upper-class, four-structure residence, including an *oratorio* excavated by Thompson (1954a), was also situated close to the civic–ceremonial core area of Mayapan. Two smaller structures associated with the complex probably housed dependents and another may have served as a kitchen, a storehouse, or an apiary. The fourth structure was independent of the complex, probably constructed before the other three were built.

Another elite household at Mayapan located less than 100 m from the Temple of Kukulcan probably was the residence of a chief or a priest of outstanding importance (Thompson and Thompson 1955). The large main building seemingly served as the residence of the most important members of this elite family. The long back room contained a small altar. The structure also housed a tomb, and a shrine was recorded in the center of its *plazuela*. An additional structure on the north side of the court faced directly toward the main building. Another structure smaller than the main building perhaps served younger sons and daughters as a residential unit.

It would appear that a close relationship existed between elite and non-elite residences in both Coba and Mayapan. In Mayapan, for example, Thompson and Thompson (1955) suggest that a fairly plain building excavated by them represents the house of the *caluac* (overseer), who served the residents of the main building. Apparently, Landa's (1941:26) statement that the houses of the overseers were farther from the city center than the homes of their masters may not always have been true. The appearance of both vaulted and pole-and-thatch buildings in close association at Mayapan suggests a closer social association between the elite and the nonelite than thought before. This complex also includes a building, located apart from a central shrine, used for religious rites. Although oratories and idols were kept in the houses of lords, priests, and other leaders where they conducted their prayers, made offerings in private, and kept vessels and statues containing the cremated remains of their ancestors (Landa 1941:108, 131), Thompson and Thompson (1955) report that the conservative Maya in Quintana Roo housed crosses or images of saints in a separate family oratory called a *chan iglesia* (small church) or *oratorio* (Villa Rojas 1945:97). Although in modern-day Yucatan the family altar is placed in the home, people traditionally built shrines for their saints outside their residential structures (Redfield and Villa Rojas 1934:131). This would indicate that worship on the household level could have been conducted either in the home or in a separate structure during prehistoric times.

ETHNOHISTORIC EVIDENCE:
RESIDENTIAL PATTERNS

Sixteenth-century Spanish census reports on the Maya emphasize that multifamily residence was the typical household form on Cozumel Island and areas near Pencuyut, Yucatan (Roys *et al.* 1940, 1959). Landa (1941:41) states that households not only consisted of more than one nuclear family, but of more than one residential structure. For example, newly married couples built houses opposite the house of their father or father-in-law (where they lived during the first year of marriage). The analysis by Roys *et al.* (1940) of the 1570 Spanish census reports on Cozumel concluded that either nuclear or extended families could be housed in one structure. Unfortunately, ethnohistorical and ethnographical data reporting on the number of households in a town or village do not necessarily reflect the number of structures occupied by a family. However, archaeological data provide the number of structures

per household without giving membership figures. In other words, the term
household does not necessarily correlate with the term *structure*. A household
frequently contained more than one structure that may have served a variety
of functions. Puleston (1973) argues, however, that while it may be that a
house refers to a household of more than one structure and, therefore, several
nuclear family domiciles, the X-Cacal settlement described by Villa Rojas is
of single structures housing more than one nuclear family.

Sixteenth-century census materials from the partly Christianized island of
Cozumel suggest that the extended family household was common among the
Maya (Roys *et al.* 1940). This may represent an indigenous pattern of several
families living in a single structure as suggested by Puleston (1973), a pattern
that had been abolished by the Spanish elsewhere in Yucatan. The sixteenth-
century census rolls (San Miguel and Santa Maria, Cozumel) provide information on the names of married couples, widowers, widows, and most older
children in the settlements. Each house was said to contain the head of a family,
his wife, and from one to seven other married couples. A letter from Fray
Lorenzo de Bienvenida to Felipe II written in 1548 seemingly supporting this
model states

> Your Highness shall know that in this land there is hardly a house which contains only
> a single *vecino* [citizen or householder]. On the contrary, every house has two, three,
> four, six, and some still more; and among them there is one paterfamilias, who is head
> of the house [Roys *et al.* 1940:14].

Although the census material does not indicate the relationship or connection between the different families living in the same household, certain possibilities can be suggested by comparing their surnames. Maya sons and
daughters inherit their father's surname and a woman retains her own patronymic after marriage; a man bearing the same patronymic as that of the
head of the house could be his brother, son, or nephew. A woman with such
a name might be the head's sister, daughter, or niece. A man bearing the
patronymic of the household head's wife could be her brother or her nephew;
in the case of a woman, her sister or her niece. In many households, we also
find married couples listed where neither spouse has the patronymic of the
head of the family nor that of his wife. In some elite households, those individuals not sharing the same patronymic may have been unrelated retainers
or servants. In that there is no indication of these peoples' status, it will be
difficult to form an adequate picture of Maya social organization in preconquest times.

The analysis by Roys *et al.* (1940) of the 1570 data from the island of
Cozumel and the census information from Pencuyut collected in 1583 demonstrates that two patterns of residential organization were in effect among
the sixteenth-century Maya. Unlike the pattern of multiple-family single structures found at Cozumel, the pattern at Pencuyut consisted of a multiple-family
household with members living in a cluster of smaller buildings, according to

Spanish decree. In contrast to the residence patterns at Cozumel where no house with less than two married couples was found in 1570, the residence pattern at Pencuyut in 1583 consisted of many residential units with less than two married couples living in the same structure.

There exist, however, only a few archaeological examples of Maya household units that consist of but one structure. Archaeological evidence tends to indicate multiple structures were supported on platforms organized around a courtyard. Present-day Maya families also develop multistructural household units, including buildings used variously as dormitories, cook houses, or storage and ancillary sheds for various domestic activities. The number of structures associated with a household usually depends on the length of time the couple has been married and their accumulated wealth. Although household compounds that consist of few structures probably represent nuclear family households, those formed of multiple structures probably represent extended family units in one stage of their domestic cycle. Smaller and even less complex units were probably the domiciles of newlywed couples. Furthermore, lower-class housing would tend to be identified more with smaller compounds. Lower-class newlyweds who break away from the natal household would probably have been associated with the simplest households, whereas established, wealthy families would occupy larger and more complex compounds.

ETHNOGRAPHIC EVIDENCE: THE COMPLEXITY OF THE RESIDENTIAL PATTERNS

Resident patterns discernible in the village of Chan Kom (Redfield and Villa Rojas 1934) document the complexity of the household unit. Although the prevalence of nuclear families in the village may reflect the pioneer nature of this community, the ideal organization of family units is expressed by the people to be the extended family. However, this extended pattern of household organization was seldom realized in Chan Kom where the prevailing family type was an economically independent, small, parental family. Few extended families lived together to form a cooperative economic unit and many newlywed couples lived in a separate home.

Larger family units in Chan Kom consisted of a married couple and their children and, in some cases, an unmarried relative of a spouse. There were 10 families in Chan Kom that were exceptions to small and simple households: (1) three housed the spouses and children of two brothers; (2) four households were composed of one or more married sons under the parental roof; (3) one housed a married brother and a married sister; (4) a daughter and her husband lived with the wife's parents in another household; and (5) in the last case a married uncle and his brother's married son lived in one household. In all cases, the households are composite, or multiple family, households. All the families were economically independent: each couple kept its property separate from the others. They did, however, contribute to a common kitchen (Redfield and Villa Rojas 1934).

An exception to the norm at Chan Kom was the existence of one extended family unit that functioned as a household unit during Redfield and Villa Rojas's fieldwork (1934) there and a second family that was undergoing dissolution. The first family consisted of a man, his wife, seven unmarried children, three married sons, and the wives and children of these couples. This group constituted a 19-person household as well as a single economic unit. These two families were headed by two of the prominent elders in the village. They were pioneers in the founding of the community and distinguished by wealth, property, and moral character (Redfield and Villa Rojas 1934:87–91).

Two factors are significant in the enumeration of familial organization in the village of Chan Kom. The Maya household organization was variable, including a range in family organization from simple, nuclear families to complex extended families; the residential district of ancient Coba also shows distinct variability in the configuration of household units. In the second place, the extension of the family to include a large number of members was associated with wealth, property, moral character, and esteem. In other words, larger household units in ancient Coba (and elsewhere in the Maya area) probably were correlated with wealth, property, and high status, and smaller households with a comparative lack of these qualities.

One of the most important studies on household composition in Yucatan was conducted in Ticul, which

> is a community of merchants and corn farmers, and of a thousand craftsmen who labor in a multitude of small workshops, producing shoes, hats, and pottery for a broad regional market. It is also the *cabecera,* the head town of a county-like *municipio,* and maintains jurisdiction over the affairs of local government of some 2,000 rural dwellers, the inhabitants of nearly forty small communities scattered over the municipality [Thompson 1974:1].

Ticul functions as an economic, political, and demographic center in Yucatan. In this respect, it is not unlike Coba operating some 14 centuries earlier. The organization of the *solar* in Ticul and the conventional dwelling compound of families clearly show variation in modern households. This unit may consist of a nuclear family or an extended kin group composed of three or four generations of partrilineally related kinsmen who form an economically interdependent household unit with their spouses and children. This unit is the

> spatial locus of domestic group process, the place where families grow and fission over time, where each successive generation cycles through recurrent phases of expansion and contraction, with each phase producing a characteristic family composition that differs from that of all other phases in the process [Thompson 1974:27–28].

The documentation of each phase of domestic organization at Ticul (Thompson 1974) as different from any other phase has implications for the reconstruction of household units in ancient Coba. The household clusters apparent in the residential zone at Coba reflect the organization of the family groups at only one period in time: the most extended period previous to abandonment of the house site. This point in time represents, however, only one phase of the domestic cycle.

HOUSEHOLD COMPOSITION OF ANCIENT COBA

The analysis provided here focuses on the organization of the household in ancient Coba, based on Zone I survey data. These data include all structures located north of the great artificial platform that supports the Coba Group B (Thompson *et al.* 1932).

Archaeologic, ethnohistoric, and ethnographic research demonstrates that Maya households most frequently consisted of more than one structure. These buildings were used as shrines, sleeping quarters, kitchens, storage houses, or animal pens. There exist 356 platform and/or structure clusters hypothesized to have functioned as household units in Zone I of Coba. These units were associated either by being encircled within a house-lot wall or located 30 m (or less) from the main platform group and isolated from any other group. These clusters were categorized into three classes:

1. Platforms supporting structure foundations. These platforms were sometimes associated with others (with and without apparent structure foundations) or with structures adjacent to the main platform.

2. Clusters of structures without substructural platforms but associated with platforms supporting no apparent structure foundations.

3. Clusters of structures with neither substructural platforms nor associated platforms.

Clusters with vaulted architecture were considered elite households ($N=57$). Clusters including unvaulted rectangular and/or apsidal buildings were classified as commoner households ($N=229$). The tabulation of these two household types reflects the pyramidal organization of Maya society with the few households associated with vaulted buildings occupying positions at the top of the social hierarchy, in comparison to numerous commoner households without vaulted architecture in all residential districts at the bottom of the social hierarchy.

Analysis: Structures and Their Function

The breakdown of household units by the number of structures associated with each compound is shown in Table 9.1. Although no complete interpretation of household organization can be finalized prior to the excavation of these complexes, spatial analysis enables us to offer an interim definition of household units.

The 73 clusters of one-structure households in Zone I probably represent small, nuclear families split from larger units. Only four units with vaulted architecture occur as single structures. A house-lot wall and metate are associated with one of these and apparently represent a simple household of elite status. Another unit has a metate but no house-lot wall and is also considered an elite residential unit. Two units with no house-lot wall nor any metates are not considered residential structures and probably served as local shrines or burial mounds.

Of the 83 household units with two associated structures only two (2%) include structures of the same size. The difference in size probably indicates that they also functioned differently. Although it is possible that some of these units housed extended families, it is more likely that the two structures were used as a dormitory and a kitchen. Both structures could have served as the loci of other household activities as well (Folan 1978: personal communication).

It is significant that a cluster of three structures ($N=88$) represents the most frequent class of commoner compounds. They housed a nuclear family, a cooperative family (possibly sisters and/or brothers), or parents and married children. These structures would have been used for sleeping, eating, and storing household goods. Seventy-five units were composed of buildings of various sizes. It is suggested that these buildings were used for different purposes. Thirteen (15%) included two structures of the same size. If structures of the same size performed the same function, then 15% of those units with three

Table 9.1   Breakdown of Household Units by the Number of Structures Associated with Each Compound

Number of associated structures	Elite household	Commoner household	Total
1	4	69	73
2	6	77	83
3	9	79	88
4	7	32	39
5	12	28	40
6	5	7	12
7	4	6	10
8	5	0	5
9	0	0	0
10	1	1	2
11	1	0	1
12	0	0	0
13	1	0	1
14	1	0	1
15	1	0	1
	57	299	356

structures had either two sleeping rooms, two kitchens, or two storage rooms. Of the 13 households that had two structures of the same size, seven had smaller buildings and one larger structure, whereas six households had larger buildings with a single smaller structure. The data on households with two associated structures of the same size in a cluster of three buildings indicate the addition of either a small kitchen, storeroom, or a large dormitory. The added structure could have been used for sleeping quarters. If it were larger, the additional members added to the household would be socially equal to those occupying the original structure (space per person remaining equal). If the structure were smaller, the number of additional members added would have been of a lower status. The smaller units may have housed newly married sons or daughters or may have housed an overflow of children that could not be accommodated in the original sleeping quarters.

Of the 39 units consisting of four associated structures, 10 (26%) included several structures of the same size. Of the 10 units, two were larger structures of equal size and seven intermediate size structures of the same size. Only one unit was composed of two large structures and two small structures of the same size. The largest structure in the unit is considered to have been the head of the household's dormitory. The intermediate rooms are thought to have been the sleeping quarters of the head of the household's married children. The smallest rooms associated with the unit were either kitchens or storage rooms with other combinations of structures and functions possible.

Of 40 units with five associated structures, 13 (33%) include some structures of the same size, one unit has larger structures of the same size, 10 units have intermediate-size structures, and two units have smaller structures. The larger rooms in the complex probably represent the sleeping quarters of the household head; intermediate structures were occupied by members of the extended family, and the smaller structures were kitchens and/or storerooms.

Of the 12 units with six structures, nine (75%) included some structures of the same size. Nine units had seven structures; six (67%) included structures of the same size. The pattern of compounds with six or seven structures is similar to the organization of the three-to-five-structure households already discussed. The spatial organization of larger household units indicates they could have housed extended families.

There were 11 households with more than seven associated structures. Six households associated with vaulted architecture include metates, thus indicating a domestic function. Although one compound has no metates, it does not exhibit special architectural or spatial features, indicating a non-residential function. Three other clusters apparently served civic or ceremonial functions. They are large, complex units, including vaulted architecture built on high substructural platforms, and located in close proximity to either the core area or in a similarly advantageous location such as adjacent to a major *sacbe*. It is possible that these platforms served dual functions as civic-ceremonial areas and elite residential units. Only one of these did not include an example of vaulted architecture, perhaps representing the domicile of a wealthy, extended, commoner family.

Analysis: Household Membership

It has been suggested that the Maya lived in extended family units in single-house dwellings (Roys *et al.* 1940, 1959). To test this hypothesis at ancient Coba, the roofed-over area for all households was calculated and combined with Naroll's (1962) figure, estimating that each person required approximately 10 m^2 of space within residential units on a worldwide basis.

In this manner, it was determined that roofed-over space in household units of one structure measured 1803 m^2. Using Naroll's (1962) 10:1 ratio, the 73 single-structure units would have housed a total of 180 persons. By accepting this figure, the average number of persons per household at Coba would have numbered only 2.5 people, representing at most a small nuclear family. There were only three single-structure households with 50 m^2 or more of roofed-over space in our sample. In only one case did a unit include up to 78 m^2 of space. This sample contained a vaulted structure and metates, and may have housed an extended elite family located near the center of the city. The remaining one-structure components either served as shrines or in some other capacity as suggested by Tourtellot (1976) for Seibal.

Compounds with two associated structures were analyzed to determine whether they were used predominantly by nuclear or extended families. Roofed-over space in households with two structures measured 3997 m^2. Using Naroll's (1962) ratio, these units could have housed 399.7 persons. In the northern test zone at Coba, there exist 83 household units that had two structures. Family size, based on Naroll's calculations, would have been 4.8 people per household, thus more or less representing the size of a Maya nuclear family. In 7 cases out of 83, one structure of the two was large (50 or more m^2); two household units had two larger structures as well as vaulted architecture. Of the 83 units with two structures, four more included vaulted architecture large enough to have housed an extended family. Of the 83 two-structure units, two without vaulted architecture (representing commoner households) included one large structure and therefore could also have housed an extended family. But the majority of two-structure households in Coba that include small structures probably represent nuclear family units.

The category of three-structure households is considered to have had the potential to house nuclear or extended families. Roofed-over space totaled 6928 m^2. Using Naroll's (1962) calculation, 692.8 people could have been housed in these structures. In the northern test zone at Coba, in the 88 units with three structures, the average household membership would have been 7.9 persons. The permutations of 7.9 persons per household are numerous. Nine units represent elite households with vaulted architecture and 79 were commoner households. Of the nine households with vaulted architecture, seven included large structures (50 m² or larger). Five of the seven included metates, thereby suggesting that they were residential. The remaining two had no metates but their function is assumed to have been residential on the basis of spatial analysis. These two were located, in one case, south of Sacbe 1 adjacent to Sacbe 3, and the other is approximately 4 km north of the Coba Group B and adjacent to Sacbe 27, thus suggesting that both may have been multifunctional, serving as either administrative or ceremonial units. Of the 79 commoner dwellings, the seven including large structures (50 m² or larger) are thought to represent wealthier commoner households in Coba.

Analysis: Structure Size

It is hypothesized that the size range of structures associated with household units would permit the assignment of function to individual structures. Again, using data from Zone I, the vaulted structures there range in area from 9 to 145 m²; with a mean area of 58.61 m² and a mode of 65 m². Rectangular, unvaulted structures range in area from 5 to 182 m²; with a mean of 37.6 m² and a mode of 36 m². Apsidal rooms range in area from 1 to 63 m²; with a mean of 19.90 m² and a mode of 20 m².

Size and use of structures are considered interdependent variables. Sixteen platform groups in the northern test zone at Coba support more than one vaulted structure (Table 9.2). In all but two cases, the size of all vaulted structures within the same unit differed. These variations probably signify differential use of structures by household members. The most prestigious architecture may have served as residential structures as well as shrine buildings similar in function to those described by Thompson (1954a) at Mayapan.

A similar pattern of structural size variation was also exhibited by groups of rectangular, unvaulted, and/or apsidal structures. The area of rectangular structures had a modal measurement of 36 m², but two other classes with areas of 21 and 50 m² also exhibited high frequencies ($N=31$ and $N=27$, respectively). The distinction between these may represent utilization of the structures by three different social groups.

Differences in structure size also indicate differential use of structures contained in the same household unit. Areas of unvaulted rectangular structures were investigated to determine if any pattern could be discerned. Of 18 households, including only unvaulted, rectangular structures, 14 included rectangular structures of different sizes while four had structures of the same size. Of the four, only two structures were of the same size; additional structures were either larger or smaller.

The area of apsidal structures associated with household complexes varied from 1 to 63 m². If size alone is significant in determining functional possibilities, this would indicate a wide range of primarily domestic functions for these structures including shelter.

The argument that structure area helps to define use is supported by the

Table 9.2 Area of Vaulted Structures by Household

Platform number	Number of vaulted structures	Area of vaulted structures (m^2)
1	3	70, 110, 120
8	2	15, 48
18	2	60, 65
24	4	85, 102, 126, 145
90	3	52, 54, 54
232	3	32, 36, 55
290	2	36, 65
329	3	24, 55, 65
375	3	40, 55, 60
432	2	28, 65
492	4	28, 32, 40, 80
562	2	36, 63
968	8	45, 50, 50, 63, 65, 85, 115, 138
1023	3	24, 32, 65, 115
1096	2	9, 85
1340	2	50, 65

spatial configuration of households in Chan Kom (Redfield and Villa Rojas 1934: Figure 9) where household structures are not only of different sizes but are used differentially. This pattern was later observed in the modern village of Coba (Folan 1975). Thompson (1954a) noted that the household complex excavated at Mayapan also exhibited a similar pattern.

CONCLUSIONS

The analysis of the data collected in the northern test zone at Coba is fundamental for the reconstruction of the Maya household unit and its organization. This analysis provides a base for the determination of household membership and a more precise reconstruction of the demographic parameters of the ancient city.

Household organization studied from Zone I at Coba exhibits a pattern suggesting that the favored household composition was the extended family living in households of 3 to 15 associated structures. Of the household units with over 7 associated structures, all (save one) include vaulted architecture. This indicates that those units formed by larger platforms, more structures, and elite architectural construction, served as elite residences and/or as civic–ceremonial areas, whereas household units without vaulted architecture served as common residences.

The archaeological, ethnohistoric, and ethnographic evidence documents that the typical Maya household unit consisted of more than one structure. This observation is supported by data on residential household complexes in Zone I at Coba where structure size correlates with structure function as in the case of modern-day Yucatec household patterns. In other words, the head of the household occupies the largest structure whereas kitchen and store-rooms are smaller. The married children of the head of the household occupy intermediate-sized units signaling their subordinate position to the head.

The preceding construct of the household unit in Coba based on spatial analysis has served to evaluate the organizational pattern of the residential population at a large Maya center, thus providing us with further insights into the sociopolitical and demographic past of Coba and other cities located throughout the Maya area.

Chapter 10

Cottage Industry
and Guild Formation
in a Classic Maya
Metropolis

Ellen R. Kintz

INTRODUCTION

One of the most significant factors in the growth of an urban center is the ability of the labor force to produce economically valued items for internal consumption and external trade. Therefore, lowland Classic Maya centers, now known to be large and complex in form and function, must have included economic production as one of their major activities.

Surveys of Classic Maya cities have documented the large variety of craft items produced by them. Beyond the unskilled labor force necessary for the construction of monumental centers, architects and engineers planned the city and its buildings while stone cutters labored in the quarries (Folan 1978a:75–79). Plaster was made and applied to the buildings, murals were drawn by artists, and stelae were carved by sculptors, while pottery, feathered headdresses, ankle adornments, animal skin cloaks, necklaces, cloth for clothing, musical instruments, masks, and other ritual as well as political symbols were produced for the ultimate benefit of the elite (Adams 1970:487–550; Becker 1973:396–406).

Maya centers like Coba, Tikal, Bonampak, Seibal, Dzibilchaltun, Palenque, and Copan were not only political and religious centers but economic and production centers as well. This is evidenced by their size and settlement pattern as well as the specific style and adornment of their architecture and associated material culture.

Much has been written on the social organization of the enigmatic Maya

149

(Chapman 1957; Coe 1965; Fletcher 1978; Fletcher and Kintz 1976; Folan 1975 1976, 1977b, 1978c; Folan *et al.* 1979; Hammond 1972, 1975; Harrison 1968; Haviland 1965, 1966, 1970a; Kintz 1978; Kurjack 1974; Landa 1941; Marcus 1976; Morley 1956; Pollock *et al.* 1962; Proskouriakoff 1961; Puleston 1973; Roys 1943, 1957; Thompson 1954b, 1970; Vogt 1964; Wilk 1977; Willey *et al.* 1965), but until now, insufficient data have been compiled for an in-depth study of their economic production. The focus of this chapter is an analysis of the residential districts that surround the Coba core area to define, in a preliminary way, the location and form of economic production and specialization practiced there on the household, neighborhood, and ward level as part of two basic production units: cottage industries and guild organizations.

Descriptions of economic activities in preindustrial cities as well as production in less complex societies reveal that the social configuration of these units share certain similarities on a worldwide basis (Burgess 1928; Calnek 1974; Chitra 1948; Millon 1976; Miner 1953; Prem 1974). Data on the spatial configuration of productive units are, however, rarely reported. Some exceptions are the results of a massive Teotihuacan mapping project suggesting that craft specialists lived as well as produced their wares in the same compounds (Millon 1976; Spence 1981). Over 500 workshops have been located in the residential precincts of this ancient city (Millon 1976). Sanders (1965) has suggested that the Teotihuacan population was organized by kinship units forming small wards such as those reported for the Aztec capital of Tenochtitlan (Calnek 1976). Larger units were probably organized as *calpullique*. Adams (1966:90) also hypothesized that during the Early Classic period at Teotihuacan localized concentrations of obsidian debitage and ceramic material points to a correlation between kinsmen, residential groups, and craft production.

Folan's (1981d) settlement pattern analysis of the Early Postclassic civic–religious center of Huamango, Municipio de Acambay, Estado de Mexico, also located numerous workshop areas within its core area. One of the largest of these was situated behind the principal ceremonial–religious structure next to what appears to have been the residential area of the priest, who seem to have had a foot in both sacred and secular activities in this Otomi community.

Although much controversy exists over the structure of the *calpulli*, Calnek (1974:194), Ixtilxochitl (1952:187), Monzon (1949:50–51), and Prem (1974) suggest some correlation between household, neighborhood, and ward and craft production units in highland pre-Columbian settlements. Calnek (1974) equates *calpulli* production units with a guild structure, although he concludes that more data are required to ascertain the sociological implications of these organizations. These craftsmen of the royal palace represented the master craftsmen probably drawn from wards throughout the city. Adams states that in Tenochtitlan

> *capullis* frequently specialized in certain crafts and professions, providing a characteristic guild-like aspect to craft production. Ixtilxochitl speaks . . . of more than 30 crafts

practiced by the inhabitants of Tenochtitlan, each with its own quarter—a view whose exclusiveness is challenged by other authorities [1966:89].

According to Carrasco (1971), ward divisions in the Aztec capital housed traders, craftsmen, and farmers. In some, a single craft item was produced while in others a variety of items were manufactured; all this activity emphasized that craft production took place not only in the palace but also in the wards of highland Mexican towns and horticultural areas outside the city core area.

Research at Tikal (Coe 1962:502–503) included the investigation of 45 small structures in the residential zones northeast of the Great Platform. Some of the structures thought to represent workshop areas were associated with quantities of flint objects or flakes. In another area of the Maya Lowlands, the results of investigations at Colha (Hammond 1974a; Hester *et al.* 1980; Wilk 1977) also concluded that major flint-working areas were interspersed among the elite and commoner households in the residential precincts. Possibly, elite families residing in these areas controlled the production, marketing, and transportation of goods produced there (Wilk 1977).

Miner's study (1953) of preindustrial Timbuktu, Mali, West Africa, demonstrated that ethnic barrios were traditional craft production areas. Craftsmen were organized into hereditary guilds of slippermakers, tailors, and masons. The guilds were maintained by supernatural sanctions, physical force, popular consensus, and the right to select apprentices. This description is not unlike that of the *calpulli* in ancient Mexico. It is hypothesized that this type of economic organization is typical of preindustrial cities including Classic Maya urban centers. Trade stimulated the importation of raw materials and the manufacture of goods for exportation. The production units were organized on the basis of kinship. Craftsmen related to one another lived in extended households, neighborhoods, or barrios as segregated groups and worked together as such.

ANCIENT COBA: A COMPLEX OF WARD, NEIGHBORHOOD, AND HOUSEHOLD

The Classic Maya center of Coba is well known for its complex system of *sacbeob* radiating out from the city center to elite residential groups (Machukani and Xmakabah on the periphery) as well as to large outposts (Ixil and Yaxuna located far beyond the periphery) at the limits of the regional state. Household units located between the *sacbeob* within the urban areas of Coba that we investigated presented a unique opportunity to test for the internal segmentation of the city into geographically discernible ward, neighborhood, and household units (Folan 1975, 1976).

The architectural remains of residential precincts inhabited by the Maya include vaulted and unvaulted structures as well as platforms with and without apparent superstructures. Although the original form of both the vaulted and unvaulted structures is readily inferable, platforms without apparent super-structures offer no clues regarding their above-floor construction. It is as-sumed, however, that they may have been roofed-over with *guano* like many contemporary Yucatec structures, yet lacking the pole walls characteristic of the modern Yucatec dwelling (Figure 10.1).

Data Summary

If the form of economic production in Coba was based on a cottage-in-dustry concept, the constellation of features associated with its household units should reflect those economic activities. It is hypothesized that platforms with no apparent room foundations represent loci of economic specialization in Coba, and that their distribution would reflect economic specialization in the form of cottage industries and/or guild formations.

It is assumed that both elite and nonelite households participated in the production of various commodities in Coba, and that settlement pattern data from all residential districts should support the view that production occurred not only near palace structures in the core area of the city but also in the residential zones surrounding the core (Figures 10.2 and 10.3).

My initial analysis of platforms with no apparent structural foundations focused on Zone I where 157 of these platforms were mapped within various contexts. Whereas 26 of these platforms occurred in association with 17 elite compounds, 69 formed part of 60 commoner households.

Of the 26 platforms with no apparent superstructures associated with the 17 elite compounds, 7 of these comparatively small compounds were com-

FIGURE 10.1   Present-day houses in Coba showing *guano* roofs and pole walls. (Photograph by V. Fadziewicz.)

FIGURE 10.2 Metates, perhaps representing a cottage-industry complex in the residential zone of Coba. (Photograph by V. Fadziewicz.)

FIGURE 10.3 A tailor, an example of cottage industry in present-day Coba. (Photograph by V. Fadziewicz.)

posed of one to three structures whereas 10 are comparatively larger compounds of 4 to 15 associated structures.

Of the 69 platforms with no visible superstructures associated with commoner household units, as many as 43 of the smaller households composed of one to three structures were associated with platforms with no visible superstructures, whereas only 16 larger commoner households composed of four to eight structures were recorded with similar platforms.

Platforms with no apparent superstructures were located both south and north of Sacbe 1 in Coba in association with elite households. For example, the four platforms with no visible superstructures associated with elite compounds situated south of Sacbe 1 and close to the core area were assumed to represent workshops. They were directly attached to larger platforms supporting vaulted architecture that housed elite members of the society. In a similar manner, the 22 platforms with no visible superstructures recorded north of Sacbe 1 outside the core area (in association with elite household compounds) were also assumed to represent workshops directly attached to elite household units similar to those to the south of the same sacbe.

Of the 17 elite compounds, including platforms with no visible superstructures, the seven relatively smaller units suggest that these households served upper-class, nuclear family groups. The 10 larger units, however, ranging from

4 to 15 structures, are assumed to have housed larger social groups including extended elite families and their servants. The occurrence of platforms with no visible superstructures associated with both small and large elite households would further demonstrate the occurrence of economic specialization among both nuclear and extended elite family units in Coba whether located close to the core or toward the periphery of the city.

In contrast, the majority (N = 43 or 72%) of the smaller commoner households grouped with platforms with no visible superstructures were composed of only one, two, or three associated structures that, presumably, housed lower-class, nuclear family groups. The 17 larger commoner households associated with platforms with no visible superstructures were composed of four or more associated structures, probably representing larger lower-class extended family groups. This, as in the case of the elite households, seems to suggest the occurrence of economic specialization among both nuclear and extended commoner family units in Coba.

Of the total number of platforms with no visible superstructures, 39% (N = 60) were found in relative isolation. The platforms included two or three of these units in six locations and could have served as storehouses, interbarrio marketing areas, local administrative or religious gathering points, or loci for workshops involved in the production of commodities. In a like manner, it is also thought that the 32 platforms with no visible superstructures located in relative isolation in the area 2800–4100 m north of Lake Macanxoc probably do not represent craft production sites. They are not associated with residential units, do not cluster as guild formations are prone to do, and are situated in the lower-class precincts of the city that housed very few craftsmen. Therefore, it is thought that these platforms may have served to store goods.

Six other platforms with no visible superstructures occurring in relative isolation adjacent to Sacbeob 3 and 27 may have served as toll stations or for storing goods entering or leaving the city, because their architectural configuration is not similar to the association of these type platforms to either household or guild forms.

One significant factor resulting from this analysis is the discovery of considerable variation in the contextual occurrence of platforms with no visible superstructures. As demonstrated, they may occur as part of elite and commoner households in the residential precinct of Coba or in clusters of two or three units isolated from other architectural features. In some cases, they are found adjacent to major *sacbeob* or occur singly in relative isolation, dispersed throughout the residential zone.

There appears to be considerable variation in the organization of households associated with platforms with no visible superstructures. If these platforms represent loci of economic specialization, then they represent a broad variation in the status of individuals involved in the production of goods. For example, those platforms associated with elite compounds seem to be distributed among the larger more often than the smaller compounds. However, the total number of larger commoner households with platforms with no apparent superstructures is smaller than the total number of smaller commoner households with these platforms. Only 17 of 60, or 28%, of the commoner households with platforms with no apparent superstructures were larger units, possibly housing extended families. In contrast, 72% of the commoner households with platforms exhibiting no apparent superstructures include only one to three associated structures possibly housing nuclear families. It would seem, that larger elite and smaller commoner households were those most often recorded with platforms exhibiting no apparent structures. It is argued, therefore, that if these units mark the location of craft production, this could mean that large elite compounds controlled these activities to their economic advantage while smaller commoner households found it necessary to supplement their income by handicraft production.

The association between households and platforms with no apparent superstructures also appears in the 12 additional zones surveyed by William Folan, Nicolás Caamal Canche, Jacinto May Hau and Lynda Florey Folan. All platforms with no apparent superstructures ($N = 862$) in these zones are presented in Table 10.1. The analysis of these survey data to determine if an elite or nonelite household compound was located in the immediate area of each of these platforms indicated that all zones showed both types of compounds associated with platforms with no apparent superstructures dispersed throughout these residential areas.

Although the areas covered by each of these zones are not equal, it can be said that Zones I, II, III, IV, and XIII produced the highest raw frequencies of platforms with no superstructures. Some suggestions can be made to account for this distribution beside their square areas in comparison to the other

Table 10.1   Frequency of Platforms with No Apparent
Superstructures for Zones I-XIII

Zone	Area of zone (km^2)	Raw frequency	Corrected frequency platforms (km^2)
I	2.9	157	54.1
II	1.7	247	145.3
III	4.0	212	53.0
IV	1.9	79	41.6
V	0.2	20	100.0
VI	0.7	14	20.0
VII	0.5	32	64.0
VIII	0.3	11	36.7
IX	1.0	1	0.5
X	0.3	3	10.0
XI	0.3	1	3.3
XII	1.0	10	10.0
XIII	4.1	47	11.5
		862	

eight zones. Zone II, the western zone, contains a high frequency of *sascaberas* (ancient quarries) associated with many platforms with no apparent superstructures (Folan 1978a). Obviously, there must be some connection, as yet unspecified, between quarrying activities and platforms with no apparent superstructures. Zone III, the southern area, is much like the northern zone in its architectural configuration. Here, however, many of the platforms with no apparent superstructures not only are associated with *sascaberas* but altars as well. In Zone IV, to the east, many of the platforms with no apparent superstructures are also found with altars, thus suggesting that some of these platforms may have been linked with special ceremonial functions associated with quarrying activities.

In Zone XIII, Telcox, where there exists a prevalence of structures formed on bedrock, platforms with no apparent superstructures were not associated with altars or *sascaberas*. Here the majority of the 47 platforms of this type are linked with commoner households. This association also occurs in Zones I, II, III, IV, XI, and XIII where more platforms are found with commoner households than those of the elite. The reverse is true in Zones V, VII, VIII, and X. In that Zones V, VII, and VIII are limited to the elite core area of Coba, this factor alone could influence this pattern. Zone X, adjacent to the Macanxoc group, is situated near a large body of water which may account for the occurrence of the higher number of elite residences and the platforms with no apparent superstructures found here. In Zone IX, however, elite and commoner households exhibit approximately an equal ratio of occurrence with platforms with no apparent superstructures.

Excluding those platforms (adjacent to *sascaberas,* altars, or abutting *sacbeob)* with no apparent superstructures, a considerable number of these platforms are found associated with elite households, commoner households, isolated and/or occurring in clusters in the same general area. The highest number of these platforms grouped together (10) is in association with an elite compound. However, the most frequent configuration of platforms with no apparent superstructures is two, occurring in the same general area (75 clusters). Platforms also occur in clusters of 3 ($N = 26$), 4 ($N = 10$), 5 ($N = 3$), and 8 ($N = 1$). If these platforms are zones of economic specialization such as those reported at Colha (Hester *et al.* 1980; Wilk 1977) or Tikal (Coe 1962), their production activities could not only represent cottage industries but larger units as well.

In Zone II, the western zone, there occur 54 instances where more than one platform with no apparent superstructure is found in the same general area. In Zone III, the southern zone, there are 31 clusters of more than one platform of this type, and in Zone IV, the eastern zone, 16 clusters were noted. Other zones include from zero to four instances of platform clusters with no apparent superstructures. If these and similar platforms mark the location of economic production units, this could be interpreted to mean that Coba fulfills the criteria of a developed urban settlement (Sanders and Price 1968:46) com-

posed of a large heterogeneous population with economic specialization practiced within the 13 zones of the city mapped by us.

GUILDS

Chinese guilds studied by Burgess (1928) offer some comparative material
with which to judge the organization of similar groups in ancient Maya society. The guilds can be portrayed most accurately as trade, professional, and
handicraft organizations. Burgess (1928) also states that the organization of
these associations varied widely. They included religious fraternities, professional organizations, craftsmen, commercial entrepreneurs, social groups,
economic groups, and merchants.

Given the complex settlement pattern at Coba, it is likely that similar com-
mon-interest groups would be dispersed throughout its residential zone. Analysis of household locations in Zone I and elsewhere identified household
clusters (Kintz 1978) reflecting this type of organization pattern. Burgess (1928)
isolates guild halls as a nexus of social interaction; these may be reflected in
the clusters of household units in Coba that exhibit elite architecture or in the
large commoner compounds that include many unvaulted buildings and platforms without visible superstructures. It is likely that groups similar to Chinese
guild associations may have operated in ancient Maya centers such as Coba
during the Classic period.

CONCLUSIONS

Early Maya economic producers were primarily oriented toward satisfying
the needs of the elite, and were probably housed in or adjacent to temples and
palaces as in Teotihuacan and Huamango. The consummate social complexity
associated with pilgrim–shrine–religious–civic–commercial centers is matched
by a high level of occupational specialization and production activities. It is
hypothesized that these activities, while continuing to operate in the palace–temple precincts, also shifted to the residential districts by the Late Classic—if not sooner—and that it was here we located them in Coba.

Residential economic production may have evolved out of extended family
groupings, territorial affiliations, and fraternities tied to occupational expertise. Certainly the Maya (Rattray 1981) and Oaxaca barrio at Teotihuacan
represent such a group (Millon 1976:225); other religious, family, or territorial
units must have been organized in a like fashion as productive units in Classic
Maya urban areas.

Based on these facts, it is believed that the following factors should be considered when reconstructing Classic Maya society:

1. Economic production must have been a major activity in Classic Maya centers.

2. If cottage industries and guild formations were production units, then remains of these activities should be recordable.

3. Platforms with no apparent room foundations are anomalies common to all residential precincts in Coba. Although it is probable that these served diverse purposes—some unspecified role in association with quarries, altar bases, or toll stations—they also may represent raised, thatched-roof work areas of craftsmen living in the suburban areas of the city, a pattern documented for economic production in the Mesoamerican highlands (Adams 1966; Calnek 1974; Carrasco 1971; Folan 1981c; Millon 1976; Prem 1974; Sanders 1965).

4. Finally, excavation of these units and the adjacent areas is required to test this hypothesis and document more fully the economic organization of the Classic Maya society.

Chapter 11

Class Structure
in a Classic Maya City

Ellen R. Kintz

INTRODUCTION

An assessment of Classic Maya social organization depends largely on knowledge of its regional centers, including their socially stratified, heterogeneous population.

Research at Tikal (Puleston 1973) and Dzibilchaltun (Kurjack 1974) has demonstrated that Maya cities were large and highly populated (Haviland 1969, 1972a,b) with both the elite and common classes living within the boundaries. Although many students have characterized Maya society as rigidly divided into noble, commoner, and slave classes (Kurjack 1974:7), archaeological investigations at Coba, as well as ethnohistorical data, do not support this view. It is hypothesized that within these three classes there existed an internal ranking system based on occupational activities. For example, a noble political ruler ranks higher than a noble priest, a priest higher than a trader within the same class. A similar system of internal ranking also can be made for commoners.

Adams (1970) defined Classic Maya class structure on the basis of occupational specialization, including the degree of complexity and amount of time demanded by their practice. At the top would be political leaders, priests, and war leaders. Those craftsmen in frequent contact with the elite would be ranked higher than craft specialists without these contacts. The next in line consisted of service personnel and/or part-time craftspeople such as stonecutters, knappers, and masons. The lowest status included those people with no distinguishable skills. Adams also noted that occupational specialization is only one index of ranking with other factors (political, religious, and social) also operating to influence social position. Fortunately, the political leadership of the Classic Maya has been clarified by the analysis of glyphic inscriptions (Marcus 1976; Proskouriakoff 1960, 1963, 1964) as well as by ethnohistoric reports (Roys 1957, 1962, 1972; Scholes and Roys 1968). However, Culbert (1971:41) states that "any attempt to comment knowledgeably about the kind and mechanisms of status differentiation [among the Classic Maya] must rely upon theory rather than fact. The range of variation and size of samples available is too limited to test such premises and specific ideas."

By 1977, large sections of Coba, Tikal, and Dzibilchaltun had been mapped in great detail, with research efforts at Coba culminating in a reassessment of Classic Maya social organization. William Folan's initial survey efforts in 1974 (Folan and Stuart 1974) and subsequent reports (Folan 1975, 1976) established that Coba encompassed approximately 63–70 km², which is approximately the size of Tikal, the major Classic period regional capital located in the southern lowlands. Folan's analysis of 6000 structures and features at Coba established it to be of urban proportions. Subsequent analyses also suggested that the approximately 50,000 people living at Coba were organized into neighborhoods and barrios active in various forms of specialization (Folan 1975, 1976; Kintz 1978).

Subsequent work on the Classic Maya, combined with ethnohistoric information and ethnographic studies on the modern Maya, has provided additional information on Maya class structure that, in some cases, has permitted associations between status and settlement among the ancient Maya (Adams 1970; Eaton 1975; Folan 1975, 1976; Harrison 1970; Kurjack 1974; Landa 1941; Marcus 1976; Morley 1956; Proskouriakoff 1960; Rathje and Sabloff 1975; Redfield and Villa Rojas 1934; Roys 1943, 1957; Thompson 1974; Thompson *et al.* 1932; Tourtellot 1976; Wauchope 1934, 1938; Wilk 1977; Winter 1974). Based on this information, it has been hypothesized that Classic Maya society was more complex than generally recognized and that it is now possible to comment more knowledgeably about the differentiation of the society into upper, middle, and lower classes (Borhegyi 1956; Culbert 1974:67) rather than gross categories of elite as opposed to commoner (see Thompson 1954b).

The household compound is the unit of investigation used here to elucidate the social differentiation of the Classic Maya. This compound is composed of high-energy vaulted and/or lower-energy unvaulted architecture. In many instances, a substructural platform supports these structures with ancillary buildings frequently adjacent to the platform.

Although household units initially were categorized as pertaining to elite or nonelite groups based on the presence or absence of vaulted architecture (Folan 1975, 1976; Kintz 1978), it was subsequently determined that, within

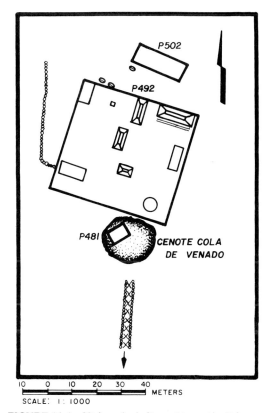

P502

P492

P481   CENOTE COLA
       DE VENADO

10   0   10   20   30   40
                            METERS
SCALE: 1: 1000

FIGURE 11.1   High-ranked elite unit in residential zone.

these two classes, there existed considerable variation in their spatial dimensions as well as in the number of structures associated with household units.
In other words, the analysis of household units not only differentiated the
upper from the lower class but also substantiated the internal ranking of each
class. Furthermore, it was possible to demonstrate an overlap between the less
affluent elite and the more affluent commoner households. As a result of the
detailed analysis of residential compounds in Coba, it was hypothesized that
variation in substructural platform size and number of structures associated
with each platform represents a heterogeneous population stratified into
classes. These classes were established through a frequency analysis of vaulted
structures and platforms, rectangular and apsidal–round unvaulted structures,
and platforms with no apparent structures associated with other platforms or
structures and features.

Here, the analysis focuses on people ranked below rulers, high priests,
war captains, and high-status traders, and above lower-class people such as

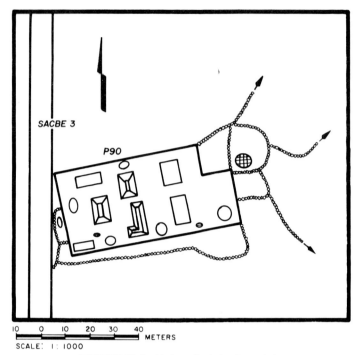

SCALE: 1 : 1000

FIGURE 11.2   High-ranked elite household.

relatively unskilled service personnel or part-time specialists. This middle-class, commoner population was also internally ranked into two major subdivisions. The upper segment consisted of wealthier middle-class people—not members of the nobility but able to obtain political positions above their statuses (Roys 1972). Apparently, the system was also regulated so that these people were at times purged from these elevated positions (Roys 1972). They would include individuals such as petty traders who could acquire wealth and improve their social status or artisan–craftsmen who produced for elite consumption. These craftsmen were members of larger lineage or guild organizations based in the residential precincts of Coba (Kintz 1978). They, like traders, were also in a position to acquire wealth and improve their social positions. The lower segment of the middle class consisted of relatively unskilled service personnel or part-time craft specialists who had little chance of improving their status.

Table 11.1 provides a list of occupations practiced in a city such as Coba, and Table 11.2 provides an assessment of where people of various classes, statuses, or roles would reside in the city. Figures 11.1–11.12 provide a visual comparison of households, documenting overlap or fluidity between social classes as reflected in the size and complexity of their quarters.

Table 11.1   Social Classes of the Classic Maya Reconstructed from Ethnohistoric Reports[a]

Upper class	Middle class	Lower class	Lowest class
Noble by lineage or reputation	*Asmen uinic* "medium man"	Construction workers	Slaves (*ppentac munach*)
Political administrator (*Halach Uinic, batab, nucil uinic, holpop*)	Petty trader	Artisans producing for the general population (knappers, weavers, spinners, tanners, potters, metate makers)	
Political assistant (*ah kulel, tupil, ah tzibhun*)	Skilled artisans (closest to the elite (feather worker, potter, tanner, weaver, spinner, stone carvers, jade workers, shell workers, etc.)	Farmers	
Religious leader (*ah kin mai or ah can mai, chac, balam, ah kin, ah kin ek*)	Cultivator of special products (bees, cacao, vanilla, tobacco, rubber, incense, etc.)		
Religious assistant (vestal virgins, *ah kulel, ah kayom*)			
Religious specialist (*chilan, ah uay, coot, a uay chamac, h-memob, yerbatero*)			
Warrior (*Batab*, nacom, soldier, member of the Cult of the Dead)			
Trader (long-distance traders)			

[a] From Landa 1941; Morley 1965; Roys 1943, 1967, 1972; Scholes and Roys 1968; Thompson, 1970.

TABLE 11.2 Social Organization and Residential Pattern of the Classic Maya Based on Ethnohistoric Reports from the Sixteenth Century

Title	Description	Residential Pattern
Ah chibal, almhenil	Noble by lineage or reputation (Roys 1972)	Depending on rank, individuals reside in the civic-religious center or in the residential precincts closest to the core; compound may be associated with other households of the same lineage
Halach uinic	"True Man," territorial ruler, also called *ahau*, great lord, ruler-priest (Morley 1956; Thompson 1970; Scholes and Roys 1968; Roys 1943)	Individual housed in the civic-religious core of the city; housing reflects elite status; vaulted buildings reflect high-energy input for construction
Batab	Village chief or ruler; feudal relationship to *halach uinic*; inherited position (Morley 1956) also had a religious aspect (Thompson 1970), served as a war captain (Morley 1956; Roys 1943, 1967)	Individual village chief did not reside permanently in the major civic-ceremonial city; was possibly housed in the center of the city when on report to the territorial ruler; apartment complexes in the civic-religious center of the city would serve to house political subordinates as well as religious pilgrims, visiting war leaders, and visiting traders
Nucil, nucil uinicob, nucbe uinicob	The elders or principal men of a town, nobles, heads of subdivisions of a town (Scholes and Roys 1968; Roys 1972)	Individuals either resided in the civic-ceremonial core and were associated with higher-ranked political administrators or, more probably, lived in residential zones in large, complex compounds with vaulted architecture and served as the co-ordinating political, economic, and religious focus for a barrio
Holpop	"Those at the head of the mat," lineage heads (Roys 1943), masters of the *popolna* or men's house, chief singers and chanters, mouthpiece for the people to the lord (Morley 1956; Landa 1941)	Individuals resided in the residential precinct; as lineage head would be housed in one of the larger compounds in a residential cluster; depending on the amount of acquired or inherited wealth, the household would have vaulted structures or rectangular and/or round apsidal unvaulted residential buildings (e.g., household focus for barrio or neighborhood clusters)
Ah cuch cab	Special councilor; below *batab* in status; number 2–3 per settlement; stood at head of subdivision of town	Individuals housed in the residential precincts of the city, housing reflects elite status, either vaulted buildings or larger com-

Term	Description (references)	Residence
	(barrio head? lineage head?) (Scholes and Roys 1968; Roys 1943; Morley 1956)	pound with rectangular and round/apsidal unvaulted structures; household may be in association with special feature such as water source, altar, quarry and/or sacbe
Ah kulel	Deputy, accompanied batab, assistant to batab, number 2–3 per settlement, ranked above tupil but below batab, also assistant to priests (Morley 1956; Scholes and Roys 1968; Roys 1943, 1967)	Housed either in the residential precincts or adjacent to the household of the batab or priest, individual resided in major cities and also in minor towns
Tupil	Town constable; bottom of law enforcement structure (Morley 1956), subordinate to ah cuch cab (deputy)	Resided in the residential precinct, household complexity equal to, greater than or less than other household dependent on rank of barrio; possibly attendent regulating traffic on sacbeob with residence adjacent to transportation system
Ah tzibhun	Town clerk (Landa 1941)	Probably resided in the residential precincts but worked in the civic-ceremonial center of the city
Ah kin mai or ah can mai	High priest	Resided in civic-ceremonial center of the city adjacent to temples; housed in vaulted buildings, compounds; probably had storehouses for ritual accouterments (e.g., compound to south of Iglesia, Coba, Group B)
Chac	High priest (?) (Landa 1941), god impersonator (Roys 1967)	Resides in the civic-religious core of the city adjacent to temples
Balam	Priest (Landa 1941), jaguar priest of the Itza (Roys 1967), Postclassic priesthood	Housed in the civic-religious center of the city, special dormitories adjacent to the large temples (e.g., located on series of platforms and structures in the Coba Group B or in other civic-religious precincts at the center of the site)
Ah kin	Priest (Thompson 1970), priest (Morley 1956; Scholes and Roys 1968; Roys 1943, 1967; Landa 1941)	Lived either in the civic-religious center of the city or practiced ritual on the barrio or neighborhood level; may be associated with large complex compounds with vaulted architecture and altars or other special features in the residential zone (e.g., compound in Zone I, the North, Cenote Cola de Venado)
Ah kin ek	Priest (Landa 1941)	Member of the priestly hierarchy, probably resides in dormitory adjacent to the temples or practiced ritual on the barrio or neighborhood level

TABLE 11.2 (*continued*)

Title	Description	Residential Pattern
Vestal Virgins	Tended the sacred fire in the temples, lived near the temples (Thompson 1970)	Housing adjacent to temples; these individuals were killed if it was discovered that their behavior was not chaste; it is probable that their residential areas were restricted access areas (e.g., location of vaulted compounds on high platforms in the Coba Group B)
Chilam	Diviner (Landa 1941; Thompson 1970), prophet mouthpiece or interpreter of the gods (Roys 1967)	Lived in the civic–religious center of the city or in civic–religious compounds associated with the barrios of the city (e.g., Zone I, Cenote Cola de Venado)
Ah uay coot	Sorcerer (Landa 1941)	Probably lived in the residential precincts; part-time practitioner?
A uay chamac	Wizard who could turn himself into a fox (Roys 1967)	Probably lived in the residential precincts; part-time practitioner?
Ay kayom	Chanter or singer, assisted priests (Scholes and Roys 1968)	Probably resides in the civic–religious core of the city in modest structures in association with the dormitories of the high priests
H-memob, ah men (h-men)	Maya priests (Roys 1967), curers, diviners, worked on community rites connected with fields and forests (Thompson 1970)	Probably lived in the residential precincts; part-time practitioner?
Yerbatero	Herbalist (Landa 1941)	Resided in the residential precincts, part-time occupation?
Nacom	Elected war captain (Morley 1956), priest executioner, practiced human sacrifice (Landa 1941); sometimes treated as a god (Roys 1967)	For the 3-year period an individual held this position, he would live in the civic–religious core of the city
Holil och	Warrior chief (Roys 1967)	Resides in the civic–religious core of the city, may be warrior-ruler; may reside in the residential precincts at the head of a barrio of associated soldiers?
Soldier	Men who formed part of the fighting legions	These probably reside in the barrio section organized along kinship lines forming fighting units similar to those of the Aztec *calpulli* or the organization of the legions could cross cut settlement sections (barrio, neighborhoods)

Cult of the Dead	Warriors are of two types: leaders and common soldiers; those who are members of the Cult of the Dead probably worship together in temples in the core area of the city, have some amount of prestige and reside in larger, more complex, house compounds as a reflection of their position; common soldiers probably reside in simpler households in the residential precincts
Warriors — Probably an organized group of warriors who revered past heroes	
Pplom — Merchant	If a member of the nobility, the individual resides in the civic-religious core of the city in the palace structures associated with the rulers of the settlement; if not, resides in the residential precincts of the city, either in compounds with vaulted structures or in larger compounds with unvaulted structures, reflecting the wealth of the household
Ayikal — Rich man (Landa 1941)	Wealthier individuals, whether nobles or commoners, were housed in buildings reflecting the high-energy input and high-cost outlay of their residential compounds construction; housing of this social group can only be inferred from comparison with other houses in the neighborhood, barrio, or larger spatial areas in the ancient city
Ah chembal uinicob — Groups or names of commoners (Morley 1956)	Resides in the residential precincts of the city
Memba uinicob — Groups or names of commoners (Morley 1956)	Resides in the residential precincts of the city
Pizil cah — "Commoner" (Roys 1957)	Lives in the residential precincts of the city
Macequal, macehual, mazeual (Nahuatl) — Commoner, not a noble (Scholes and Roys 1968; Landa 1941)	Lives in the residential precincts of the city
Azmen uinic — Upper fringe of commoner class; "medium man" between principal and plebian; middle status (Roys 1943: 34); sons of nobles and low-born mothers (Roys 1943) middle status	Individual had elevated position with respect to the commoner population and status would be reflected in the household size and organization; probably lived in close proximity to the civic-religious core in either medium-sized compounds with vaulted architecture or in larger compounds with unvaulted buildings

(continued)

169

TABLE 11.2 (*continued*)

Title	Description	Residential Pattern
Yalba uinicob	"Small man," "I am small or low in stature or I am a common and plebian man" (Roys 1972: 34; *Diccionario de Motul* 1929: 440–441) lower status group of plebians	Commoner of low rank; lived furthermost from the core of the city
Camsah (Ah)	Teacher (Landa 1941)	Possibly resided in the civic-religious core of the city, status relative to material taught and to whom; if a teacher of nobles' children, status above that of other social classes and other material taught
Chic	Clown	Served the elite, lived in the residential precincts or in the core of the city as a retainer to larger, more complex, wealthy households
Guatepol	Prostitute in Nicaragua (Landa 1941)	Served the elite and commoner populations depending on rank, resided in the core area or in the barrios
Ah chuen	Special craftsmen of various types	Depending on the occupation, whether important to the elite, on the degree of complexity of skill, and the time demanded by the practice, these individuals would reside in the palace or in the residential areas
Featherworker	Occupational specialization, high degree of skill; time demanded for work dependent on the needs of the elite; goods produced for—and consumed by—the elite (Landa 1941)	May have been housed in the civic-religious center of the city in association with palaces; may have been a specialization practiced on the barrio level
Idol carver, altar carver	Involved some degree of skill; production for elite use or ceremonial affairs (Landa 1941)	Individuals either lived in residential precincts in coordinated barrio units as guild organizations, cottage production units or household production specialties; possibly dormitories and workshops located in civic-ceremonial area as part of palace industry

Tanner	Individuals would process skins; two types of production were carried on: one for household level use, and one for skins worn by the elite as a symbol of rank (Landa 1941)	The household-level production located in the residential precincts, the other type of production for elite consumption was in the form of palace industries, guild production, and/or cottage industry
Weapon maker	These individuals would manufacture weapons for use in war or possibly in religious rituals; in addition, they would also produce weapons for hunting (Landa 1941)	Possibly some of the production was done in the palace area or near the temples and other forms of manufacturing was accomplished on the household level (i.e., production of weapons used in hunting by members of the family) or on the barrio level as part of guild specializations or cottage industry activities
Weaver	Two types of practitioners; one practiced this craft for the production of household textiles; the other, for the production of textiles for elite consumption (Landa 1941)	The household-level production was carried on in the residential precincts and the other in the form of palace industry, guild production, and/or cottage industry
Spinner	Provides threads for textile manufacture (Landa 1941)	Two types of practitioners: one practiced this craft for the production of household textiles, the other for the production of threads used in the clothing of the elite. The household level production was carried out in the residential precincts; the other, in the form of a palace industry
Beekeepers	Individuals who kept bees for the production of honey and wax (Roys 1967), an important occupation in ancient Coba	Resided in the residential area; possibly those walled households in these areas would permit sufficient space for beekeeping
Builder	Those individuals involved in the building of civic-religious architecture, low complexity of skill (Landa 1941)	Lived in simple households in the residential precincts
Ppentac (male slave)	Worked for the elite and wealthy commoners, many were female or children of war captives (Roys 1943)	Resided and worked in modest structures associated with elite compounds or larger commoner households; dormitory was furthest away from the dormitory of the head of the household and his family within the boundaries of the solar

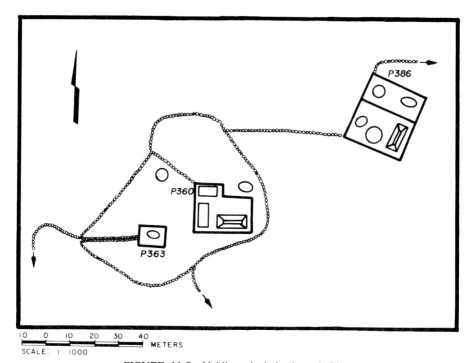

SCALE: 1:1000

FIGURE 11.3   Middle-ranked elite household.

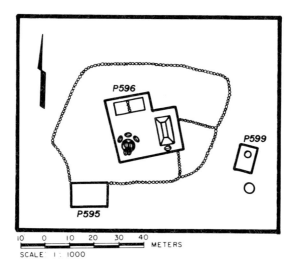

SCALE: 1:1000

FIGURE 11.4   Middle-ranked elite household.

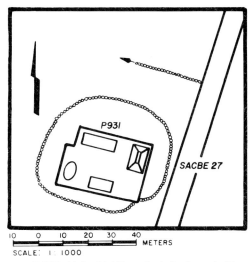

FIGURE 11.5 Middle-ranked elite household.

Variation in household form and function as well as the complex pattern of social stratification can be defined in Coba through the configuration of structures, platforms, and features defined in Zones I–XIII. These platform areas range in size from 1 to 6020 m². Of the 2523 platforms mapped in the 13 zones, the platform areas most frequently recorded measure 42–91 m². These

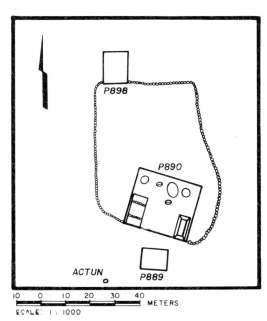

FIGURE 11.6 Middle-ranked elite household.

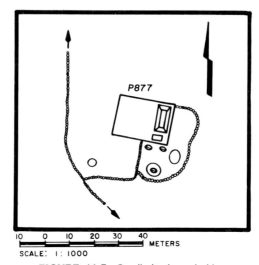

FIGURE 11.7   Small elite household.

probably served as substructures for less wealthy, smaller, commoner households or substructures for ancillary units adjacent to and associated with the
larger *plazuela* complexes of the more wealthy elite and commoners living in
the city.

Platforms supporting structures occur most frequently in the modal class,
42–91 m^2. They also are found in high numbers measuring 12, 15, 20, 24, 35,
117, 130, 221, 374, 391, and 598 m^2. Although, in some cases, these size differences demarcate functional variances, it is suggested that they represent
distinctions in household status. The lowest-ranked individuals resided on the
smallest platforms, while wealthier members of the society were associated

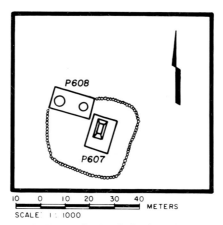

FIGURE 11.8   Small elite household.

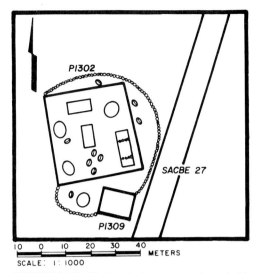

FIGURE 11.9 High-ranked commoner household.

with larger units. Between the lowest and highest were those of middle-class households.

In addition to household platform size, the number of structures associated with a household also reflects social status. Platforms support from 0 to 14 apparent superstructures. Only nine platforms in all 13 zones are associated

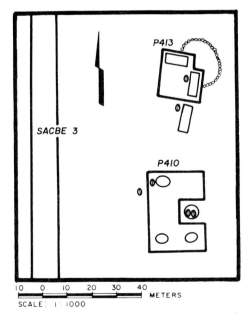

FIGURE 11.10 Middle-ranked commoner household.

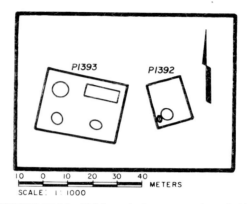

FIGURE 11.11   Middle-ranked commoner household.

with 10 or more superstructures. Of these, eight included vaulted structures; one supported unvaulted buildings only. Some of these larger groups represent civic–religious centers associated with the core area of the city and are related to political–economic–religious barrio functions while others represent upper-class households.

Platforms supporting five to nine structures probably represent the elite as well as nonelite households or persons able to generate multistructural compounds but unable to afford vaulted structures. The latter group seemed to represent middle-class artisans, petty traders, lineage heads, or ward-level political figures.

Finally, platforms including from one to four structures were those occurring most frequently. It has been argued elsewhere (Kintz 1978) that these platforms were multifunctional. They served to support lower-class household units, the households of newly married couples, and units ancillary to larger, more complex *plazuela* groups serving as kitchens, storehouses, or dormitories for servants.

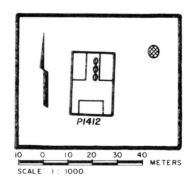

FIGURE 11.12   Small commoner household.

CONCLUSIONS

Platform size and associated structures demonstrate that the social structure of the Classic Maya included upper, middle, and lower classes akin to the structure of Maya society reported for the sixteenth century. Once detailed excavation of these units can be carried out, this hypothesis can be put to the test based on the comparative content, quantity, and relative value of their associated artifacts.

Chapter 12

Neighborhoods and Wards in a Classic Maya Metropolis

Ellen R. Kintz

INTRODUCTION

Diego de Landa (1941) has described sixteenth-century Maya towns as being centered about the temples with priests, nobles, and the wealthy residing nearby and the lower-class members living on the town's periphery. This account and subsequent analyses of precolumbian settlement patterns in the lowland Maya area have been central to the definition of Maya organization (Bullard 1954, 1960; Coe 1965; Fletcher 1978; Folan 1969b, 1975, 1976; Folan *et al.* 1979; Hammond 1972; Haviland 1965; Kintz 1978; Kurjack 1974; Landa 1941; Pollock *et al.* 1962; Puleston 1973; Roys 1962, 1972; Willey 1956a,b; Willey *et al.* 1965). The settlement pattern of complex Maya centers during the Classic period is represented by a general model of concentric zones (Folan 1975, 1976; Hammond 1972; Kintz 1978; Kurjack 1974; Puleston 1973).

It is further hypothesized that at Coba a mosaic pattern of household clusters representing small, coordinated neighborhood divisions is contained within and crosscutting these concentric zones. Bullard's study (1960:336) of Maya settlement patterns in northeastern Peten, Guatemala, also defined areas where the frequency of some buildings exhibited a high density with an average distance between households measuring 50–75 m, as well as areas of low density with distances between households measuring 150 m or more. Additionally, some Peten architecture in high-density zones may have included small shrines (Bullard 1960:367). Studies in the Belize Valley, British Honduras (Willey 1956a,b), although a broader territory, once again offers evidence of a high- and low-density household settlement pattern, whereas Hammond's (1975) work at Lubaantun suggests that site was organized in concentric rings composed of religious, ceremonial, and residential zones from the center of the site to the periphery. Puleston's (1973:18–35) settlement pattern analysis of Tikal demonstrated the amoeboid irregularity of its epicentral and residential zones, reflecting differential settlement density within the civic–ceremonial core and the residential ring. A more recent evaluation of the Tikal settlement pattern (Arnold and Ford 1980) has concluded, however, that the concentric zone model does not represent settlement at that site. But the restriction of the Arnold and Ford analysis to the central 9-km^2 core area seems insufficient to test the value of this pattern as does their inability to distinguish vaulted from unvaulted architecture in their limited sample (Folan *et al.* 1982).

Folan (1975, 1976) and Kintz (1978) documented the settlement pattern of Coba as being organized in general concentric circles with the area adjacent to Lakes Macanxoc and Coba considered a downtown area made up of "mixed ceremonial, administrative and some habitational buildings and plazas" (Folan 1975). The suburban area at Coba was divided into two zones:

1. An inner suburban area is described as being "closest to the site center and . . . characterized by the distribution of a few administrative and ceremonial structures among a great many habitational and utilitarian units located on platforms in association with numerous multipurpose linear, wall-like features" (Folan 1975; Fletcher 1978).

2. The outer suburban zone was an area "characterized by a noticeable thinning of all architectural features including multipurpose walls" (Folan 1975).

The rural hinterland continued beyond this zone for up to 14 km toward the north (Folan 1975, 1976).

This settlement model was defined by Folan following the survey of Zones I–XIII at Coba by Folan, Nicolás Caamal Canche, Jacinto May Hau, and Lynda Florey Folan. Subsequently, Caamal, Fletcher, Kintz, and May resurveyed Zone I. All architecture and other features associated with house mounds were remapped; the reanalysis of Zone I enabled us to conclude that architecture in this zone was not only *generally* distributed in concentric circles, in accord with Folan's initial statement (Folan 1975; Kintz 1978), but included household clusters of small, coordinated neighborhood divisions that more exactly reflect the organization of Coba.

The analysis of survey data from Classic Tikal (Haviland 1965; Puleston 1973) and Dzibilchaltun (Kurjack 1974; Kurjack and Garza 1981) as well as Postclassic Mayapan (Bullard 1954) demonstrates that residential units as well as architecture representing civic–religious activities were clustered in residential zones. The extrapolation and application of these findings to the settlement pattern in residential precincts at Coba suggested that the low- and high-density configurations of its residential zones probably demarcate the neighborhood (*china*) and ward (*cuchteel*) forms of organization described by Roys (1957:7) for the sixteenth-century Maya. William Folan brought the term *china* to my attention as more clearly reflecting the sociological organization of some units in Coba as explained more fully in the subsequent analysis.

Two basic assumptions are made with respect to the reconstruction and analysis of household units in the residential districts at Coba. The first concerns the form of household groups. Residential units were defined mainly on the basis of platforms and structures enclosed within house-lot walls (Fletcher 1978; Folan 1976; Kintz 1978), with unwalled architectural associations similar in design to walled households also considered residential units. The second assumption is that these households pertain to the Late Classic period on the basis of their architectural style, dated stelae, and the ceramics collected from excavations of several house-lot walls (Ball 1977: personal communication). Furthermore, household units have been defined and analyzed, assuming that all units were contemporary. It is known that all structures at Coba do not date to this early period as there existed a rather important Postclassic occupation at the center (Brainerd 1958, Robles 1980; Thompson *et al.* 1932). Although not all Classic architecture was built in a day or within a generation, neither architectural nor ceramic analyses on house mounds at Coba currently offer data sufficient to delineate shorter occupation periods essential to resolve this dilemma.

ANALYSIS

The most elemental barrier to social interaction is space itself. The greater the distance between household units, the more limited the interaction and, conversely, the less the distance between units, the greater the interaction. It is hypothesized that the localization of household units with respect to water sources or quarries as well as the spatial association of units reflects social status, economic organization, and/or factors of political control. In other words, social activities contributed toward the organization of households into clusters. The mapping of high- and low-status households in Coba revealed patterns that permit their identification and interpretation as participating in neighborhood and ward types of organizations within residential zones.

The 78 survey lines, ranging in length from 324 to 1282 m at 50-m intervals from the north shore of Lake Macanxoc to the *sacbe* terminal of Xmacaba in the northern periphery of the city recorded from one to nine household groups per line. This pattern provided an expected average of approximately 160 m between households, based on survey line lengths and the amount of households recorded per line. The distances between nearest neighbors to the north, south, east, and west of the 353 household units in Zone I provided a total of 1392 measurements (Table 12.1). Of the 1392 measurements, 983 were 70

TABLE 12.1   Frequencies of Distances between Zone I
Households Based on 1392 Measurements

Distances (m)	Frequencies	Distances (m)	Frequencies
0- 9	20	170-179	5
10- 19	86	180-189	16
20- 29	121	190-199	7
30- 39	170	200-209	9
40- 49	165	210-219	2
50- 59	159	220-229	2
60- 69	132	230-239	2
70- 79	130	240-249	2
80- 89	83	250-259	2
90- 99	69	260-269	5
100-109	60	270-279	0
110-119	34	280-289	0
120-129	40	290-299	0
130-139	22	300-309	2
140-149	21	310-319	0
150-159	11	320-above	2
160-169	13		

m or less (70.6%), thereby indicating that a majority of the household units in the northern zone were more closely associated than the expected 160-m distance.

It is assumed that the distances between these households represent variations in social isolation between households and, as such, were the first indicators of intrazonal boundaries between neighborhoods and wards in Coba. Therefore, quantitative data on distances between households would demonstrate that some households were in close proximity to each other, thus forming clusters; others were more isolated from each other, thus forming single units.

The tally of distances between household units is thought to provide an index of connectivity. Those units in close proximity are considered to have had the closest social interaction. On the other hand, those units more than 70 m apart are considered to have experienced a more distant social interaction. All households within 70 m of each other were connected on the map (Figure 12.1). This resulted in the formation of 35 clusters, including 8 elite and 27 commoner compounds in relative isolation. All 8 elite compounds are situated south of the San Pedro complex at the northern terminus of Sacbe 3; whereas all but two of the 27 commoner compounds in relative isolation are situated to the north of this same complex (Table 12.2).

The clustering of household compounds in Zone I forms a pattern. Elite compounds are either isolated or in association with commoner household units. Relatively isolated units with high-status, vaulted architecture probably

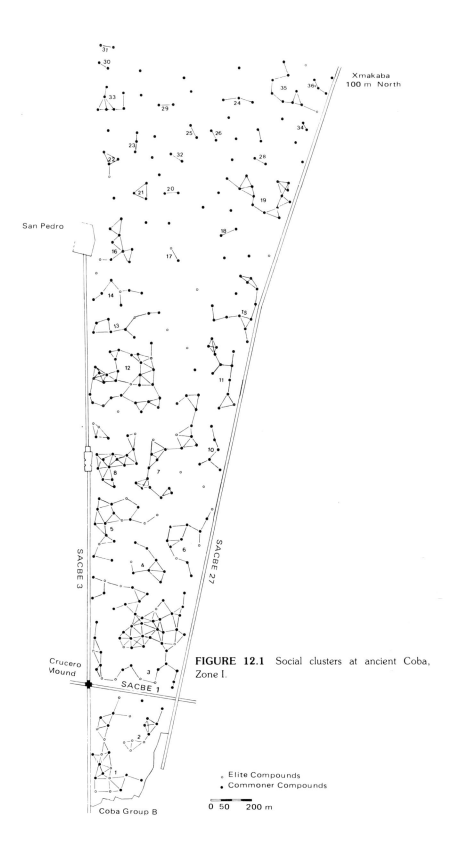

FIGURE 12.1 Social clusters at ancient Coba, Zone I.

San Pedro

Xmakaba
100 m North

SACBE 3

SACBE 27

SACBE 1

Crucero
Mound

Coba Group B

○ Elite Compounds
● Commoner Compounds

0 50   200 m

TABLE 12.2 Zone I: Clusters of Elite and Commoner Compounds, Location, and Description

Cluster number	Cluster Composition			Location	Description
	Elite	Commoner	Total		
1	9	11	20	South of Sacbe 1, west boundary adjacent to Sacbe 3, south boundary adjacent to edge of Great Platform.	Elite households and commoner households are grouped together.
2	4	5	9	South of Sacbe 1, east boundary adjacent to Sacbe 27, south boundary adjacent to edge of Great Platform.	Elite households tend to be grouped together as do commoner households within this cluster.
3	9	45	54	North of Sacbe 1. Lies along Sacbeob 3 and 27 running north, in the center of the two sacbeob.	The largest cluster located in the northern zone. Elite units near Sacbe 1. Elite compounds placed to serve as focal points for surrounding commoner households.
4	1	7	8	Located in the central zone between Sacbeob 3 and 27, approximately 600 m north of Sacbe 1.	This, and others like it, represent a cluster of commoner households with an elite household.
5	5	12	17	Lies along Sacbe 3 approx. 600–900 m north of Sacbe 1 and extending to the central area approximately 300 m to the east.	Cluster 5 seems larger and more complex than 4. More prestigious architecture is present in the cluster.

6	3	9	12	Adjacent to Sacbe 27 approximately 600–900 m north of Sacbe 1.	This cluster is more complex than cluster 4; it consists of three architectural compounds with vaulted architecture. The commoner households occur in groups of 2–3 or 4 units. Two elite compounds are located in close proximity to Sacbe 27.
7	2	19	21	Lies in the central zone between Sacbeob 3 and 27, 900–1500 m north of Lake Macanxoc.	This cluster represents another variation on the internal organization of groupings. The unit is large but has only two groups with vaulted architecture. Furthermore, the commoner units are more discrete in their association. It appears that the commoner households form five subunits.
8	1	14	15	East of Sacbe 3, approximately 30 m and extending 220 m into the central area between Sacbeob 3 and 27, 900 m north of Lake Macanxoc.	An elite compound is at the northern boundary of the cluster. Commoner units are tightly linked and discrete groups of commoner units are not apparent except possibly on the southern boundary of this cluster.
9	2	2	4	Immediately north of cluster 8, adjacent to Sacbe 3.	This represents the smallest cluster of elite and nonelite household units identified south of San Pedro.

(continued)

TABLE 12.2 (continued)

Cluster number	Cluster composition			Location	Description
	Elite	Commoner	Total		
10	0	6	6	Location 1100–1300 m north of Sacbe 1 adjacent to Sacbe 27.	This cluster consists solely of commoner households. To the south lies the complex and prestigious Cenote Cola de Venado group and another compound with vaulted architecture.
11	0	12	12	Location 80 m north of cluster 10 and approximately 60 m to the west of Sacbe 27.	This cluster consists of at least two internal commoner household groupings.
12	2	28	30	Located 1375 m north of the Crucero Mound adjacent to Sacbe 3 and extending approximately 300 m to the east of Sacbe 3.	This cluster represents one of the larger units. One elite household is central to the cluster and another is near the northeast boundary of the group. Discrete groups of commoner households are present.
13	1	8	9	Located approximately 80 m north of cluster 12, adjacent to Sacbe 3.	One of the smaller clusters with an elite compound as a possible focus. Four commoner households form an internal cluster on the western boundary.
14	1	6	7	Located approximately 75 m north of cluster 13 adjacent to Sacbe 3.	One of the smaller clusters; a compound with vaulted architecture serves as a central focus.
15	0	12	12	The center of the cluster lies approximately 170 m north of cluster 11, part of the cluster lies near Sacbe 27, and extends as far as 240 m west of Sacbe 27.	This large cluster consists of commoner households divided into two internal commoner household groups.

Cluster				Location	Description
16	9	8	1	Location approximately 100 m east of San Pedro at the north end of Sacbe 3.	Elite households occupy southern terminal link of the cluster. Clustering of commoner households present.
17	2	1	1	Location approximately 210 m east of cluster 16.	Association between an elite and commoner household.
18	2	2	0	Location approximately 200 m north of cluster 15 and 220 m west of Sacbe 27.	Assocation between two commoner households.
19	14	14	0	Location approximately 300 m north of cluster 15 and adjacent to Sacbe 27.	This represents the largest cluster north of San Pedro. It consists totally of commoner households. Three discrete internal commoner groups are present.
20	2	2	0	Location approximately 240 m west of cluster 19.	Association between two commoner units.
21	3	3	0	Location approximately 100 m west of cluster 20.	Association between three commoner units.
22	4	3	1	Location approximately 200 m north of cluster 16.	Cluster of commoner units with prestigious vaulted architecture.
23 and 24	3	3	0	Location north of San Pedro.	Similar to cluster 21.
25 thru 32	2	2	0	Located north of San Pedro.	Similar to cluster 18.
33	7	7	0	Located north of San Pedro.	One of the larger units located north of San Pedro; consists solely of commoner units.
34	2	2	0	Located approximately 300 m north of cluster 19 and only 70 m west of Sacbe 27.	Similar to cluster 18 but has greater access to major transportation route.
35	9	8	1	Located approximately 80 m north of cluster 33. The southeast boundary of the cluster lies 25 m west of Sacbe 27.	This cluster is more dispersed than most other clusters. Commoner household internal groupings present.
36	3	3	0	Located approximately 190 m north of cluster 33 and adjacent to Sacbe 27.	Similar to cluster 21 and commands access to major transportation route.

served intrabarrio religious or political coordinating activities at this level (Folan 1975) with those elite units associated with commoner dwellings probably serving as foci for the coordinated control of *china* or *cuchteel*. The commoner households in these units were probably related to each other on the basis of kinship and controlled by elite families. It is therefore hypothesized that these neighborhood units represent extended family groups exercising political, social, and economic functions in Coba.

Those commoner households without vaulted architecture found near the core area in relative isolation probably served as high-status, middle-class independent households. The households on the periphery of the city were probably those of low-status, small, nuclear families primarily involved in limited agricultural pursuits and low-status service occupations. Commoner households without vaulted architecture also occur with other commoner households. It is hypothesized that these households represented political, economic, and social units based on kinship ties coordinated by lineage heads. They functioned as cooperative work units practicing one or more forms of economic specialization. Socially, they were responsible for coordinating the economic wealth of the entire group while they also participated in common religious activities.

If some clusters represented neighborhoods, it is hypothesized that they were organized as lineages or name groups as reported for six provinces of Yucatan in 1584 and 1688 (Roys 1957:8–9). These lists include residents by name and their numbers within provinces with the exception of the Cupul of Cupul ($N=15$), the Iuit of Hocaba ($N=40$) and the Chel of Ah Kin Chel (no listing), who were sparsely represented in the provinces ruled by them.

Assuming that these groups represented localized royal lineages, they provide us with a rough estimate of the number of people belonging to town wards. The calculations of *china* and *cuchteel* populations in the residential zone at Coba can be compared with these figures. Following ethnographic evidence from Coba (Folan 1975) and Chan Kom (Redfield and Villa Rojas 1934: 91), as well as Wauchope's (1938:145) evaluation of archaeological data, it is estimated that an average of 5.6 persons occupied each household (Table 12.3). Analysis of these data demonstrate that of the 36 neighborhoods in Zone I of Coba, 15 are associated with low populations (less than 15 persons), 9 with medium populations (greater than 15 but less than 40) and 12 with high populations (greater than 40). The larger clusters are near the core area of Coba where residential units are more tightly packed. The intermediate-sized neighborhoods are in the zone to the north of the core, whereas the concentration of small clusters, consisting mainly of only two households, are in the outer zone of the city. While the small- and medium-sized clusters may be similar to the neighborhood name–group lineages described by Roys (1957:7–9), the larger units may represent the wards (*cuchteel, cuchabal*) (Roys 1957:7), which exercised some degree of autonomy under the control of headmen residing in the larger households.

TABLE 12.3   Population Size of Neighborhoods and Wards, Zone I

Neighborhood or ward number	Frequency elite households	Frequency commoner households	Total number households	Population size[a]
1	9	11	20	112.0
2	4	5	9	50.4
3	9	45	54	302.4
4	1	7	8	44.8
5	5	12	17	95.2
6	3	9	12	67.2
7	2	19	21	117.6
8	1	14	15	84.0
9	2	2	4	22.4
10	0	6	6	33.6
11	0	12	12	67.2
12	2	28	30	168.0
13	1	8	9	50.4
14	1	6	7	39.2
15	0	12	12	67.2
16	1	8	9	50.4
17	1	1	2	11.2
18	0	2	2	11.2
19	0	14	14	78.4
20	0	2	2	11.2
21	0	3	3	16.8
22	1	3	4	22.4
23	0	3	3	16.8
24	0	3	3	16.8
25	0	2	2	11.2
26	0	2	2	11.2
27	0	2	2	11.2
28	0	2	2	11.2
29	0	2	2	11.2
30	0	2	2	11.2
31	0	2	2	11.2
32	0	2	2	11.2
33	0	7	7	39.2
34	0	2	2	11.2
35	1	8	9	50.4
36	0	3	3	16.8

[a] Population size = Total number of households × 5.6.

CONCLUSIONS

Although we have been primarily concerned with the characterization of Classic Coba as an ancient city, the intrazonal differentiation of social groups in the northern residential zone documents that the population was organized in contiguous neighborhoods and wards. This then would tend to support Kur-jack's (1974:80) hypothesis that "clusters of ruins must have been related to the organization of . . . groups that made up Maya society.'' The clusters nearest the core consisted of upper-class elite served by commoner retainers. In the intermediary zone, elite compounds served not only as political and economic units coordinating the activities of the associated members of the ward, but also as religious centers. On the periphery, small clusters of commoner households generally represented lower-class housing organized on a nuclear family basis.

In summation, the preliminary analysis of neighborhood and ward organization in Zone I documents the complexity of the zones surrounding the city core area. Although a general concentric model is characteristic of the settlement pattern at Coba (Folan 1975, 1976; Folan *et al.* 1979; Kintz 1978), a more exacting interpretation of the sociological organization of the populations residing in this ancient city remained to be ascertained. Thus, the differentiation of intrazonal clusters, neighborhoods, and wards in Coba reflect more precisely the political, economic, and social organization of this city than any offered before or since.

Chapter 13

A Reconstruction of the Prehistoric Population at Coba

Ellen R. Kintz and Laraine A. Fletcher

INTRODUCTION

The size and composition of the resident population of Classic Maya centers have been factors under investigation for many years with high population figures estimated for large regional centers such as Tikal and Dzibilchaltun. It is our goal here to offer a construct of the resident population at Coba during the Late Classic to provide a demographic model of the city suitable for comparison to other cities in Mesoamerica in general, and the Maya zone in particular.

The data base for this population construct consists of structure counts for 13 zones surveyed at Coba as well as a separate corpus of data from Zone I and VI of discrete household compounds containing variable numbers of associated structures. This analysis follows methods introduced by Folan (1975), who initiated the preliminary population estimates for the city using the methodologies of Naroll (1962), Haviland (1969, 1970a), and Puleston (1973) as well as his own investigations in modern Coba. In addition to estimates based on structure counts, calculations are presented using an analysis of Zones I and VI household compounds together as a basis for projecting population figures for the entire city.

Control for noncontemporaneous occupation of household compounds in Coba is possible through the adjustment of structure counts based on demographic reconstruction done elsewhere in the Maya area (Haviland 1969, 1970a; Puleston 1973). Rationales for various reductions in the number of

structures occupied at any one time in the history of the city are discussed
in greater detail.

Ceramics excavated by the Coba Archaeological Mapping Project to date
the linear features and associated architecture at Coba were identified by Joseph Ball (1977: personal communication) as pertaining predominantly to the
Late Classic (Tepeu I) in basic agreement with Coba's architectural styles and
stelae dates. Further analysis on ceramics by Fernando Robles (1980), Instituto
Nacional de Antropología e Historia, Mérida, should define more clearly the
temporal dimensions of the center.

According to Puleston (1973:150), divisions in ceramic types at Tikal do
not provide sufficient evidence to ascertain whether structures dating to a particular period were coeval. However, the overall density of structures in the
residential zone at Tikal (Puletson 1973) does provide sufficient data to indicate, on the basis of population size, that Tikal was indeed a city. Sanders
and Price (1968:165), on the other hand, have proposed that household units
were noncontemporaneous to the extent that the status of Tikal was dimin-
ished as an urban center with a population of only 2000 or 3000 at any given
time. Although Sanders and Price suggested that Tikal was the largest of the
lowland Maya centers, Coba, Calakmul, and Naranjo, for example, operated
as Classic period regional centers (Marcus 1976), probably controlling an area
akin to that controlled by Tikal. Certainly, the sociopolitical organization of
the Lowland Maya as described by Sanders and Price more than 10 years ago
requires reevaluation in light of recent work in the Maya area (see Adams 1981
and Adams and Jones 1981).

Initially, the problem of determining the population of any prehistoric city
lies in locating its structures and features for a complete count. Second, a
determination of the number of structures functioning as domestic units must
be made; following this, it must be determined which of these were coeval. It
is probable that at least some surveyed structures were not yet built or were
abandoned during the Late Classic time span, as stated by Folan (1975:40–47).
Various arguments have been offered against the residential stability of the
ancient Maya; one of the most pervasive was based on the necessity of the
Maya to shift residences due to the exigencies of a swidden-type agriculture
regime. Puleston (1973:155), however, suggests the Maya may have exploited
productive kitchen gardens, thereby making this settlement pattern shift less
essential. Because Coba is located in a lake district, pisciculture was another
production possibility for intensive exploitation of a high-protein source, possibly contributing to the stability of its population. Although the Coba area
has yet to be investigated with respect to drained fields, these were possibly
constructed adjacent to the lakes (Folan 1976) and could have supplemented
the agricultural productivity of the area.

Haviland (1969:429; 1970a:191) provides evidence to support the continuous occupation of many Late Classic house ruins at Tikal. For example,
although structures were frequently altered, the ceramic complexes associated

with them show little change. When small structures were refurbished, old floors and walls were still used, suggesting the continuous occupation of structures. Middens also show continuous deposition. If a site had been abandoned, soil would have accumulated with a subsequent layering of middens obvious, but such is not the case in Tikal.

Although abandonment of a household may have been a preferred pattern following a death and burial, space limitations in a densely occupied zone may have made it possible for a family to remain in a house by cleansing themselves of the spiritual dangers via ritual absolution (Folan 1969b; Puleston 1973). House rituals are still practiced by the modern Maya prior to moving into a new house or upon the reoccupation of houses where deaths have occurred. Landa (1941:130) stated for the Contact period that houses were abandoned after burials except when there were a great number of people living in the compound. If the unit consisted of many members, the house would not be abandoned as the survivors would constitute a viable economic unit and would continue to carry on the functions of the familial group. This hypothesis could be tested by correlating the number of burials per household unit with the size of the unit—a reflection of membership size. Haviland (1970a), for example, found that burials in house-mounds were rarely disturbed. This suggests that the location of the burials was remembered by those living in these domestic structures at the time of the burial. For example, as many as 11 nonoverlapping burials have been located in a single platform at Tikal (Puleston 1973:152–153), thus suggesting that burial under household floors was not accompanied with the abandonment of the structure as has been suggested for historic times (Folan 1969b).

Another factor to consider in an assessment of Maya demographics is dual residence. It is possible, for example, that the distribution of architecture in the residential zones at Coba represents house compounds with kitchen gardens near the core and *nai nal* (milpa houses) near the periphery of the surveyed zones adjacent to the core. Puleston (1973:159) has argued against this pattern for Tikal. For reasons similar to those suggested by Puleston, this pattern does not seem to apply to Coba.

For Coba and Tikal, a pattern of dual residence is unlikely for two reasons. First, some of the units on the periphery of the surveyed zone once thought to be *nai nal* structures are similar in construction to those units near the center designated as residential. Also, there would be little need for a *nai nal* to be built on an elevated platform. Modern *nai nal* constructed in milpa fields surveyed in Zone I at Coba were less complex than the majority of prehistoric household compounds located in the periphery of the surveyed areas. Second, and more important, the compounds located at the peripheries of the surveyed zones exhibit house-lot walls forming *solares*. These, it has been suggested, represent household enclosures used for the development of kitchen gardens rather than storage houses adjacent to milpa plots.

Sixty-five of the designated household units in the periphery of Zone I (*N*

= 112) were built on substructural platforms and were indistinguishable from household compounds in the innermost areas around the core of the city. Of these peripheral compounds, 36 had house-lot boundary walls of stone, while 29 could have had perishable walls, both a distinctive feature of the *solar* unit. The substructural platform represents a large amount of energy not normally expended to build a structure serving solely storage purposes. Substructures, or platforms with no visible superstructures, are associated with 15 of the apsidal, round, and/or rectangular structure groups on the periphery and again represent energy outputs not consistent with the building of a temporary residence or corn storage unit. Remaining are 32 household units consisting of apsidal, round, or vaulted structures with no associated platforms. These include 18 cases of single structures, 11 cases of two associated structures, and 3 cases of three associated structures. Of these, 7 have house-lot boundary walls and 7 metates. Their spacing among other household units with platforms and house-lot boundary walls suggests they represent the residential dwellings of Coba's middle and lower classes. Moreover, the zones in the periphery of the survey areas probably were not used for agricultural fields but represent the less densely populated outer ring of an urban settlement. And finally, there was an insufficient number of structures on the periphery of the city to accommodate more than a very small percentage of the households located in the area close to the core as *nai nal*.

One further problem that may introduce error into the reconstruction of ancient demographic figures is the possibility of hidden house mounds. This is more of a problem in the central lowlands than it is at Coba where soil accumulation is slight. Reports on Tikal (Puleston 1973:164) and Seibal (Tourtellot 1976:8) have mentioned that the excavation of house-mound clusters produced more structures than had been mapped previously. Furthermore, the final survey in Zone I was the result of 1 year's training of Caamal and May in survey techniques by Folan, and after the collection of data on 6000 structures and features had been accomplished before detailed mapping in the northern zone was begun.

INITIAL POPULATION ESTIMATES AT COBA

Initial analysis of Coba's population by Folan (1975) included Haviland's (1970a) calculation for population size at Tikal and Naroll's (1962) formula for estimating population size on the basis of one person per 10 m² of roofed-over space. Haviland suggested that the house platforms recorded at Tikal were small and concluded that they represented nuclear family habitations. He suggested 5.0–5.7 individuals per family or per household structure.

Folan's (1975) calculation of population size in ancient Coba included not only the data collected on the ancient platforms and structures but a comparison drawn from data collected on habitation and population size in the

modern village of Coba. He calculated that the roofed-over space of all structures (vaulted and unvaulted, rectangular, apsidal and round, including roofed-
over space on platforms with no visible superstructures) equaled approximately 136,000 m² for the north, south, west, and east survey zones (Folan
1975). Naroll's (1962) formula thus yielded an approximate population density
of 2000 people per km² based on total roofed-over space (136,000 m²) for the
heavily packed and populated inner and outer suburban areas.

By testing the population figures—using Haviland's (1970a) and Naroll's
(1962) formulae against the known population figures for modern Coba—
Folan found that Haviland's formula overestimated and Naroll's formula
underestimated population figures for the modern village. Based on data from
contemporary Coba, Folan (1975) suggested that approximately 55% of the
structures in ancient Coba were contemporaneous habitations rather than 80%
as suggested by Haviland for Tikal. Folan (1975) concluded that population
estimates need take into account not only noncontemporaneity based on long
ceramic periods but abandonment of some structures during the same period
by people moving from town to hamlet. Folan, therefore, concluded that by
calculating a maximum contemporaneous occupancy of 55% and 5.7 individuals per family a figure of 1400 persons per km² for Zones I, II, III, and IV
would represent a reasonable estimate of Coba's population during the Late
Classic for, once again, the high-density suburban zone.

With data tabulated for all 13 zones surveyed at Coba, a more comprehensive estimate of the ancient population is possible, using several distinct methods. One method includes the data from all survey zones at Coba and parallels
Folan's (1975) preliminary analysis—using Naroll's (1962) method and adding
Folan's procedures for control over noncontemporaneity of households. A
second method focuses on Zones I and VI and the individual household compound as the unit of analysis. Concentrating on household compounds for
Zones I and VI facilitates the analysis as various structures (kitchens, storehouses) hypothetically can be excluded providing a range of possible population figures.

Naroll (1962) suggested that, despite considerable variation in dwellings,
human populations on an average maintain an optimal requirement for roofed-
over space. Therefore, the dwelling space of an archaeological settlement can
be measured and used to estimate its prehistoric population. There are, however, at least two basic problems with using an estimate of one person per 10
m² of space. First, the societies Naroll investigated to arrive at this figure are
located in North America, Oceania, South America, Africa, and Eurasia. It
is questionable if the organization of all these societies is comparable to that
of the ancient Maya. Here the arguments presented by Casselberry are ger-
mane:

> Formulae derived from data based on temporary or small circular structures, square
> log structures or permanent apartment-like structures, cannot be used to compute the
> population of, for example, semi-permanent farmers who are polygynous and have

several structures enclosed within a compound. In short, it is argued that each dwelling type must be examined separately [1974: 117–122].

Second, it is probable that there is considerable variation in the space utilized by different subgroups in Maya society such as the upper, middle, and lower classes. Other problems present in the utilization of Naroll's (1962) formula will be discussed in more detail and adjustments will be made where possible. It can be said, however, that the advantage of using Naroll's method is that it provides a rapid calculation of ancient demographic figures, resulting in a magnitude within which the population may be viewed.

POPULATION ESTIMATES
FOR CLASSIC PERIOD COBA

Urban Coba encompasses approximately 63 km² and the 13 zones surveyed by members of the Coba Archaeological Mapping Project total approximately 21.3 km² or 33% of the entire city (Table 13.1). Survey Zones I and VI are combined in the following tables. The initial site survey undertaken by Folan (1974–1975) established the 13 survey zones (see Figure 1.3). The northern transect between Sacbes 3 and 27 is composed of two survey zones: Zone I is located north of Sacbe 1; Zone VI is that portion south of Sacbe 1 and north of the Great Platform supporting the Coba Group B. Zone VI originally included a portion of the downtown administrative area with large, vaulted palace complexes, temples, and administrative structures associated with the religious, economic, and political functions of the city. This northern test area was resurveyed by Caamal, Fletcher, Kintz, and May in 1975–1976, and

TABLE 13.1   Areas of the 13 Zones
Surveyed at Coba

Zone	Area (km²)
I	2.8
II	1.7
III	4.0
IV	1.9
V	0.2
VI	0.7
VII	0.5
VIII	0.3
IX	1.9
X	1.9
XI	0.3
XII	1.0
XIII	4.1
	21.3

Zone I was redefined. For the purpose of this demographic analysis, the data from the second survey are utilized—representing the residential precinct and excluding the predominantly nonresidential administrative building complexes of the city core area from the calculations. For these reasons, most tables presented here show Zones I and VI combined.

POPULATION ESTIMATES
BASED ON ALL 13 ZONES

Additionally, the total amount of roofed-over space was calculated for all 13 zones surveyed, including vaulted and unvaulted rectangular, apsidal, and round structures (Table 13.2). A second tally included the structures already mentioned as well as all platforms with no visible superstructures. Based on these figures, the application of Naroll's (1962) formula (without controlling for noncontemporaneity) yields a rough population figure of 24,962 for Coba, with platforms without visible superstructures included in the tally and a population figure of 17,040 for the 13 zones if platforms with no visible superstructures are excluded. By projecting these figures for the entire site, a population of 75,643 is calculated if platforms without visible superstructures are included and 51,636 if these platforms are excluded. A 45% reduction for noncontemporaneity and nonresidential roofed-over space yields a figure of 13,729 (platforms without visible superstructures included) for the 13 zones and a projected population of 41,603 for the entire city. A second calculation, which excludes the platforms without visible superstructures, yields a population of 9372 for the 13 zones and a projected population figure of 28,400 for the entire city.

Calculations were made using Folan's formula deducting 45% from the total number of structures, thereby controlling for noncontemporaneity and those structures not used as residences. The number of structures is then multiplied by 5.7 inhabitants per household. When only vaulted, unvaulted rectangular, round, and apsidal structures are included in the sample, the estimated population for the 13 zones is 18,023 (Table 13.3). If the platforms without visible superstructures are included, this amount increases to 20,675 (Table 13.4). Again, these figures only represent the 33% of the city surveyed. Projecting these figures for the entire city, we arrive at 54,615 (excluding platforms without visible superstructures) and 62,652 with these platforms included.

POPULATION ESTIMATES
BASED ON ZONES I AND VI

Because discrete household compounds were mapped in Zones I and VI, separate calculations were computed, based on these data. The structures that were included in the calculations were those considered to have been household

TABLE 13.2 Roofed-over Space in Square Meters for Zones I-XIII

Features	I (+ VI)	II	III	IV	V	VII	VIII	IX	X	XI	XII	XIII	Totals (m²)
Apsidal/round	14,471	5,345	8,885	4,784	35	2,460	483	5,324	984	137	1,561	9,105	53,574
Rectangular unvaulted	5,566	12,316	12,375	8,838	518	7,158	3,995	6,783	390	205	1,505	2,306	61,955
vaulted	12,037	6,860	11,713	1,869	6,496	4,273	1,899	5,451	1,003	141	981	2,152	54,878
Subtotals	32,074	24,521	32,973	15,491	7,049	13,891	6,377	17,558	2,377	483	4,047	13,563	170,404
Platforms: no visible superstructures	22,708	19,865	12,466	5,840	1,979	4,029	1,824	2,979	283	63	2,531	4,649	79,216
Totals	54,782	44,386	45,439	21,331	9,028	17,920	8,201	20,537	2,663	546	6,578	18,212	249,620

TABLE 13.3 Population Estimate Based on Structure Counts for Zones I-XIII,
Excluding Platforms with No Visible Superstructures

	I (and VI)	II	III	IV	V	VII	VIII	IX	X	XI	XII	XIII	Total area (m²)
						Total number of structures							
Vaults	93	93	179	40	40	85	38	101	22	3	14	30	738
Unvaulted rectangular	321	403	517	384	16	231	122	192	12	6	44	66	2,314
Apsidal/round	723	252	466	232	2	118	23	272	44	7	85	465	2,689
Total	1,137	748	1,162	656	58	434	183	566	78	16	143	561	5,741
(−45%)	625	411	639	364	32	239	101	311	43	9	79	309	—
× 5.7 persons	3,563	2,343	3,642	2,075	182	1,362	576	1,773	245	51	450	1,761	18,023

TABLE 13.4 Population Estimate Based on Structure Counts for Zones I-XIII, Including Platforms with No Visible Superstructures

| | Total number of structures | | | | | | | | | | | | Total area (m²) |
	I (and VI)	II	III	IV	V	VII	VIII	IX	X	XI	XII	XIII	
Vaults	93	93	179	40	40	85	38	101	22	3	14	30	738
Unvaulted rectangular	321	403	517	384	16	231	122	192	12	6	44	66	2.314
Apsidal/round	723	252	466	232	2	118	23	272	44	7	85	465	2.689
Platforms: no structure	162	243	211	78	20	32	11	29	11	1	10	46	854
Total	1,299	991	1,373	734	78	466	194	594	89	17	153	607	6.595
(−45%)	714	545	755	404	43	256	107	327	49	9	84	334	—
×5.7 persons	4,070	3,107	4,304	2,303	245	1,459	610	1,864	279	51	479	1,904	20.675

TABLE 13.5   Number of Structures Per Household Unit and Total
Square Meters of Roofed-over Space in Zones I and VI

Number of structures	Roofed-over space (m^2)
1	1,803
2	3,997
3	6,928
4	4,455
5	5,134
6	2,177
7	2,315
8	1,107
9	0
10	615
11	639
12	0
13	806
14	409
15	505
	30,890

complexes only. These tabulations included structures from household compounds ranging from one to 15 structures. Roofed-over space in Zones I and VI
equals 30,890 m^2 (Table 13.5). Using Naroll's (1962) method to calculate the
number of persons resident in the zone results in a figure of 3089. Compounds
with two or more structures were considered to have included a kitchen that
should be excluded from the calculation to which Naroll's formula would be
applied. The total number of square meters, excluding structures considered
kitchens, totaled 26,157 m^2. The household floor area was again decreased for
those households exhibiting three or more structures to control for households
that included both a kitchen and an ancillary storehouse. The roofed-over area
following this adjustment is 21,435 m^2. The tabulation for correlated square
meters, excluding the smallest structure per household as a probable kitchen
and the two smallest structures per household as a probable kitchen and storehouse appears in Table 13.6.

If the residential population at Coba occupied a circle of 360° surrounding
the civic–ceremonial core, and the northern test area, Zones I and VI, comprised
approximately $\frac{1}{20}$ of the total urban area, or about 5%, then if the gross figure
of 3089 persons for Zones I and VI is approximately correct, the entire city
could have supported 20 times that or a population of 61,780. If we correct
for those structures that were kitchens, Zones I and VI had a residential population of 2,615.7 persons and the residential zone of Coba could have had
a total population of approximately 52,314. If kitchens and storehouses were
excluded then the reduced population figure for Zones I and VI is 2143.5 and
the entire site could have contained 42,870 persons.

TABLE 13.6 Number of Structures per Household Unit and Total Square Meters of Roofed-over Space, Excluding "Kitchens," and Excluding "Kitchens and Storehouses" in Zones I and VI

Number of structures	Total m^2	Total m^2 "kitchens"	Corrected m^2 excluding "kitchens"	Total m^2 "kitchens" and "storehouses"	Corrected m^2 excluding "kitchens" and "storehouses"
1	1,803	0	1,803	0	1,803
2	3,997	1,598	2,399	1,598	2,399
3	6,928	1,531	5,397	3,784	3,144
4	4,455	623	3,832	1,640	2,815
5	5,134	530	4,604	1,306	3,828
6	2,177	169	2,008	414	1,763
7	2,315	128	2,187	330	1,985
8	1,107	66	1,041	167	940
9	0	0	0	0	0
10	615	24	591	58	557
11	639	18	621	54	585
12	0	0	0	0	0
13	806	25	781	55	751
14	409	9	400	21	388
15	505	12	493	28	477
	30,890	4,733	26,157	9,455	21,435

Although these figures do not account for noncontemporaneous structures of the same time period, abandoned structures, or structures of another time period, they are very close to the figure of 44,287 arrived at for the entire city, using figures from the 13 zones on roofed-over space and adjusting the total by a reduction of 45% following Folan. A higher figure of 62,652 for the entire city is produced by using Folan's method of adjusting the total structure count by 45% and then multiplying by 5.7 persons per structure.

ETHNOHISTORIC AND ETHNOGRAPHIC DATA

The population data collected during the Contact period reflect the social disruption in Yucatan brought about by the conquest, the subsequent breakdown of native political organizations, as well as massive population decreases due to the introduction of European diseases. Whatever changes occurred between the Classic and Contact periods (and some changes must have occurred as demographic conditions are sensitive to changes in social, economic, and political structure), it is assumed within a reasonable range, that the ethnohistorical and ethnograpic materials from Yucatan are consistent with Classic Maya patterns of household organization.

Census material collected in 1570 from Cozumel (Roys et al. 1940) provides a list of household members including the head of the house, his wife, male tributaries, and their wives. The membership in some households also indicated that the sons, brothers, or nephews of the head of the house were commonly included in the household (Roys *et al.* 1940:14). Nine of the 17 households listed exhibited this pattern. Four of the 17 households had another woman in the compound that shared the same name as the wife of the head—either a sister, daughter, or niece of the wife. Relevant data on household membership are also obtained from the census material from Pencuyut (Roys *et al.* 1959). Figures on household size in Cozumel, Tizimin–Boxch'en, Dzonotchuil, Tecay, Tixacauche, as well as Pencuyut, are listed—including the number of houses in each town and the average number of inhabitants per house (Table 13.7). It is not clear, however, whether the "house" referred to in the ethnohistoric literature is one structure or a household compound of more than one structure. This presents a problem in the application of these figures to ancient settlements where virtually all that remains visible on the surface is collapsed architecture.

Ethnographic data from Yucatan provide a range of figures to apply in the reconstruction of ancient demographic figures. Data available, as cited by Puleston (1973:171–176), include materials collected by Redfield and Villa Rojas (1934:91), who calculated an average figure of 5.6 persons per house or household for Chan Kom. This figure has been used by Wauchope (1938:145) for Uaxactun and by Haviland (1965:19; 1969:429) for the reconstruction of the Tikal population. Haviland, however, later reduced his figure from 5.6 to 5.0 people per house (1972a:138), basing this reduction on his reconstruction of household statistics from the Cozumel 1570 census material from which he derived a norm of 3.7 married couples per house. Each married couple, he suggests, had four surviving children based on skeletal materials recovered from Tikal as well as modern Maya populations studied by Steggerda (1941). The combination of one elder couple, 2.7 young children and four children per couple yields a total of 18.2 persons per household. This breaks down to an average of 4.9 persons per nuclear family. The average figure of 5 people

TABLE 13.7 Number of Houses and Average Number of Inhabitants per House during the Ethnohistorical Period[a]

Town	Number of houses	Average number of inhabitants/house
Pencuyut	81	8.42
Tizimin-Boxch'en	56	9.89
Dzonotchuil	76	8.66
Tecay	37	7.48
Tixcacauche	59	8.32
Cozumel Island	39	11.43

[a] From Roys *et al.* 1959: Table 2.

per house is used for population calculations on the basis of the still unproved assumption that "each individual house was occupied by a single nuclear family consisting of a married couple and their unmarried offspring" (Haviland 1972a:136).

Puleston (1973:173) criticized Haviland's reconstruction, stating that the number of children per family is too high as the archaeological evidence indicates that the population from A.D. 500–700 was stable and did not increase at the rate it would have had to, based on Haviland's surviving children figures. He suggests that other categories, such as unmarried adults, widows, widowers, or childless couples may have controlled population growth while also increasing household membership size. Puleston (1973), therefore, suggests that the number of people per household is higher than that suggested by Haviland, while the number of children per family is lower. His assumption is based primarily on data collected by Villa Rojas (1945:43–44) from nine settlements in central Quintana Roo where the average number of people per household was 6.07, a figure higher than that listed for more acculturated communities in Yucatan.

Following Haviland's argument, an average of five members per house (per structure) can be used to calculate the population residing in Zones I and VI at Coba, based on a total of 1117 structures associated with the 356 household compounds in those zones. Assuming that all structures were residential, 5585 persons could have lived in these zones. Controlling for kitchens by excluding one structure from each household compound that had two or more associated structures, the corrected number of structures would be 830. If each structure housed a nuclear family of five, then 4150 persons could be said to have lived in Zones I and VI. Correcting for kitchens *and* storehouses, then 634 structures would remain in Zones I and VI for a population of 3170. If these three figures are projected for the entire city, of which Zones I and VI represents only 5%, we get an estimated population of 111,600 (no controls), 83,000 (controlling for a kitchen), and 63,400 (controlling for a kitchen and one storehouse). These projected figures seem high when compared with the projected figures from our other calculations.

A variation is to assume a certain percentage of the structures as being nonresidential. Puleston (1973:194–196) corrected his structure count by considering 16% of the structures at Tikal as nonresidential, making his corrected figure for structures occupied during the Late Classic approximately 1120 for the northern and southern survey strips. On this basis, he calculated that the density of Late Classic residential structures was approximately 100 structures per square kilometer.

In comparison, at Coba, the 1117 structures in Zones I and VI were associated with household compounds. Considering 16% of the structures as nonresidential leaves 938 residential structures. Controlling for temporal variation, following Puleston's analysis of the Tikal data, 99% would be Late Classic, giving a figure of 928 structures. In that Zones I and VI are approximately 3.5 km², this would produce a density of 265 structures per square kilometer.

To present a range of population figures calculated on the basis of 265 structures per square kilometer, material cited above from ethnohistorical and ethnographic household composition are tabulated (Table 13.8). The projected population figures based on the density of structures per square kilometer seem high in comparison to other estimates in that they range from 81,487.5 to 186,280.4. One controlling factor that cannot be accounted for at Coba is the amount of land unsuitable for settlement. This land would include ancient quarries (*sascaberas*), cenotes, lowlands subject to flooding, and swamplands. These areas, however (with the exception of the numerous *sascaberas* in Zone II)—as far as can be discerned—are minimal and most of the zones surveyed at Coba showed remarkable consistency in the continuous distribution of architecture.

Household units (N = 356) in Zones I and VI include from one to 15 associated structures. Using the materials provided by Roys (*et al.* 1959:Table 2), the population of this zone was calculated on the basis of his figures from six colonial towns (Table 13.9). Also included is the distribution of household

TABLE 13.8 Ethnohistorical, Ethnographic, and Archaeological Figures for Household Composition Utilized to Reconstruct the Population of Residential Zones I and VI at Coba

Source	Average number inhabitants per house	Projected population figures based on 265 structures/km²	
		Zones I and VI[a]	Entire residential zone[b]
Ethnohistorical			
Pencuyut	8.42	7,809.6	137,225.0
Tizimin-Boxch'en	9.89	9,173.0	161,182.3
Dzonotchuil	8.66	8,032.2	141,136.4
Tecay	7.48	6,937.7	121,905.3
Tixcacauche	8.32	7,716.8	135,595.2
Cozumel Island	11.43	10,601.3	186,280.4
Ethnographic			
Chan Kom	5.6	5,194.0	91,226.0
X-Cacal	6.07	5,629.9	98,925.8
Archaeological			
Wauchope (1938)	5.6	5,194.0	91,266.0
Haviland (1965)	5.0	4,637.5	81,487.5
Puleston (1973)	6.07	5,629.9	98,925.8

[a] Population for Zones I and VI = Area of northern zone (3.5 km²) × average number of inhabitants per house × structures per km² (265).

[b] Population of entire residential zone = average number inhabitants per house × structures per km² (265) × area of entire residential zone (61.5 km²).

TABLE 13.9 Calculation of the Residential Population of Ancient
Coba Based on Figures for Occupants Per Household during
the Ethnohistorical Period

Number of persons per household	Population for Zones I and VI	Population for residential zone
8.42	2,997.52	59,950.4
9.89	3,520.84	70,416.8
8.66	3,082.96	61,659.2
7.48	2,662.88	53,257.6
8.32	2,961.92	59,238.4
11.43	4,069.09	81,381.6

units by number of structures per household to evaluate the figures presented
(Table 13.10). The two figures calculated from the ethnohistorical data,
81,381.6 and 70,416.8, appear to be too high. These reconstructions are based
on a family size of 9 to 11, with possibly two to three sleeping quarters and
an ancillary kitchen and storehouse or two for a total of four to seven structures per household. The number of persons per household would have possibly included two married couples and from five to seven children or possibly
a household membership consisting of three married couples and a total of
from three to five children.

At Coba, the most frequently reported number of structures per household is three. Only 31% of all household units located in Zones I and VI consist
of four to 15 structures per household. In other words, the median number of

TABLE 13.10 Number of Structures per Household
and Their Frequency of Occurrence in Zones I and VI

Number of structures	Frequency
1	73
2	83
3	88
4	39
5	40
6	12
7	10
8	4
9	0
10	2
11	2
12	0
13	1
14	1
15	1
TOTAL	356

structures per household could have housed a range of inhabitants from a small nuclear family to a household with two married couples with one to three children, respectively, for a total household membership of possibly 10. Therefore, it is suggested that 9.89 or 11.43 represent the upper extreme range of family membership as derived from ethnohistorical data. Thus the figures that range from 52,314 to 61,780 for the total population of Coba seem to approximate occupation of the city based on Folan's (1975) and Naroll's (1962) formula as well as on ethnohistorical materials.

A TRIAL ESTIMATE OF CLASSIC MAYA PALACE POPULATIONS AT COBA

A preliminary estimate of the resident population of the Coba Group B (Thompson *et al.* 1932) completes this initial reconstruction of Classic demographic parameters at Coba. The aim of this section is not to present a precise population figure but to suggest an order of magnitude for the population of the core area.

Adams (1974a) has argued that some palace compounds in the administrative precincts at ancient Maya centers served as residential structures for the elite and their retainers. He states that clusters of palace rooms, including those rooms exhibiting benches (for sleeping areas), occasionally display a constellation of domestic features indicating that palaces were probably partially domestic as well as administrative.

Using Naroll's (1962) factor for the A–V palace at Uaxactun, Adams (1974a) calculated that 214 persons would have been accommodated in the structure. However, the multifunctional nature of these palace structures— domestic, administrative, storage—would reduce the number of people per unit. In light of this, he suggests the metered area should, therefore, be reduced to account more accurately for the nonresidential roofed-over space component. Bench areas could be used to calculate the resident population in the palace compounds. Using length and width of benches in structure A–V at Uaxactun, Adams (1974a:288–298) calculated that either 95 adults or 190 children could be accommodated in the structure. Of course, this projection does not represent reality since the structure most certainly did not house only adults or only children. Fortunately, Adams had also calculated from data collected in the conservative and more traditional villages of east central Quintana Roo (Villa Rojas 1945:3) that children formed about 33% of the population. Using the X–Cacal proportions, the Uaxactun A–V palace could have housed 114 persons: 76 adults and 38 children.

Turning to the Coba data and applying Naroll's (1962) formula, the 94 structures surveyed in the Coba Group B measure 8011 m², meaning 801.1 persons would have been accommodated in the group. Concurring with Adams (1974a), this figure is probably high. Although data on bench areas are not available at Coba, correction of the structure counts and roofed-over space can be made using the factors calculated for Uaxactun as well as by comparisons with palace compounds at other sites in the Maya zone. Using Adams's (1974a) material, the following calculations can be made with the Coba Group B data. Adams's corrected population figure of 114 was 53% of his figure based on roofed-over space. The figure calculated from Naroll's function for the Coba Group B was 801 persons, 53% of which provides a corrected population of 425. However, the Coba figure may still be high because each of the 94 structures was considered a residential unit. A reduction is necessary for structures that were nonresidential in character. Adams (1974a) suggests that only 59% of the rooms in the A–V palace area at Uaxactun were residential. A tally of the metered area of the Coba Group B structures demonstrated that the average room size was 40 m². The number of additional rooms—calculated by dividing the total roofed-over area (8011 m²) by the averge room size (40 m²)—provides a gross room count of 200. This number is utilized as the number of rooms in the Coba Group B and a correction factor is applied, following Adams, to exclude probable nonresidential structures. In other words, 59% ($N = 118$) of the total number of rooms in the Coba Group B will be considered residential. Following Adams's (1974a:289) estimate of 2.53 persons of both sexes and all ages per room, the Coba Group B residential rooms could have housed a maximum population of 298.54 people.

The Coba Group B represents only ⅔ of the civic–ceremonial zone supported on the large, substructural platform known as the Great Platform. This platform also supports the Chumuk Mul Group, which is at least partially residential, and the Nohoch Mul Group, which may also have housed a percentage of the center's elite and retainer population. In gross figures, we can say that the Great Platform at Coba could have supported approximately 400 persons, including the elite priests, aristocracy, and their retainers.

CONCLUSIONS

As mentioned, Folan (1975) introduced two variations instructive for calculating prehistoric populations in the Maya area. Analyzing data on the population resident in modern Coba and associated household units, he found that family size averaged 5.7 persons (1975:18) and that only 55% of the structures in the village were occupied at a given time. Although Folan pointed out the difficulty in comparing population centers of different sociopolitical complexity, his analysis did suggest that abandoned structures represent a significant variable in the reconstruction of population size. In his analysis, family membership is higher and structures occupied is lower than the figures presented by Haviland (1972a:136). In the calculation of population figures from Folan's outline, 5.7 members per family is used for the reconstruction of ancient populations at Coba with only 55% of the structures considered contem-

TABLE 13.11   Population Estimates for Coba: Data from Zones I-XIII
for Roofed-Over Space and Structure Counts

Description of method	Zones I-XIII no platforms	Projected entire site	Zones I-XIII with platforms	Projected entire site
Naroll (1962) 10 m^2 roofed-over space per person; no adjustments	17,040	51,636	24,962	75,643
Naroll (1962) with adjustment (-45%)	9,372	28,400	13,729	41,603
Folan (1975) structure count (-45%)	18,023	54,615	20,675	62,652

poraneous and used as dormitories. Applying this formula to Coba by subtracting 45% of the 1117 structures in Zones I and VI, 614 structures would be considered dormitories. Multiplying this figure by 5.7 persons results in 3499.4 for the population of Zones I and VI. Multiplying this by 20, the projected population for the entire site would be 69,996. Again, comparing this figure to the one derived from Folan's method but with data from the 13 zones and projecting it for the entire site, we see similar results: 69,996 compared to 62,652.

TABLE 13.12   Population Estimates for Coba: Data from Zones
I and VI for Household Compounds as the Unit of Analysis

Description of method	Zone I	Projected for entire site
Naroll 10 m^2 roofed-over space per person; no adjustments	3,089	61,780
Naroll adjustment for one kitchen	2,615.7	52,314
Naroll adjustment for one kitchen, one storehouse	2,143.5	42,870
Folan structure count (-45%), family size 5.7 persons	3,499.4	69,996
Haviland structure count; control for one kitchen; family size 5 persons	4,150	83,000
Haviland structure count; control for one kitchen, one storehouse; family size 5 persons	3,170	63,400

In conclusion, the initial demographic figures calculated by Folan (1975) were most instructive in establishing the urban proportions of Coba on the basis of population figures alone. His calculations leave no doubt as to the magnitude of the population density at Coba (Table 13.11 and Table 13.12). We believe the discussion of demographic figures at Coba will orient others to a more comprehensive understanding of other conclusions drawn about this urban center. We will not underestimate the problems inherent in calculations of prehistoric demographic figures and are prepared to reevaluate the figures as more data are collected from Coba in areas not covered by our survey. Possibly the most significant comparison that has been drawn is that between Coba and the better-known city of Tikal. That these and other large cities were regional centers (Adams 1981; Folan 1975; Marcus 1973) and have now been shown to have had large, heterogeneous populations are sufficient causes for a thoughtful reevaluation of the political, economic, and agricultural bases of Classic Maya society.

In sum, we suggest that conservative figures of between approximately 40,000 and 60,000 be considered as a realistic range for the population at Coba during the Late Classic.

Chapter 14

Summary
and Conclusions

William J. Folan

COBA: A DEVELOPMENTAL MODEL

In this book, we have developed and tested a model of a Classic Maya city based on such factors as size, social complexity, and economic diversity. But, as could be expected, Coba did not develop into the capital of a regional state overnight. Given the successes of MacNeish *et al.* (1981) in discovering an early preceramic occupation on the east coast of the peninsula, coupled with Hammond's (1974b) definition of early semisedentary or sedentary horticultural, ceramic-producing settlements, it seems reasonable to speculate that the habitation of the Coba area also may have begun at an early date. Perhaps a few band-level peoples dedicated to hunting and gathering (Folan 1979) or tribal-level peoples dedicated to horticultural activities arrived in the Coba area and formed a camp or hamlet sometime during the early Kukican Period (? B.C.–A.D. 250) (Folan 1978c:Table 1; (see Table 14.1, this volume). Such settlement may have coincided with the same cool–humid period in which the Olmec were developing into a state-level society on the Isthmus of Tehuantepec. But whereas the Olmecs abandoned La Venta during the following period (beginning ca. 400 B.C.) of comparatively higher temperatures and lower humidity, people remained in Coba to form an early village society. They remained perhaps due to Coba's location in a zone of fairly high precipitation, at least during the early years of its growth (Wilson 1980:24). The inhabitants of Coba have been associated with a ceramic type during this developmental period that

211

TABLE 14.1 Periods of Cultural Development in Coba[a]

Time periods	Maya area: general	Coba cultural periods	
2000 B.C.–A.D. 250	Early to Late Preclassic	Kucican (early village)	Coba was the site of one or more farming villages during this period.
A.D. 250–A.D. 600	Early Classic	Pakchen (early urbanization)	Coba was developing into an urban center during this time.
A.D. 600–A.D. 800	Late Classic	Machukani (middle urbanization)	Coba was now a metropolis and the capital of a larger regional state with Peten connections, especially Naranjo.
A.D. 800–A.D. 1000	Terminal Classic	Xmakabah (late urbanization)	Coba continued to operate as an urban center at this time and the capital of a regional state with lessening Peten connections and increasing Gulf Coast associations.
A.D. 1000–A.D. 1250	Early Postclassic	Kanakax (Early Protohistoric)	Coba had already been invaded by Itza people who probably used it as a civic-ceremonial center at this and later times.
A.D. 1250–A.D. 1441	Middle Postclassic	Manaachi (Middle Protohistoric)	Coba's power had been mostly lost to people from the east coast and Mayapan.
A.D. 1441–A.D. 1546	Late Postclassic	Chumuk Mul (Late Protohistoric)	Coba was now a pilgrimage center visited by both coastal and inland people. The move was still toward the coast.
A.D. 1546–Present	Recent	San Pedro (historic)	Coba remained a pilgrimage center with few people still living, farming, and hunting in its territory, as they have done up to the present day.

[a]Source: based on Folan 1978c: Table 1.

has been classified by Robles C. (1980) as Añejo (Chicanel, Chicanna). These ceramics, however, have been found only in small quantities.

It was not until the Pakchen period (A.D. 250–600) that Coba began to develop into a chiefdom-level society arriving at a city–state status during the last centuries of this developmental period (Folan 1978c:Table 1) (see Table 14.1). At this time, Coba residents utilized a ceramic type classified by Robles C. (1980) as Blanco (Cochuah, Tzakol).

The maximum period of development of Coba as a civic–religious–economic center and metropolis did not occur, however, until its Machukaani period (A.D. 600–800) (Folan 1978c:Table 1) (Table 14.1) when a cooler, more humid interval returned to the peninsula (Gunn and Adams 1981; Folan *et al.* 1980). At that time Coba represented one of the most important regional centers dotting the coastal zone of the peninsula (Folan 1975). This is the period to which Joseph Ball (1977:personal communication) dated the majority of the linear features in Coba sampled by us (Tepeu I); Robles (1980) later associated this period with his Palmas ceramic type (Tepeu I and II), found there in impressive quantities. Coba continued as the capital of a regional state that ultimately included between 5000 and 8000 km² of territory (Folan 1976). We suggest that it was primarily during this period that Coba took on the form described in this work, including its maximum formation of population, wards, neighborhoods, and guilds situated within the 63–70-km² area surveyed by us and serviced by its multiple *sacbeob* and other routes of communication.

Following these periods of considerable activity and political importance, Coba entered into apparent decline, manifested by a reduction in its political and economic importance around A.D. 900–1000 (Folan 1978c:Table 1) (Table 14.1). Coba probably functioned at this time as a chiefdom rather than as the state-level society it had been during its previous Machukanni period. Robles C. (1980) identifies his Oro (Cehpech) wares with the years associated with this warmer, drier interval.

Despite many references to several important personages in Coba in the history of Chichen Itza (Folen 1976), there is little evidence of a large population in Coba during the maximum development of this important civic–religious center. The Maya apparently continued to dominate the moister coasts of Quintana Roo and the southern part of the peninsula, leaving the drier northwest area of the peninsula to the Toltec invaders.

Following the shift from a comparatively dry to a more humid period during Manaachi times (A.D. 1200–1441), Coba continued to demonstrate close relationships with the east coast of the peninsula as well as strong ties to Mayapan (Folan 1978c:Table 1) (Table 14.1). It was during this period that the Coba residents built numerous temple-shrines in the core area of Coba in association with the La Iglesia and La Ixmoja group, as well as with other groups outside the core area at places such as Pakchen. Coba residents were now associated with a Seco ceramic type (Tases), according to Robles C. (1980).

Following this humid period, the downfall of Mayapan, and the Balkanization of the peninsula into more or less independent provinces, Coba lost the major part of its power as a political and economic unit. It did continue, however, to be a major pilgrimage center serving both coastal and interior peoples during its Chumuk Mul period (A.D. 1441–1541).

During the historic San Pedro period (Folan 1978c:Table 1) (Table 14.1), from the conquest of the peninsula by Spaniards to the present century, Coba continued to be a religious center with a few families living on limited farming incomes combined with hunting and collecting activities, much as their ancestors lived during Coba's early, Preclassic occupation over 2000 years before.

TESTING THE MODEL

Although the chronology and associated social forms discussed here seem reasonable enough in light of what is now known of the specific history of human habitation on the peninsula of Yucatan, as well as general knowledge of urban and state development, regional or local development must be tested whether the models of development focus on Coba or elsewhere.

Problem-oriented excavation to locate the earliest inhabitants of Coba is essential if encampments of egalitarian, band-level hunting and gathering people, and incipient tribal-level horticulturists are to be discovered in the Coba area. Remains of the hunter–gatherers will probably be found in the form of lithic materials similar to those so far discovered by MacNeish *et al.* (1981) and Velázquez Valadéz (1980) to the south, and probably will be found close to water-bearing caves and seasonal *akalches* still used as water sources by present-day residents and travelers.

The remains of early and fully developed tribal-level horticulturists, or at least indications of their presence, can be determined through large, open-pit excavations and through the analysis of the flora collected from the bottoms of the many aquatic features dotting the Coba area. Although one would expect to find fairly permanent habitations among fully developed tribal-level horticulturists, there should exist little or no indication of rank differences or public buildings.

It would seem that the development of Coba into a nonegalitarian chiefdom-level society came before its development into a city-state type of organization. Although Freidel (1981b:375), for example, associated the shift (ca. 300 B.C.) from nucleated egalitarian to dispersed nonegalitarian residential patterns at Cerros with accommodation to changing social relations rather than to changing ecological factors, this event may well have been associated with climatic change from a cool–humid to a warmer–drier episode. This shift was apparently of benefit to the people of Cerros, as it is marked by an increase in monumental construction and cosmopolitan art. This may also have been the case in Coba where one should look not only for changing population distribution and public architecture but also for rank differences based on habitation size and elaboration, plus artifact content, suggesting that households of differing degrees of importance existed within the same community. Public architecture and households should also be distributed in a concentric fashion typical of preindustrial towns, as also seems to be the case at Preclassic Komchen in Northwestern Yucatan (Andrews V 1981).

Evidence suggesting a shift from a locally based chiefdom level to a regional-state form of organization should be associated with the appearance of elaborate palace-type architecture, as has been often suggested by Sanders (e.g., 1981), in addition to an increase in the size and quantity of religious architecture (made possible through corvée labor). Other cultural remains should also indicate a higher degree of stratification among households.

Careful dating of the Coba *sacbeob* could provide an additional clue toward differentiating between city and regional state organization. What seems a reasonable indicator of political and territorial conservatism or expansionism in Coba is reflected by the apparent early development of the Coba Group B, coeval with what may be considered a local system of *sacbeob*. This suggests a city-state form of organization in contrast to the development of the Nohoch Mul Group associated with later ceramic types (Robles 1980). In that the latter group is associated with a more extensive system of *sacbeob* (including the 6-km-long intracity *sacbe* to Kukican and the 100-km intercity *sacbe* to Yaxuna), this strongly suggests a regional (in contrast to a more local) city-state form of development. This also seems true of the 20-km *sacbe* connecting Coba with Ixil during Late Classic times (Folan and Stuart 1974; Robles 1976).

The best test of a regional organization in contrast to a city-state organization will, however, be possible only after deep excavations in the major groups at Coba to locate buried stelae, murals, and other glyphic and nonglyphic materials. These will indicate not only degrees of ranking systems but also the relative role of Coba during its early development as an urban center. This is in contrast to its role during the Late and Terminal Classic as the capital of a regional state. Investigations of this type should not only provide us with emblem glyphs but with additional information such as personages involved in elite activities, much like the investigations of Marcus (1976), Proskouriakoff (1963), and Schele (1978) in the Central and Southern Lowlands. Cleaning the facades of buildings and their subsequent consolidation simply does not satisfy the need for obtaining the type of information essential to understand better the development of Coba.

It seems reasonable to suggest that an intensive effort be made to locate and define all sites within the Coba region to determine through, for example, their stelae, relative size and location, and occurrence of scarce goods, which sites can be considered politically and commercially dependent upon others.

Another well-known method to determine Coba's development during any one period is through the systematic excavation of test pits from the core area to the limits of the urban area. One should discover a more restricted range of habitation during Early (rather than Late) Classic times and fewer materials associated with the earlier in contrast to the later period. In comparison to the Late Classic, a more restricted range of Terminal and Postclassic materials should also be found, with fewer materials, indicating a reduced population and a decline in the importance of the city during these periods.

In order to test for the existence of barrios or wards within the urban limits of Coba, each of the divisions produced by the *sacbe* system must be carefully mapped and test-excavated to determine whether the existence of wards can be supported by the type and distribution of structures discovered within these divisions. If wards do exist, their associated architecture should suggest at least a degree of local political and religious autonomy, separate from other areas of the city. For example, barrio formation should be associated with outstanding forms of civic–religious architecture—such as the Cola de Venado and Uitzil Mul groups—distributed in a measured fashion over the urban zone and forming parish-like nodes already defined by us in Coba (Folan 1975; Kintz 1978; see also Chapter 12, this volume) and earlier by Culbert (1974) in Tikal.

Within these wards, there will be found groups of households clustering closer together than other households in the same general area, suggesting the existence of neighborhoods within the barrios (discussed in detail by Kintz in Chapter 12).

Household composition can best be determined through the presence of linear features, deliminating them much in the same way that barrios may be framed by *sacbeob* (Folan 1975, 1976) (see also Chapters 6 and 7, this volume). If linear features are not recognizable on the surface, they should be located through excavation. Once the various households have been defined within each barrio, the shape and general composition of their buildings as well as the contents of each must be determined and quantified in order to state with a reasonable degree of accuracy whether a particular type of structure was intended for civic–religious functions, culinary purposes, or for residences, storage, manufacturing, or other uses.

Once the barrios, neighborhoods, and households are defined, their relationships to each other (as well as to their architectural and artifact content) should aid the definition of guild areas. For example, one would expect to find a greater frequency of metates of a certain shape and size and associated debitage in a manufacturing zone (Folan 1976) than in other areas of the city where they were distributed. A source of the stone used in their formation should also be located near their place of distribution.

Population is another matter worthy of further investigation: when the total area of roofed-over space available in Coba during a given time period is known, the possibilities of determining its population will improve greatly. What must be looked for during the excavation of buildings forming households are items such as the number of cooking areas associated with each household, because each family will usually have access to its own hearth for culinary purposes. The location and quantity of sleeping platforms (Landa 1941:86) in each household should also be determined (Adams 1974a) as an aid toward calculating population size. Once the area of roofed-over floor space, building types, number and distribution of hearths, and sleeping platform area is defined, the size of the Maya household and population of the urban area at a given time will become less of a problem. However, no great surprises are anticipated along these lines.

The question of climatic change is also testable in Coba. In addition to the information that can be obtained based on limnological studies (*see* Dahlin *et al.* 1980 for El Mirador), the *sacbeob* of Coba also offer a testing ground because their construction and location in low, now-flooded areas can indicate fluctuating water levels in Coba during different climatic intervals. What may be discovered is that Sacbes 8 and 11 were built during a comparatively warm–dry period whereas Sacbes 14 and 15 were formed during a comparatively cooler and more humid interval.

Finally, the testing of our model of Coba as a regional, urban center divided into barrios, neighborhoods, guilds, and households —all affected by climatic change—is the least of the many problems that exist in Maya archaeology. Virtually every aspect of the Maya past is recoverable if and when we have the funds and properly trained multidisciplinary personnel available for forming the models and carrying out the detailed excavations and analyses necessary for testing. Following these indispensable prerequisites, the Maya past will come to form part of contemporary expectations for a more knowledgeable tomorrow. We may add that, in our opinion, work at Coba has taken us further down the path toward a more complete understanding of preindustrial societies in Mesoamerica and elsewhere.

Bibliography

Adams, Richard E. W.
    1969   Maya archaeology 1958–1968: a review. *Latin American Research Review* 4(2):3–45.
    1970   Suggested classic period occupational specialization in the Southern Maya Lowlands. *Monographs and Papers in Maya Archaeology. Papers of the Peabody Museum of Archaeology and Ethnology, Harvard University* 61:437–502.
    1973   The collapse of Maya civilization: a review of previous theories. In *The Classic Maya Collapse,* edited by T. Patrick Culbert. Albuquerque: New Mexico Press.
    1974a   A trial estimation of classic Maya palace populations at Uaxactun. In *Mesoamerican archaeology: new approaches* edited by Norman Hammond. Austin: University of Texas. Pp. 285–296.
    1974b   Preliminary reports on archaeological investigations in the Rio Bec area, Campeche, Mexico, edited by R. E. W. Adams. *Middle American Research Institute, Tulane University,* New Orleans. Reprint from Publication 31:103–146.
    1977a   *Prehistoric Mesoamerica.* Boston: Little, Brown
    1977b   Rio Bec archaeology and the rise of Maya civilization. In *The origins of Maya civilization,* edited by R. E. W. Adams. Albuquerque: University of New Mexico Press.
    1981   Settlement patterns of the central Yucatan and southern Campeche regions. In *Lowland Maya settlement patterns,* edited by Wendy Ashmore. Albuquerque: University of New Mexico Press. Pp. 211–258.
Adams, Richard E. W., W. E. Brown, Jr., and T. Patrick Culbert
    1981   Radar mapping, archaeology, and ancient Maya land use. *Science* **213:** 1457–1463.
Adams, Richard E. W., and Richard C. Jones
    1981   Spatial patterns and regional growth among classic Maya cities. *American Antiquity* **46**(2):301–322.

Adams, Robert McC.
1966   *The evolution of urban society.* Chicago: Aldine.
Aguilera Herrera, N.
1959   Suelos. *In* Los recursos naturales del sureste y su aprovachamiento, edited by
                E. Beltrán. *Instituto Mexicano de Recursos Naturales Renovables* Part 2, Vol.
                2, pp. 3–24.
Allen, P. H.
1956   *The rain forests of Golfo Dulce.* Gainesville: University of Florida.
Altschuler, Milton
1958   On the environmental limitation of Maya cultural development. *Southwestern
                Journal of Anthropology* **14**(2):189–198.
Anderson, Edgar
1952   *Plants, man and life.* Berkeley: University of California Press.
1954   Reflections on certain Honduran gardens. *Landscape* **4**(1):21–23.
Andrews, Anthony P.
1977   Reconocimiento arqueológico de la costa norte del Estado de Campeche. *Bol·
                etín de la Escuela de Ciencias Antropológicas de la Universidad de Yucatán,*
                Año 4, No. 24:64–77
1978   Puertos costeros del postclásico temprano en el norte de Yucatán. *Estudios de
                Cultura Maya* **11**:75–93.
Andrews IV, E. Wyllys
1938   Some new material from Cobá, Quintana Roo, Mexico. *Ethnos* **3**(2):33–46.
1943   The archaeology of southwestern Campeche. *Carnegie Institution of Washing-
                ton, Contributions to American Anthropology and History,* No. 40.
1961   Review of *Prehistoric ceramics and settlement patterns in Quintana Roo, Mex-
                ico,* by William T. Sanders. *American Antiquity* **27**:123–124.
1962   Excavaciones en Dzibilchaltun, Yucatán 1956–1962. *Estudios de Cultura Maya*
                2:149–183.
1965   Explorations in the Gruta de Chac, Yucatan, Mexico. In *Archaelogical inves-
                tigations on the Yucatan Peninsula,* Middle American Research Institute, Pub-
                lication 31. New Orleans: Tulane University. Pp. 1–22.
1968   Dzibilchaltun: A northern Maya metropolis. *World Archaeology* **21**(1):36–47.
1970   Balankanche, throne of the tiger priest. *Middle American Research Institute,*
                Publication 32, Tulane University, New Orleans.
1973   The development of Maya civilization after abandonment of the southern cit-
                ies. In *The Classic Maya Collapse,* edited by T. Patrick Culbert. Albuquerque:
                University of New Mexico Press.
Andrews IV, E. Wyllys, and A. Andrews
1975   A preliminary study of the ruins of Xcaret, Quintana Roo, Mexico with notes
                on other archaeological remains on the central east coast of the Yucatán Pen-
                insula. *Middle American Research Institute,* Publication 40, Tulane University,
                New Orleans.
Andrews IV, E. Wyllys, and Andrews V, E. Wyllys
1980   Excavations at Dzibilchaltun, Yucatán, Mexico. *Middle American Research In-
                stitute,* Publication 48, Tulane University, New Orleans.
Andrews V, E. Wyllys
1981   Investigaciones recientes en Komchen, Yucatán. Paper presented at La XVII
                Mesa Redonda, Sociedad Mexicana de Antropología, San Cristóbal de las
                Casas, Chiapas.
Andrews, George F.
1969   *Etzna, Campeche, Mexico: settlement patterns and monumental architecture.*
                Eugene: University of Oregon.
1975   *Maya cities: placemaking and urbanization.* Norman: University of Oklahoma
                Press.

Arnold, Dean E., and B. F. Bohor
1975   Attapulgite and Maya blue: an ancient mine comes to light. *Archaeology* 28:23-29.
1977   An ancient clay mine at Yo'kat, Yucatán. *American Antiquity* 42(4):575-582.
Arnold, Jeanne E., and Anabel Ford
1980   A statistical examination of settlement patterns at Tikal, Guatemala. *American Antiquity* 45(4):713-726.
Ashmore, Wendy (editor)
1981a   *Lowland Maya settlement patterns.* Albuquerque: University of New Mexico Press.
1981b   Some issues of method and theory in Lowland Maya settlement archaeology. In *Lowland Maya settlement patterns.* Albuquerque: University of New Mexico Press. Pp. 37-70.
Ball, Joseph
1974   A coordinate approach to northern Maya prehistory: A.D. 700-1200. *American Antiquity* 39(1):85-92.
Barrera Marín, Alfredo
1976   El parque nacional y arqueologico de Cobá, Quintana Roo. *Boletin del INAH,* Epoca II, Enero-Marzo, Mexico.
Barrera Marín, Alfredo, Alfredo Barrera Vásquez, y Rosa Maria Lopez Franco
1976   *Nomenclatura etnobotánica Maya.* Instituto Nacional de Antropología e Historia, Secretaria de Educación Pública, Colección Científica, México, D.F.
Bartlett, Harley H.
1956   Fire, primitive agriculture and grazing in the tropics. In *Man's role in changing the face of the earth,* edited by W. L. Thomas. Chicago: University of Chicago Press. (Originally published 1935.)
Becker, M. J.
1971   *The identification of a second plaza at Tikal, Guatemala and its implications for ancient Maya social complexity.* Ph.D dissertation, Department of Anthropology, University of Pennsylvania. University Microfilms, Ann Arbor.
1973   Archaeological evidence for occupational specialization among the Classic period Maya at Tikal, Guatemala. *American Antiquity* 38(4):396-406.
Benavides Castillo, Antonio
1976a   *El systema prehispánico de communicaciones terrestres en la región de Cobá, Quintana Roo, y sus implicaciones sociales.* Tésis profesional Escuela Nacional de Antropología e Historia, Universidad Nacional Autónoma de México, Mexico, D.F.
1976b   Cobá, Quintana Roo. Reporte de actividades en Coba: un sitio Maya en Quintana Roo. *Cuadernos de los Centros* (Mexico) No. 26: 1-103.
Bergthórsson, Päll
1969   An estimate of drift ice and temperature in Iceland in 1,000 years. *Jöküll (Journal of the Icelandic Glaceological Society)* 19:94-101.
Berlin, Heinrich
1965   The inscription of the Temple of the Cross at Palenque. *American Antiquity* 30:330-342.
Berry, B. J. L.
1961   City size distribution and economic development. *Economic Development and Cultural Change* 9:573-588.
Blalock, H. M.
1960   *Social statistics* (2nd ed.). New York: McGraw-Hill.
Blom, Frans
1932   Commerce, trade and monetary units of the Maya. *Middle American Papers, Middle American Research Institute,* Publication 4, pp. 531-556, Tulane University, New Orleans.

1946   Apuntes sobre los ingenieros mayas. *Irrigación en Mexico* **27**(3):5–16.

Borhegyi, Stephan F. de
1956   The development of folk and complex cultures in the southern Maya area. *American Antiquity* **21**:343–356.
1965   Settlement patterns of the Guatemala highlands. In *Handbook of Middle American Indians* (Vol. 2), edited by R. Wauchope. Austin: University of Texas Press.

Boserup, Esther
1965   *The conditions of agricultural growth.* Chicago: Aldine.

Brainerd, George W.
1956   Changing living patterns of the Yucatan Maya. *American Antiquity* **22**:162–64.
1958   The archaeological ceramics of Yucatan. *University of California, Anthropological Records* 19, Berkeley and Los Angeles.

Bronson, B.
1966   Roots and subsistence of the ancient Maya. *Southwestern Journal of Anthropology* **22**:251–279.

Brookfield, Harold C.
1972   Intensification and disintensification in Pacific agriculture. *Pacific Viewpoint* **13–14**:30–48.

Bryson, Reid A. and Thomas J. Murray
1977   *Climates of hunger; mankind and the worlds changing weather.* Madison: University of Wisconsin Press.

Bullard, William R., Jr.
1952   Residential property walls at Mayapan. *Carnegie Institution of Washington, Department of Archaeology, Current Report* 3.
1954   Boundary walls and house lots at Mayapan. *Carnegie Institution of Washington, Department of Archaeology, Current Report* 13.
1955   The Maya community of prehistoric times. *Archaeology* **8**:18–25.
1960   Maya settlement pattern in northeastern Peten, Guatemala. *American Antiquity* **25**:355–372.
1962   Settlement patterns and social structure in the southern Maya lowlands during the Classic period. *35th International Congress of Americanists,* Mexico.
1964   Settlement patterns and social structures in the southern Maya lowlands during the Classic period. *35th Congreso Internacional de Americanistas. Actas y Memorias* 1:279–87.
1970   Topoxte, a Postclassic Maya site in the Peten, Guatemala. *Papers of the Peabody Museum of Archaeology and Ethnology, Harvard University* 61.

Bullard, William, G. R. Willey, J. B. Glass, and J. C. Gifford
1965   Prehistoric Maya settlements in the Belize Valley. *Papers of the Peabody Museum of Archaeology and Ethnology, Harvard University* 54.

Burgess, John Stewart
1928   *The guilds of Peking.* New York: Columbia University Press.

Caamal Canche, Nicolás
1974–1976 Field notes taken in Coba, Quintana Ròo (several volumes). Notes in possession of Folan, Fletcher, Kintz and Stuart.

Calnek, Edward
1974   The Sahagún texts as a source of sociological information. In *Sixteenth-century Mexico.* Edited by M. S. Edmonson. Albuquerque: University of New Mexico Press.
1976   The internal structure of Tenochtitlan. In *The Valley of Mexico: studies in pre-Hispanic ecology and society,* edited by Eric R. Wolf. Albuquerque: University of New Mexico Press.

Carr, R. F., and J. E. Hazard
    1961   Map of the ruins of Tikal, El Petén, Guatemala. *Tikal Reports, Museum Monographs* 11. Philadelphia: The University Museum.

Carrasco, Pedro
    1971   Social organization of ancient Mexico. In *Handbook of Middle American Indians,* edited by R. Wauchope. Austin: University of Texas Press. Pp. 349-375.
    1981   Comment on Offner. *American Antiquity* 46(1):62-68.

Caso, Alfonso
    1963   Ancient agricultural farmsteads in the Rio Bec region of Yucatan. *Contributions of the University of California Archaeological Research Facility,* Berkeley, 27:56-82.

Casselberry, S. E.
    1974   Further refinement of formulae for determining population from floor area. *World Archaeology* 6(1):117-122.

Chapman, Anne M.
    1957   Port of trade enclaves in Aztec and Maya civilizations. In *Trade and market in early empires,* edited by K. Polanyi, C. Arensberg, and H. Peterson. Glencoe, Illinois: Free Press. Pp. 114-153.

Chi, Gaspar Antonio
    1941   *Relación sobre los costumbres de los indios* [*1582*], translated by R. L. Roys. In Landa's Relación de las Cosas de Yucatán, translated and edited by Tozzer. *Papers of the Peabody Museum of American Archaeology and Ethnology,* 18, pp. 230-232. Harvard University.

Chitra, V. R.
    1948   *Cottage industries in India.* Madras: Silpi.

Clavigero, F. J.
    1817   *Storia antica del Messico,* translated into English by Charles Cullen. Philadelphia: Thomas Dobson.

Codice de Calkini
    1957   *Versión de Alfredo Barrera Vásquez.* Mexico: Gobierno del Estado de Campeche.

Coe, Michael
    1962   Social typology and the tropical forest civilizations. *Comparative Studies in Society and History* 4:65-85.
    1963   Cultural development in southeastern Mesoamerica. *In* Aboriginal cultural development in Latin America: an interpretative review, edited by Betty J. Meggers and C. Evans. *Smithsonian Miscellaneous Collection* 146:27-44.
    1965   A model of ancient community structure in the Maya lowlands. *Southwestern Journal of Anthropology* 21:97-114.

Coe, Michael, and William Coe
    1949   Some new discoveries at Coba. *Carnegie Institution of Washington, Notes on Middle American Archaeology and Ethnology,* 93.

Coe, William R.
    1957   Environmental limitations on Maya culture: a reexamination. *American Anthropologist* 59(2):328-335.
    1962   A summary of excavation and research at Tikal, Guatemala, 1956-1961. *American Antiquity* 27(4):179-507.
    1965   Tikal, Guatemala: an emergent Maya civilization. *Science* 147:1401-1419.

Cogolludo, Fray Diego López
    1957   *Historia de Yucatán, México.* Editorial Academia Literaria 5ª edición, México.

Colección de Documentos Inéditos
    1895   Second series, Vols. 9 and 11. Real Academia de la Historía, Madrid.

Collier, George A.
1975   *Fields of the Tzotzil.* Austin: University of Texas Press.
Cook, O. F.
1909   *Vegetation affected by agriculture in Central America.* U.S. Department of
            Agriculture, Bureau of Plant Industry, Bulletin 145. Washington D.C.: U.S.
            Government Printing Office.
1921   Milpa agriculture, a primitive tropical system. *Annual Report of the Smith-
            sonian Institution,* 1919, Washington, D.C., pp. 307–326.
Cooke, C. W.
1931   Why the Maya cities of the Peten District, Guatemala, were abandoned. *Jour-
            nal of the Washington Academy of Sciences* 21:287.
Cortes de Brasdefer, Fernando
1981a   La zona habitacional de Coba. Paper read at the XVII Mesa Redonda de la
            Sociedad Mexicana de Antropología en San Cristóbal de las Casas, Chiapas.
1981b   La extensión de Coba. Paper read at the XVII Mesa Rodonda de la Sociedad
            Mexicana de Antropología en San Cristóbal de las Casas, Chiapas.

Covarrubias, M.
1946   *Mexico South.* New York: Knopf.
Cowgill, George
1964   The end of Classic Maya culture: a review of recent evidence. *Southwestern
            Journal of Anthropology* 20(2):145–159.
Cowgill, U. M.
1961   Soil fertility and the ancient Maya. *Transactions of the Connecticut Academy
            of Arts and Sciences,* New Haven, 42:1–56.
1962   An agriculture study of the southern Maya lowlands. *American Anthropologist*
            64:273–286.
1971   Some comments on manihot subsistence and the ancient Maya. *Southwestern
            Journal of Anthropology* 27:51–63.
Cowgill, U. M., and G. E. Hutchinson
1963   Ecological and geochemical archaeology in the southern Maya lowlands.
            Southwestern Journal of Anthropology 19:267–286.
Crumley, Carole I.
1976   Toward a locational definition of state systems of settlement. *American An-
            thropologist* 78:59–73.
Culbert, T. Patrick
1973   *The Classic Maya Collapse.* Albuquerque: University of New Mexico Press.
1974   *The lost civilization: the story of the Classic Maya.* New York, Evanston, San
            Francisco, London: Harper.
1977   Early Maya development at Tikal, Guatemala. In *The origins of Maya civili-
            zation,* edited by R. E. W. Adams. Albuquerque: University of New Mexico
            Press.

Dahlin, Bruce
1981   Climate and prehistory on the Yucatan Peninsula. Unpublished paper in pos-
            session of the author.
Dahlin, Bruce H., John E. Foss, and Mary Elizabeth Chambers
1980   Project Acalches: reconstructing the natural and cultural history of a seasonal
            swamp at El Mirador, Guatemala; Preliminary results. *In* El Mirador, Peten,
            Guatemala: An Interim Report, edited by Ray T. Matheny. *Papers of the New
            World Archaeological Foundation* No. 45, Brigham Young University, Provo,
            Utah.
Dawson, John A.
1969   Some early theories of settlement and size. *Town Planning Institute Journal*
            55:444–448.

Denton, George, and Widjorn Karlén
    1973   Holocene climatic variation. Their pattern and possible cause. *Quaternary Research* **3**(2):155–205.
Diccionario de Motul
    1929   Maya-Español atribuído a Fray Antonio de Ciudad Real y arte de lengua Maya por Fray Juan Coronel, edited by Juan Martínez Hernandez. Sixteenth-century manuscript, missing. Copy said to be seventeenth century, in John Carter Brown Library, Providence. Reproduced by Gates.
Doehring, Donald O., and Joseph H. Butler
    1974   Hydrogeologic constraints on Yucatan's development. *Science* **186**:591–595.
Dumond, D. E.
    1961   Swidden agriculture and the rise of Maya civilization. *Southwestern Journal of Anthropology* **17**:301–316.
    1965   Population growth and culture change. *Southwestern Journal of Anthropology* **21**(4):302–324.
Eaton, Jack D.
    1975   Ancient agricultural farmsteads in the Rio Bec region of Yucatan. *Contributions of the University of California Archaeological Research Facility,* Berkeley, 27.
    1978   Archaeological survey of the Yucatan-Campeche coast. *Middle American Research Institute,* Publication 46, Tulane University, New Orleans.
Eaton, Jack D., and Joseph Ball
    1978   Studies in the archaeology of coastal Campeche, Mexico. *Middle American Research Institute,* Publication 46, Tulane, University, New Orleans.
Eddy, John A.
    1977   The case of the missing sunspots. *Scientific American* **236**(5):80–88.
Edmonson, Munroe S.
    1978   Some Postclassic questions about the Classic Maya. Paper presented at the Tercera Mesa Redonda de Palenque, Mexico.
    1982   *The ancient future of the Itza: The Book of Chilam Balam of Tizimin,* translated and annotated by Munro S. Edmonson. Austin: University of Texas Press.
Edwards, C.
    1954   Geographical reconnaissance in the Yucatan Peninsula. Rept. fieldwork carried out under ONR Contract 222(11) NR 388 067. University of California, Department of Geography.
Eisemann, E.
    1955   The species of middle american birds. *Translinn. Soc.,* New York, Vol. 7.
Ferdon, E. N., Jr.
    1959   Agricultural potential and the development of cultures. *Southwestern Journal of Anthropology* **15**:1–19.
Fettweis-Vienot, Martine
    1980   Las Pinturas murales de Coba: Período Postclásico. *Boletín de la Escuela de Ciencias Antropológicas de la Universidad de Yucatán* 40:2–50.
Fletcher, Laraine A.
    1978   *Sociocultural implication of the linear features at Coba, Quintana Roo, Mexico.* Ph.D dissertation, Department of Anthropology, State University of New York at Stony Brook.
Fletcher, Laraine A., and Ellen R. Kintz
    1976   Appendix A. Map: Coba, Quintana Roo. Preliminary report. Xeroxed manuscript. (Also published in *Boletín de la Escuela de Ciencias Antropológicas de la Universidad de Yucatán,* 22, 23, 1977.)
Folan, William J.
    1959   Excavation of Structures 33, 36, 36A, and 50, Dzibilchaltun, 1958-1960. In *Excavations at Dzibilchaltun, Yucatan, Mexico,* Andrews IV and Andrews V

	1980, pp. 169–190. Middle American Research Institute, Publication 48, Tulane University, New Orleans.
1960	Excavation of Structures 38 and 38-sub, Dzibilchaltun, Yucatan 1959–1960. In *Excavations at Dzibilchaltun, Yucatan, Mexico.* Andrews IV and Andrews V 1980, pp. 151–169. Mexico American Research Institute, Publication 48, Tulane University, New Orleans.
1969a	Dzibilchaltun, Yucatan, Mexico: structures 384, 385, and 386: a preliminary interpretation. *American Antiquity* **34**:434–461.
1969b	Sacalum, Yucatan: A prehispanic and contemporary source of attapulgite. *American Antiquity* **34**(2):182–183.
1972a	*The community, settlement and subsistence patterns of the Nootka Sound area: a diachronic model.* Uncirculated Ph.D. dissertation, Department of Anthropology, Southern Illinois University, Carbondale.
1972b	Un botellon monopodio del centro de Yucatan. *Estudios de Cultura Maya* **8**:67–75.
1974–1976	Fieldnotes taken in Coba, Quintana Roo (several volumes). Notes in possession of Folan, Fletcher, Kintz and Stuart.
1975	Coba archaeological mapping project, interim report No. 2, Coba, Quintana Roo, Mexico. August 6, 1975. Xeroxed. (Also in *Boletín de la Escuela de Ciencias Antropológicas de la Universidad de Yucatán* Enero–Abril 1977, Nos. 22, 23:29–51.)
1976	Coba Archaeological mapping project, interim report No. 3, Coba, Quintana Roo, Mexico. February 14, 1976. Xeroxed. (Also in *Boletín de la Escuela de Ciencias Antropológicas de la Universidad de Yucatán* Enero–Abril 1977, Nos. 22, 23:52–71.)
1977a	El Sacbe Coba-Ixil, un camino Maya del pasado. *Nueva Antropología* **6**:31–42.
1977b	*Uxmal, Kabah, Labna, Sayil and Xla'pak.* Accepted for publication. Ediciones Orto, Mexico.
1978a	Algunos ejemplos arqueologicos de piedras de sacrificio en Coba, Quintana Roo. *Boletín de la Escuela de Ciencias Antropológicas de la Universidad de Yucatán.* No. 31:15–42.
1978b	*Coba, Quintana Roo.* Accepted for publication. Ediciones Orto, Mexico.
1978c	Coba, Quintana Roo, Mexico: an analysis of a prehispanic and contemporary source of sascab. *American Antiquity* **43**:79–85.
1979	La organización sociopolítico de los habitantes del area Maya del norte a través del tiempo. *Boletín de la Escuela de Ciencias Antropológicas de la Universidad de Yucatán,* Año 6, No. 32:34–45.
1980	The political and economic organization of the lowland Maya. *Mexicon* **2**(5):73–77.
1981a	Flora, fauna, atmospheric and groundwater: the paleoclimatology and prehistory of Dzibilchaltun, Yucatan and environs. Submitted for publication.
1981b	San Miguel de Huamango: un centro regional del antiguo Estado de Tula-Jilotepec. In *Investigaciones Sobre Huamango y Su Región Vecina,* directed by Román Piña Chan. Gobierno Del Estado de México, Dirección de Turismo 1975–1981.
1982	Coba, Quintana Roo, Mexico: un campo de prueba para cambios climáticos. *Información, Boletín del Centro de Investigaciones Históricas y Sociales,* Universidad Autónoma del Sudeste, Campeche. Vol. 2.
in press	Una nota sobre la importancia del consumo de fruta entre los Maya del presente y del pasado. In *El Boletín de la Escuela de Ciencias Antropológicas de la Universidad de Yucatán.*
in press	Tulum, Quintana Roo, Mexico and environs: a hypothetical model of Maya

development and survival on the east coast of Yucatan through time. *Information*, Vol. 4.

Folan, William J., with Nicolás Caamal Canche and Jacinto May Hau
    1974-1976 field notes (1974-1976). Various volumes in possession of the Coba Archaeological Mapping Project.

Folan, William J., Joel Gunn, Jack D. Eaton and Robert W. Patch
    1980   Paleoclimatologic Patterning in Southern Mesoamerica. Accepted for publication in *The Journal of Field Archaeology*.

Folan, William J., Laraine A. Fletcher, and Ellen R. Kintz
    1979   Fruit, fiber, bark and resin: the social organization of a Maya urban center: Coba, Quintana Roo, Mexico. *Science* **204**:697-701.

Folan, William J., and Burma H. Hyde
    in press   Climatic forecasting and recording among the ancient and historic Maya: an ethnohistoric approach to epistemological and paleoclimatological patterning. In *Contributions to the archaeology and ethnohistory of greater Mesoamerica*, edited by William J. Folan. Carbondale: Southern Illinois University Press.

Folan, William J., Ellen R. Kintz, Laraine A. Fletcher, and Burma H. Hyde
    1981   An examination of settlement patterns at Coba, Quintana Roo, Mexico and Tikal, Guatemala: a reply to Arnold and Ford. *American Antiquity* **47**(2):430-436.

Folan, William J., and George E. Stuart
    1974   Coba archaeological mapping project, Quintana Roo, Mexico, interim report No. 1. June 24-August 17, 1974, Coba. Xeroxed manuscript. (Also published in *Boletín de la Escuela de Ciencias Antropológicas de la Universidad de Yucatán*, Nos. 22, 23:20-29 in 1977.)

Freidel, David
    1981a   Continuity and disjunction: late Postclassic settlement patterns in northern Yucatan. In *Lowland Maya settlement patterns,* edited by W. Ashmore. Albuquerque: University of New Mexico Press. Pp. 311-332.
    1981b   The political economics of residential dispersion among the lowland Maya. In *Lowland Maya settlement patterns,* edited by W. Ashmore. Albuquerque: University of New Mexico Press. Pp. 311-332.

Fustel de Coulanges, Numa Denis
    1956   *The ancient city*. Garden City, New York: Doubleday.

Gallareta Negrón, Tomás
    1981   Investigaciónes del asentamiento prehispánico de Coba. Paper read at the XVII Mesa Redonda de la Sociedad Mexicana de Antropología en San Cristobal de las Casas, Chiapas.

Gann, Thomas
    1925   *Mystery cities.* New York: Scribner's.
    1926   *Ancient cities and modern tribes: exploration and adventure in Mayaland.* London: Duckworth.

Garduño, Jaime A.
    1976   Aplicación de las normas de la primera reunión técnica consultiva de Chapultepec en las excavaciones de Cobá, en el Estado de Quintana Roo. En *Cuadernos de los Centros.* México: INAH.
    1979   El muestreo en forma de cruz en Coba. *Boletín de la Escuela de Ciencias Antropológicas de la Universidad de Yucatán* 38:29-43.

Garza, Sylvia, y Eduardo Kurjack
    1981   Aplicación de la teoría de los lugares centrales en el norte de Yucatán. Paper read at the XVII Mesa Redonda de la Sociedad Mexicana de Antropología, San Cristóbal de las Casas, Chiapas.

Gleave, M. B., and H. P. White
    1969   Population density and agricultural systems in West Africa. In *Environment*

and land use in Africa, edited by M. F. Thomas and G. W. Wittington. London: Methuen. Pp. 273–300.

Gonzalez, F. Baltasar
    1975   Coba projecto arqueológico. *Boletín de la Escuela de Ciencias Antropológicas de la Universidad de Yucatán* 12:14–19.

Gordon, G. B.
    1896   The prehispanic ruins of Copan, Honduras: a preliminary report of the explorations by the Museum, 1891–1895. *Memoirs of the Peabody Museum of American Archaeology and Ethnology.* Cambridge, Massachusetts: Harvard University, 1(1).

Grove, David
    1972   The function and future of urban centers. In *Man, settlement and urbanism,* edited by P. J. Ucko, R. Tringham, and G. W. Dimbleby. Cambridge, Massachusetts: Schenkman.

Guillemin, George F.
    1968   Development and function of the Tikal ceremonial center. *Ethnos* 33:1–35.

Gunn, Joel, and Richard E. W. Adams
    1981   Climatic change, culture, and civilization in North America. *World Archaeology,* **13**:87–100.

Haggett, Peter
    1965   *Locational analysis in human geography.* London: St. Martins Press.

Hammond, Norman
    1972   The planning of a Maya ceremonial center. *Scientific American* **226**(5):82–91.
    1973a   British Museum-Cambridge University Corozal project 1973 interim report, edited by Norman Hammond.
    1973b   Locational models and the site of Lubaantun: a classic Maya center. In *Models in archaeology,* edited by D. L. Clarke. London: Methuen. Pp. 758–799.
    1974a   The distribution of Late Classic Maya major ceremonial centers in the central area. In *Mesoamerican archaeology: New approaches,* edited by Norman Hammond. Austin: University of Texas Press. Pp. 313–334.
    1974b   Preclassic to postclassic in northern Belize. *Antiquity* **48**:177–189.
    1975   Lubaantun: a Classic Maya realm. *Monographs of the Peabody Museum, Harvard University,* Cambridge 2.
    1978   The myth of the milpa: agricultural expansion in the Maya Lowlands. In *Pre-Hispanic Maya agriculture,* edited by Peter Harrison and B. L. Turner II. Albuquerque: University of New Mexico Press. Pp. 23–34.
    1982   A late formative period stela in the Maya lowlands. *American Antiquity* **47**(2):396–403.

Hardoy, Jorge, and R. P. Schaedel (editors)
    1969   *The urbanization process in America from its origins to the present.* Buenos Aires: Editorial del Instituto.

Harris, David R.
    1978   The agricultural foundations of Lowland Maya civilization: a critique. In *Pre-Hispanic Maya agriculture,* edited by P. D. Harrison and B. L. Turner II. Albuquerque: University of New Mexico Press. Pp. 301–323.

Harrison, Peter
    1968   Form and function in a Maya "palace" group. *38th International Congress of Americanists, Stuttgart,* 1968, 1:165–172.
    1978   So the seeds shall grow: some introductory comments. In *Pre-Hispanic Maya agriculture,* edited by P. Harrison and B. L. Turner. Pp. 1–11. Albuquerque: University of New Mexico Press.

Harrison, Peter, and B. L. Turner II (editors)
    1978   *Pre-Hispanic Maya agriculture.* Albuquerque: University of New Mexico Press.

Haviland, William
    1965   Prehistoric settlement at Tikal, Guatemala. *Expedition* 7(3):14–23.
    1966   Social integration and the Classic Maya. *American Antiquity* **31**:625–631.
    1967   Stature at Tikal, Guatemala: implications for classic Maya demography and social organization. *American Antiquity* **32**:316–325.
    1968   Maya settlement patterns: a critical review. *Middle American Research Institute, Archaeological Studies in Middle America,* Publication 26, pp. 21–48, Tulane University, New Orleans.
    1969   A new population estimate for Tikal, Guatemala. *American Antiquity* **34**:429–433.
    1970a   Ancient lowland Maya social organization. *Archaeological Studies in Middle America, Middle American Research Institute,* Publication 26, pp. 95–117, Tulane University, New Orleans.
    1970b   Tikal, Guatemala and Mesoamerican urbanism. *World Archaeology* 2(2):186–198.
    1971   Occupational specialization at Tikal, Guatemala: stone-working, monument carving. *American Antiquity* **39**:494–496.
    1972a   Estimates on Maya populations: comments on Thompson's comments. *American Antiquity* **37**(2):261–262.
    1972b   Family size, prehistoric population estimates for the ancient Maya. *American Antiquity* 37:135–139.
Hester, J. A. Jr.
    1951   Agriculture, economy and population of the Maya. *Carnegie Institution of Washington, Yearbook* 51:266–271.
    1952   Agriculture, economy and population density of the Maya. *Carnegie Institution of Washington Yearbook* 52:288–292.
Hester, Thomas R., Jack D. Eaton and Harry J. Shafer
    1980   *The Colha Project, 1980 Interim Report.* Center for Archaeological Research, The University of Texas at San Antonio and Centro Studi e Ricerche Ligabue, Venezia. San Antonio, Texas.
Hewett, E. L.
    1912   The excavations of Quirigua, Guatemala by the School of American Archaeology. *Bulletin of the Archaeological Institute of America* 3:163–171.
Hirth, Kenneth G.
    1978   Teotihuacan regional population administration in eastern Morelos. *World Archaeology,* **9**:320–333.
Isphording, W. C.
    1975   The physical geography of Yucatan. *Transactions-Gulf Coast Association of Geological Societies* 25:231–262.
Ixtlilxochitl, Fernando de Alva
    1952   *Obras Históricas,* edited by Chavero. Mexico City: Editora Nacional.
Jacobs, Jane
    1969   *The economy of cities.* New York: Random House.
Johnston, R. J.
    1973   *Spatial structures.* New York: St. Martin's Press.
Joyce, T. A.
    1929   Report on the British Museum expedition to British Honduras in 1928. *Journal of the Royal Anthropological Institute* **58**:323–50.
Kampen, Michael
    1978   The graffiti of Tikal, Guatemala. *Estudios de la Cultura Maya* 11:155–179.
Kelley, David
    1962   Glyphic evidence for a dynastic sequence at Quirigua, Guatemala. *American Antiquity* **27**:323–335.

Kimber, Clarissa
    1966   Dooryard gardens of Martinique. *Yearbook Association of Pacific Coast Geographers* **28**:97–118.
    1973   Spatial patterning in the dooryard gardens of Puerto Rico. *Geographical Review* **63**:6–26.

Kintz, Ellen R.
    1978   *The social organization of a Classic Maya city: Coba, Quintana Roo, Mexico.* Ph.D dissertation, Department of Anthropology, State University of New York at Stony Brook.
    1981   Weather, water and wealth: a preliminary study of kitchen gardens, Coba, Quintana Roo, Mexico. Paper presented at the Northeastern Anthropological Association 21st Annual Meeting, Saratoga Springs, New York, March 25–29.

Kraeling, C. H., and R. M. Adams (editors)
    1960   *City invincible: a symposium on urbanization and cultural development in the ancient Near East.* Chicago: University of Chicago Press.

Kurjack, Edward B.
    1974   Prehistoric lowland Maya community and social organization: a case study at Dzibilchaltun, Yucatan, Mexico. *Middle American Research Institute,* Publication 38. Tulane University, New Orleans.

Kurjack, E. B., and S. Garza T.
    1981   Pre-Columbian community form and distribution in the northern Maya area. In *Lowland Maya settlement patterns,* edited by W. Ashmore. Albuquerque: University of New Mexico Press. Pp. 287–310.

Kurjack, Edward, and E. Wyllys Andrews V
    1976   Early boundary maintenance in northwestern Yucatan. *American Antiquity* **41**(3):318–324.

Lambert, J. D. H. and J. T. Arnason
    1982   Ramón and Maya ruins: an ecological, not an economic relation. *Science* **216** (4543):298–299.

Landa, Diego de
    1941   *Relación de las cosas de Yucatán,* translated and edited with notes by Alfred M. Tozzer. Papers Peabody Museum, Harvard University, Vol. 18, Cambridge.

Lange, F. W.
    1971   Marine resources: a viable subsistance alternative for the prehistoric lowland Maya. *American Anthropologist* **73**:619–639.

Littman, Edwin R.
    1958   Ancient Mesoamerican mortars, plasters and stuccos: the composition and origin of *sascab. American Antiquity* **24**:172–176.

Logan, Michael H., and William T. Sanders
    1976   The model. In *The Valley of Mexico,* edited by Eric R. Wolf. Albuquerque: University of New Mexico Press. Pp. 31–58.

Lothrop, Samuel K.
    1924   Tulum, an archaeological study of the east coast of Yucatan. *Carnegie Institution of Washington,* Publication 335.

Lundell, Cyrus L.
    1934   Preliminary sketch of the phytogeography of the Yucatan Peninsula. *Contributions to American Archaeology, Carnegie Institution of Washington* **12**:255–321.
    1937   The vegetation of Petén: studies of Mexican and Central American plants. *Carnegie Institution of Washington,* Publication 478.
    1938   Plants probably utilized by the old empire Maya of Peten and adjacent lowlands. *Michigan Academy of Sciences, Arts and Letters Papers* **24**(1): 37–56.

MacNeish, R. S., J. Wilkerson, and Antoinette Nelkin-Terner
    1981   *The first annual report of the Belize Archaic Archaeological reconnaissance.*
            The Robert S. Peabody Foundation for Archaeology, Andover.
McTaggert, W. Donald
    1964-1965 Comment: The reality of urbanism. In *Pacific viewpoint,* **5-6:**220-224.
Maldonado-Koerdell, Manuel
    1964   Geohistory and paleogeography of Middle America. In *Handbook of Middle
            American Indians,* edited by R. Wauchope. Austin: University of Texas Press.
Maler, Teobert
    1932   *Impresiónes de viaje a las ruinas de Coba y Chichén Itzá,* edited by Jose E.
            Rosado. Merida, Yucatan.
Marcus, Joyce
    1973   Territorial organization of the lowland Classic Maya. *Science* **18:**911-916.
    1974   The iconography of power among the Classic Maya. *World Archaeology*
            6(1):83-94.
    1976   *Emblem and state in the Classic Maya lowlands.* Washington, D.C.: Dumbar-
            ton Oaks.
Mathney, Ray T.
    1976   Maya lowlands hydraulic systems. *Science* **193**(4254):639-646.
May Hau, Jacinto
    1974-1976 Field notes taken in Coba, Quintana Roo, (several volumes). Notes in posses-
            sion of Folan, Fletcher, Kintz, and Stuart.
Meggers, B. J.
    1954   Environmental limitation on the development of culture. *American Anthro-
            pologist* **56:**801-24.
Miller, Arthur G.
    1974   The iconography of the painting in the temple of the Diving God, Tulum, Quin-
            tana Roo, Mexico: the twisted cords. In *Mesoamerican archaeology: new ap-
            proaches,* edited by Norman Hammond. Austin: University of Texas Press.
Millon, Rene
    1974a   The study of urbanism at Teotihuacan. In *Mesoamerican archaeology: new
            approaches,* edited by Norman Hammond. Austin: University of Texas Press.
            Pp. 335-362.
    1974b   Urbanization at Teotihuacan (Vols. 1 and 2). Austin: University of Texas Press.
    1976   Social relations in ancient Teotihuacan. In *The Valley of Mexico,* edited by
            Eric R. Wolf. Albuquerque: University of New Mexico Press. Pp. 205-248.
Millon, Rene, R. B. Drewitt, and G. L. Cowgill
    1973   *Urbanization at Teotihuacan, Mexico.* Vol. I, part two: maps. Austin: Univer-
            sity of Texas Press.
Miner, Horace
    1953   *The primitive city of Timbuctoo.* New Jersey: Princeton University Press.
Molloy, John, and William L. Rathje
    1974   Sexploitation among the Late Classic Maya. In *Mesoamerican archaeology:
            new approaches,* edited by Norman Hammond. Austin: University of Texas.
Montoliú, Maria
    1978   Algunos aspectos del venado en la religion de los Mayas de Yucatan. *Estudios
            de Cultura Maya* **10:**149-172.
Monzon, Arturo
    1949   *El calpulli en la organización social de los Tenochca.* Publicaciónes del Instituto
            de Historia, Ser. 1, No. 6. Mexico City: Universidad Nacional Autónoma de
            México and Instituto National de Antropología e Historia.
Morley, Sylvanus Griswold
    1956   *The ancient Maya* (3rd edition, revised by George W. Brainerd). Stanford:
            Stanford University Press.

Mumford, Lewis
    1961   *The city in history.* New York: Harcourt, Brace and World.

Naroll, Raoul
    1962   Floor area and settlement pattern. *American Antiquity* **27**:587–589.

Navarrette, Carlos, María José Con, and Alejandro Martinez Muriel
    in press   Un reconocimiento arqueológico de Coba, Quintana Roo. *Centro de Estudios Mayas.* México, D.F.: Universidad Nacional Autónoma de México.

Netting, Robert McC.
    1968   *Hill farmers of Nigeria.* Seattle: University of Washington Press.
    1977   Maya subsistence: mythologies, analogies, possibilities. In *The origins of Maya civilization,* edited by R. E. W. Adams. Albuquerque: University of New Mexico Press. Pp. 229–333.

Noyes, E.
    1932   Fray Alonso Ponce in Yucatán, 1588. *Middle American Research Series,* Publication 4, pp. 297–372, Tulane University, New Orleans.

Offner, Jerome A.
    1981a   On Carrasco's use of theoretical first principles. *American Antiquity* **46**(1):69–74.
    1981b   On the inapplicability of "oriental despotism" and the "Asiatic mode of production" to the Aztecs of Texcoco. *American Antiquity* **46**(1):43–61.

Ortiz, Monasterio R.
    1950   Reconocimiento agrológico regional de estado de Yucatán. *Bol. Soc. Mex. Geog. y Estad.* **69**:245–324.
    1955   *Los recursos agrológicos de la República Mexicana.*
    1957   *Ingenieria Hidráulica en México* (Vols. **9–11**). Sec. Recursos Hidráulicos.

Park, Robert E., E. W., Burgess, and R. D. McKenzie
    1925   *The city.* Chicago: University of Chicago.

Parsons, Jeffrey, and Norbert P. Psuty
    1975   Sunken fields and prehispanic subsistence on the Peruvian Coast. *American Antiquity,* **40**(3):259–282.

Pearse, A. S., E. P. Creaser, and F. G. Hall
    1936   The cenotes of Yucatan. *Carnegie Institution of Washington,* Publication 457.

Peniche Rivero, Piedad
    1975   Proyecto Coba, Instituto National de Antropología e Historia. Reporte No. 1 primera temporada, Mayo 17–Diciembre 10, 1974.

Peniche Rivero, Piedad, and William J. Folan
    1978   Coba, Quintana Roo, Mexico: reporte sobre una metrópolis Maya del noroeste. *Boletín de la Escuela de Ciencias Antropológicas de la Universidad de Yucatán* No. 30:48–74.

Piña Chan, Román
    1978   Commerce in the Yucatan Peninsula: the conquest and colonial period. *In* Mesoamerican communication routes and cultural contacts, edited by T. A. Lee, Jr., and Carlos Navarrete. *Papers of the New World Archaeological Foundation* No. 40, Brigham Young University, Provo, Utah.

Pirenne, H.
    1925   *Medieval cities.* Garden City, New York: Doubleday.

Pohl, Mary
    1981   Ritual continuity and transformation in Mesoamerica: reconstructing the ancient Maya cuch ritual. *American Antiquity* **46**:513–529.

Pollock, H. E. D.
    1953   Department of archaeology. *Carnegie Institution of Washington,* Yearbook 52:263–67.

Pollock, H. E. D., R. L. Roys, T. Proskouriakoff, and A. L. Smith
  1962   Mayapan, Yucatan, Mexico. *Carnegie Institution of Washington,* Publication 619.
Pong, David
  1971   Early urban forms. *Science* **174**(4006):281–282.
Poole, Sidman
  1940   A geographic reconnaissance in northern Mayaland. *Geographical Journal* **95**:121–126.
Potter, David F.
  1973   *Maya architectural style in central Yucatan.* Ph.D dissertation, Department of Anthropology, Tulane University, New Orleans.
Pounds, N. J. G.
  1969   The urbanization of the classical world. *Annals of the Association of American Geographers* **59**:135–157.
Prem, Hans
  1974   *Matrícula de Huexotzinco.* Manuscript Mex. 387 der Bibliotheque Nationale Paris: Ed., Kommentar, Hieroglyphengloffar. Graz: Akademia druk und Verlagsanst.
Price, Barbara
  1968   Cause, effect and the anthropological study of urbanism. *38th International Congress of Americanists* (Stuttgart) **4**:311–318.
  1977   Shifts in production and organization: a cluster-interaction model. *Current Anthropology* **18**:209–233.
Proskouriakoff, Tatiana
  1950   A study of Classic Maya sculpture. *Carnegie Institution of Washington,* Publication 593.
  1960   Historical implications of a pattern of dates at Piedras Negras, Guatemala. *American Antiquity* **25**(4):454–475.
  1961   The lords of the Mayan realm. *Expedition* **4**(1):14–21.
  1963   Historical data in the inscriptions of Yaxchilan, Part I. *Estudios de Cultura Maya* **4**:177–201.
  1964   Historical data in the inscriptions of Yaxchilan, Part II. *Estudios de Cultura Maya* **4**:177–201.
Puleston, Dennis
  1973   *Ancient Maya settlement patterns and environment at Tikal, Guatemala: Implications for subsistence.* Unpublished Ph.D dissertation, Department of Anthropology, University of Pennsylvania.
  1974   Intersite areas near Tikal and Uaxactun. In *Mesoamerican archaeology: new approaches,* edited by Norman Hammond. Austin: University of Texas Press. Pp. 303–310.
  1978   Terracing, raised fields and tree cropping in the Maya lowlands: new perspective on the geography of power. In *Prehispanic Maya agriculture,* edited by P. D. Harrison and B. L. Turner II. Albuquerque: University of New Mexico Press. Pp. 225–248.
Puleston, Dennis, and D. W. Callender Jr.
  1967   Defensive earthworks at Tikal. *Expedition* **9**(3):40–48.
Ramayo Lanz, Teresa
  1978   Carta al coordinator del Boletín de la Escuela de Ciencias Antropológicas de la Universidad de Yucatán. *Boletín de la Escuela de Ciencias Antropológicas de la Universidad de Yucatan* Año 6, No. 31:43–46.
Rathje, William
  1970   Sociopolitical implications of lowland Maya burials. *World Archaeology* **1**(3):359–374.

1973   Classic Maya development and denouement: a research design. In *The Classic Maya Collapse,* edited by T. P. Culbert. Albuquerque: University of New Mexico Press. Pp. 405–456.

Rathje, William L., and Jeremy A. Sabloff
1975   Changing precolumbian commercial systems. *Monographs of the Peabody Museum* No. 3. Cambridge: Harvard University.

Rathje, William L., David A. Gregory, and Fredrick M. Wiseman
1978   Trade models and archaeological problems: Classic Maya examples. *In* Mesoamerican communication routes and cultural contacts. *Papers of the New World Archaeological Foundation* No. 40. New World Archaeological Foundation, Brigham Young University Press.

Rattray, Evelyn Childs
1981   La interacción Teotihuacán-Maya: Nuevas interpretaciones. Paper read at the XVII Mesa Redonda de la Sociedad Mexicana de Antropología en San Cristóbal de las Casas, Chiapas, 23 June, 1981.

Redfield, Robert
1941   *Folk culture of the Yucatan.* Chicago: University of Chicago Press.

Redfield, R., and A. Villa Rojas
1934   *Chan Kom: a Maya village.* Chicago: University of Chicago Press.

Reina, Ruben E.
1964   The urban world view of a tropical forest community in the absence of a city, Peten, Guatemala. *Human Organization* **24**(4):265–277.
1967   Milpas and milperos: implications for prehistoric times. *American Anthropologist* **69**(1):1–20.

Reina, R., and R. M. Hill II
1980   Lowland Maya subsistence: notes from ethnohistory and ethnography. *American Antiquity* **45**(1):74–79.

Rice, Don S.
1978   Population growth and subsistence alternatives in a tropical lacustrine environment. In *Pre-Hispanic Maya agriculture,* edited by P. D. Harrison and B. L. Turner. Albuquerque: University of New Mexico Press. Pp. 35–61.

Ricketson, O. G., Jr.
1925   Burials in the Maya area. *American Anthropologist* **27**:381–401.

Ricketson, O. G., Jr., and E. B. Ricketson
1937   Uaxactun, Guatemala, group E–1926–1931. *Carnegie Institution of Washington,* Publication 477.

Robles, Ramos R.
1959   Geología y geohidrología. *In* Los recursos naturales del sureste y su aprovachamiento, edited by E. Beltran. *Instituto Mexicano de Recursos Naturales Renovables,* Part 2 Vol. 2, pp. 55–92.

Robles C., Fernando
1976   Ixil, centro agrícola de Coba. En *Boletín de la Escuela de Ciencias Antropológicas de la Universidad de Yucatán.* Año 4, No. 20, pp. 13–43.
1980   *La secuencia cerámica de la región de Coba, Quintana Roo.* Tésis profesional no publicado. Escuela National de Antropología e Historia, Universidad Nacional Autónoma de México.

Rosales de B., Margarita
1976   Análisis de la situación socioeconómica en Coba, Quintana Roo. *Cuadernos de los Centros. Coba: un sitio maya en Quintana Roo,* No. 26:128–172. Instituto Nacional de Antropología e Historia. Dirección de Centros Regionales. Centro Regional del Sureste.

Rowe, John
1967   Urban settlements in ancient Peru. In *Peruvian archaeology: selected readings,*

edited by John Rowe and Dorothy Menzel. California: Peck Publications. Pp. 293–319.

Roys, Ralph L.
1939 The titles of Ebtun. *Carnegie Institution of Washington,* Publication 505.
1943 The Indian background of colonial Yucatan. *Carnegie Institution of Washington,* Publication 548.
1957 The political geography of the Yucatan Maya. *Carnegie Institution of Washington,* Publication 613.
1962 Literary sources for the history of Mayapan. *In* Mayapan, Yucatan, Mexico, edited by H. E. D. Pollock. *Carnegie Institution of Washington,* Publication 619:25–86.
1965 *Ritual of the Bacabs.* Norman: University of Oklahoma Press.
1967 *The Book of Chilam Balam of Chumayel.* Norman: University of Oklahoma Press.
1972 The Indian background of colonial Yucatan. Norman: University of Oklahoma Press.

Roys, Ralph, France V. Scholes, and Eleanor B. Adams
1940 Report and census of the Indians of Cozumel [1570]. *Contributions to American Anthropology and History* **6**(30):1–30.
1959 Census and inspection of the town of Pencuyut, Yucatan [1583], edited by Diego Garcia de Palacio, oidor of the audiencia of Guatemala. *Ethnohistory* **6**(3):195–225.

Roys, R. L., and Edwin M. Shook
1966 Preliminary report on the ruins of Ake, Yucatan. In *Memoirs of the Society for American Archaeology* 20, edited by Raymond H. Thompson.

Ruppert, K., and J. H. Denison Jr.
1943 Archaeological reconnaissance in Campeche, Quintana Roo, and Peten. *Carnegie Institution of Washington,* Publication 543.

Ruppert, Karl, and A. L. Smith
1954 Excavations in house mounds at Mayapan III. *Current reports, Carnegie Institution of Washington* 7:27–51.
1957 House types in the environs of Mayapan and at Uxmal, Kabah, Sayil, Chichen-Itza and Chacchob. *Carnegie Institution of Washington, Department of Archaeology Current Report* 39, Cambridge.

Ruz Lhuillier, Alberto
1973 El templo de las inscripciones: Palenque. In *Colección científica,* Arqueología, No. 7. México: Instituto Nacional de Antropología e Historia.

Sabloff, J. A., and D. A. Freidel
1975 A model of a pre-columbian trading center. In *Ancient civilization and trade,* edited by J. A. Sabloff and C. C. Lamberg Karlovsky. Albuquerque: University of New Mexico Press. Pp. 369–408.

Sabloff, Jeremy A., and William L. Rathje
1975a The rise of a Maya merchant class. *Scientific American* **233**(4):73–82.
1975b A study of changing pre-columbian commercial systems: the 1972–1973 seasons at Cozumel, Mexico. *Monographs of the Peabody Museum. Harvard University* No. 3.

Sanders, William
1955 An archaeological reconnaissance of northern Quintana Roo. *Carnegie Institution of Washington, Department of Archaeology Current Report* 24: 179–224.
1956 The central Mexican symbiotic region: a study in prehistoric settlement patterns. In *Prehistoric settlement patterns in the New World* edited by G. R. Willey. Viking Fund Publication 23:115–127.

1960   Prehistoric ceramics and settlement patterns in Quintana Roo, Mexico. *Carnegie Institution of Washington, Contributions to American Anthropology and History* Vol. 12 No. 57–60, Publication 606.

1962   Cultural ecology of the Maya lowlands, Part I. *Estudios de Cultura Maya* 2:79–121.

1963   Cultural ecology of the Maya lowlands (Part II). *Estudios de Cultura Maya* 3:203–41.

1965   *Cultural ecology of the Teotihuacan Valley: a preliminary report of the results of the Teotihuacan Valley project.* Department of Sociology and Anthropology, Pennsylvania State University, University Park.

1972   Population, agricultural history and societal evolution. In *Population growth: anthropological implications,* edited by Brian Spooner. Cambridge: MIT Press. Pp. 101–153.

1973   Cultural ecology of the lowland Maya. In *The Classic Maya Collapse,* edited by Patrick Culbert. Albuquerque: The University of New Mexico Press. Pp. 325–359.

1981   Classic Maya settlement patterns and ethnographic analogy. In *Lowland Maya settlement patterns,* edited by Wendy Ashmore. Albuquerque: University of New Mexico Press. Pp. 351–369.

Sanders, William, and B. Price
1968   *Mesoamerica: the evolution of a civilization.* New York: Random House.

Sapper, K.
1896   Sobre la geografía física y la geología de la península de Yucatán. *Instituto Geológico de México Boletín* 3.

1899   Über Gebirgsbau und Boden des nördlichen Mittelamerika *Petermanns Mitteilungen,* Ergänzungsband 27, Ergänzungshefte 127.

Satterthwaite, Linton Jr.
1951   Reconnaissance in British Honduras. *University of Pennsylvania Museum Bulletin* 16(1):21–37.

Schaedel, R. P.
1970   The city and origin of the state in America. *International Congress of Americanists Proceedings Actas y Memorias* 2:1–33.

Schele, Linda
1978   Genealogical documentation on the tri-figure panels at Palenque. In *Tercera mesa redonda de Palenque* (Vol. 4), edited by M. G. Robertson and D. C. Jeffers. Pre-Columbian Art Research. Monterey, California: Hearald Printers. Pp. 41–70.

Scholes, F. V., and R. L. Roys
1968   *The Maya Chontal Indians of Acalan-Tixchel.* Norman: University of Oklahoma Press.

Schott, A.
1866   Die Küstenbildung des nördlichen Yukatan. *Petermanns Mitteilungen* 12:127–30.

Shattuck, G. C.
1933   The peninsula of Yucatan medical, biological, meterological and sociological studies. *Carnegie Institution of Washington,* Publication 431.

Shook, E., and T. Proskouriakoff
1956   Settlement patterns in Mesoamerica and the sequence in the Guatemalan highlands. In *Prehistoric settlement patterns in the New World,* edited by G. R. Willey. Viking Fund Publication 23.

Shook, Edwin
1961   Maps of the ruins of Tikal, El Petén, Guatemala. *Tikal Reports, Museum Monographs* II. Philadelphia: The University Museum.

Siemens, Alfred, and Dennis E. Puleston
  1972   Ridged fields and associated features in southern Campeche: new perspectives on the lowland Maya. *American Antiquity* **35**:441-462.
Simons, Michael P., and Gerald F. Brem
  1979   The analysis and distribution of volcanic ash tempered pottery in the lowland Maya area. *American Antiquity* **44**:79-91.
Sjoberg, Gideon
  1960   *The preindustrial city.* New York: The Free Press.
Smith, A. L.
  1929   Report on the map of environs of Uaxactun. *Carnegie Institution of Washington* Yearbook **28**:325-327.
  1962   Residential and associated structures at Mayapan. *In* Mayapan, Yucatan, Mexico. *Carnegie Institution of Washington,* Publication 619:165-320.
  1972   Excavations at Altar de Sacrificios: Architecture, settlement and burials and caches. *Papers of the Peabody Museum of Archaeology and Ethnology,* Vol. 62, No. 2, Harvard.
Smith, H. M., and E. H. Taylor
  1945   An annotated checklist and key to the snakes of Mexico. *Smithsonian Institution, United States National Museum Bulletin* 187.
  1950   An annotated checklist and key to the reptiles of Mexico, exclusive of snakes. *Smithsonian Institution, United States National Museum Bulletin* 199.
Spence, Michael W.
  1981   Obsidian production and the state in Teotihuacan. *American Antiquity* **46**:769-788.
Spencer, J. E.
  1966   *Shifting cultivation in southeastern Asia.* Berkeley and Los Angeles: University of California Press.
Spencer, J. E., and G. A. Hale
  1961   The origins, nature and distribution of agricultural terraces. *Pacific Viewpoint* **2**:1-40.
Stadelman, Raymond
  1940   Maize cultivation in northwestern Guatemala. *Contributions to American Anthropology and History* No. 33.
Standley, P. C.
  1930   Flora of Yucatan. *Field Museum of Natural History,* Publication 279, Botanical Series Vol. 3, No. 3.
Steggerda, M.
  1941   The Mayan Indians of the Yucatan. *Carnegie Institution of Washington,* Publication 531.
Stenholm, Nancy
  1973   *Identification of house structures in Mayan archaeology: a case study at Kaminaljuyu.* Ph.D dissertation, Department of Anthropology, University of Washington.
Stephens, John L.
  1963   *Incidents of travel in Yucatan* (Vols. 1 and 2). New York: Dover Publications.
Stevens, Rayfred L.
  1964   The soils of Middle America and their relation to Indian people and cultures. In *The handbook of Middle American Indians* (Vol 1), edited by R. C. West. Austin: University of Texas Press. Pp. 265-315.
Stromsvik, G., H. E. D. Pollock, and H. Berlin
  1955   Exploration in Quintana Roo. *Carnegie Institution of Washington Current Report* 23.

Stuart, George E.
1960   Survey of Dzibilchaltun. Unpublished field report on file at Middle American Research Institute, Tulane University, New Orleans.
1975   The Maya: riddle of the glyphs. *National Geographic,* **148**:768–792.
Stuart, George E., and Gene S. Stuart
1977   *The mysterious Maya.* Washington: National Geographic Society.
Stuart, George E., John C. Scheffler, Edward B. Kurjack, and John W. Cottier
1979   Map of the ruins of Dzibilchaltun, Yucatan, Mexico. *Middle American Research Institute,* Publication 47. Tulane University, New Orleans.
Stuart, L. C.
1964   Fauna of Middle America. In *Handbook of Middle American Indians* (Vol. 1), edited by R. C. West. Austin: University of Texas Press. Pp. 316–363.
Tamayo, Jorge L., and R. C. West
1964   The hydrography of Middle America. In *The handbook of Middle American Indians* (Vol. 1), edited by R. C. West. Austin: University of Texas Press. Pp. 84–121.
Thomas, Prentice M. Jr.
1975   Prehistoric settlement at Becan: A preliminary report. *Middle American Research Institute,* Publication 31, pp. 139–146, Tulane University, New Orleans.
Thompson, J. Eric S.
1928   The causeways of the Coba district, eastern Yucatan. *Proceedings of the 23rd International Congress of Americanists,* New York, pp. 181–184.
1930   Ethnology of the Mayas of southern and central British Honduras. *Field Museum of Natural History* (Chicago), Publication No. 274, Anthropological Series 17(2)
1931   Archaeological investigations in the southern Cayo district, British Honduras. *Field Museum of Natural History* (Chicago), *Anthropological Series* 17(1).
1939   Excavations at San José, British Honduras. *Carnegie Institution of Washington,* Publication 506.
1954a   A presumed residence of the nobility at Mayapan. *Carnegie Institution of Washington Current Report* 19.
1954b   *The rise and fall of Maya civilization.* Norman: University of Oklahoma Press.
1966   Merchant gods of Middle America. In *Summa Antropológica en Homenaje a Roberto J. Weitlander,* edited by A. Pompa y Pompa. Mexico, D.F.: Instituto Nacional de Antropología e Historia.
1967   The Maya central area at the Spanish Conquest and later: a problem in demography. *Proceedings of the Royal Anthropological Institute of Great Britain and Ireland for 1966,* pp. 23–37.
1970   *Maya history and religion.* Norman: University of Oklahoma Press.
1971   Estimates of Maya population: deranging factors. *American Antiquity* **36**(2): 214–216.
1974   "Canals" of the Rio Candelaria basin, Campeche, Mexico. In *Mesoamerican archaeology: new approaches,* edited by Norman Hammond. Austin: University of Texas Press. Pp. 297–302.
1976   *Maya history and religion.* Norman: University of Oklahoma Press.
Thompson, J. E. S., H. E. D. Pollock, and J. Charlot
1932   A preliminary study of the ruins of Coba, Quintana Roo, Mexico. *Carnegie Institution of Washington,* Publication 424.
Thompson, J. E. S., and Donald E. Thompson
1955   A noble's residence and its dependencies at Mayapan. *Carnegie Institution of Washington Current Report* 25:225–251.
Thompson, Richard
1974   *The winds of tomorrow.* Chicago: The University of Chicago Press.

Timms, D. W. G.
1971   *The urban mosaic: towards a theory of residential differentiation.* Cambridge:
        Cambridge University Press.
Tourtellot, Gair
1970   The peripheries of Seibal: an interim report. *Papers of the Peabody Museum
        of Archaeology and Ethnology* 61:407–419.
1976   Patterns of domestic architecture at a Maya garden city: Seibal. Paper pre-
        sented at the 41st annual meeting, Society for American Archaeology, St. Louis,
        Missouri, May 6.
Tourtellot, Gair, and J. A. Sabloff
1972   Exchange systems among the ancient Maya. *American Antiquity* 37(1):126–35.
Tozzer, Alfred M.
1907   *A comparative study of the Mayas and the Lacandones.* Archaeological Insti-
        tute of America, 1902–1905, New York.
1913   A preliminary study of the prehistoric ruins of Nakum, Guatemala. *Memoirs
        of the Peabody Museum of American Archaeology and Ethnology,* 5:
        136–197.
1941   Landa's Relación de las Cosas de Yucatan. *Papers of the Peabody Museum of
        American Archaeology and Ethnology,* 18.
Trigger, Bruce
1972   Determinants of urban growth in preindustrial societies. In *Man, settlement and
        urbanism,* edited by P. J. Ucko, R. Tringham, and G. W. Dimbleby. Cam-
        bridge, Massachusetts: Schenkman.
Turner II, B. L.
1974   Prehistoric intensive agriculture in the Maya lowlands. *Science* **185**
        (4146):118–124.
1978   Ancient agricultural land use in the Central Maya Lowlands. In *Pre-Hispanic
        Maya agriculture,* edited by P. D. Harrison and B. L. Turner II. Albuquerque:
        University of New Mexico Press. Pp. 163–189.
Turner II, B. L., and Peter D. Harrison
1978   Implications from agriculture for Maya prehistory. In *Pre-Hispanic Maya ag-
        riculture.* Albuquerque: University of New Mexico Press. Pp. 337–373.
Turner, B. L., and William C. Johnson
1979   A Maya dam in the Copan Valley, Honduras. *American Antiquity*
        44(2):299–305.
Turner, Ellen Sue, Norman Turner, and Richard E. W. Adams
1981   Volumetric assessment, rank ordering and Maya civic centers. In *Lowland Maya
        settlement patterns,* edited by Wendy Ashmore. Albuquerque: New Mexico
        Press. Pp. 71–88.
Velázquez Valadéz, Ricardo
1980   Recent discoveries in the caves of Loltun. *Mexicon* 2(4): 53–55.
Villa Rojas, Alfonso
1934   The Yaxuna-Coba causeway. *Carnegie Institution of Washington,* Publication
        463, Contribution 9.
1945   The Maya of east central Quintana Roo. *Carnegie Institution of Washington,*
        Publication 588:187–208.
1961   Notas sobre la tenencia de la tierra en los Mayas de la antigüedad. *Estudios de
        Cultura Maya* 1:21–46.
1969   The Maya of Yucatan. In *Handbook of Middle American Indians,* edited by
        R. Wauchope. 7(1):244–97. Austin: University of Texas Press.
Vivó Escoto, Jorge A.
1964   Weather and climate of Mexico and central America. In *The handbook of Mid-*

dle American Indians (Vol. 1), edited by R. C. West. Austin: University of Texas Press. Pp. 187–215.

Vlcek, D. T., S. Garza de González, and E. B. Kurjack

    1978   Contemporary farming and ancient Maya settlements: some disconcerting evidence. In *Pre-Hispanic Maya Agriculture,* edited by P. D. Harrison and B. L. Turner II. Albuquerque: University of New Mexico Press. Pp. 211–224.

Vogt, Evon

    1964   Some implications of Zinacantan social structure for the study of the ancient Maya. *Actas y Memorias del 35th Congreso Internacional de Americanistas* 1:307–19.

    1969   *Zinacantan: A Maya community in the highlands of Chiapas.* Cambridge, Massachusetts: The Belknap Press of Harvard University Press.

    1970   *The Zinacantecos of Mexico.* New York: Rinehart and Winston.

Voorhies, Barbara

    1972   Settlement patterns of two regions of the southern Maya lowlands. *American Antiquity* **74**:117–124.

    1973   Possible social factors in the exchange system of the prehistoric Maya. *American Antiquity* **38**:486–489.

Wagner, Phillip L.

    1958   Nicoya: a cultural geography. *University of California Publications in Geography* **12**(3):195–250.

    1964   Natural vegetation of Middle America. In *The handbook of Middle American Indians* (Vol. 1), edited by R. C. West. Austin: University of Texas Press. Pp. 216–263.

Walton, John

    1978   Guadalajara: Creating the divided city. In *Metropolitan Latin America: The challenge and the response,* Vol. 6, edited by Wayne A. Cornelius and Robert V. Kemper. Beverly Hills: Sage.

Watter, R. F.

    1960–1961   The nature of shifting cultivation. *Pacific Viewpoint* **1,** 2:59–99.

Wauchope, Robert

    1934   House mounds of Uaxactun, Guatemala. *Carnegie Institution of Washington,* Publication 436, Contribution 7.

    1938   Modern Maya houses: a study of their archaeological significance. *Carnegie Institution of Washington,* Publication 502.

Webb, Malcolm C.

    1973   The Peten Maya decline viewed in the perspective of state formation. In *The Classic Maya Collapse,* edited by T. P. Culbert. Albuquerque: University of New Mexico Press.

Weber, Max

    1958   *The city.* New York: Collier Books.

Webster, David J.

    1975   The fortifications of Becan, Campeche, Mexico. *Middle American Research Institute,* Publication 31, pp. 123–132. Tulane University, New Orleans.

    1977   Warfare and the evolution of Maya civilization. In *The origins of Maya civilization,* edited by R. E. W. Adams. Albuquerque: University of New Mexico Press. Pp. 335–371.

West, R. C.

    1964   The natural regions of Middle America. In *The handbook of Middle American Indians* (Vol. 1), edited by R. C. West. Austin: University of Texas Press. Pp. 363–383.

Whalen, Michael

    1976   Zoning within an Early Formative community in the Valley of Oaxaca. In *The early Mesoamerican village,* edited by Kent Flannery. New York: Academic Press. Pp. 75–79.

Wheatley, Paul
    1971   *The pivot of the four quarters.* Chicago: Aldine.

Wilk, Richard
    1977   Colha, Belize, and the evidence for large-scale craft production. Paper prepared for the Annual Meetings of the Society of American Archaeologists, New Orleans, Louisiana, April 1977.

Wilken, G. C.
    1971   Food-producing systems available to the ancient Maya. *American Antiquity* **36**:432–447.
    1972   Microclimate management by traditional farmers. *Geographical Review* **62**:543–560.

Willey, Gordon R.
    1956a   Problems concerning prehistoric settlement patterns in the Maya lowlands. In *Prehistoric settlement patterns in the New World,* edited by G. R. Willey. Viking Fund Publication in Anthropology 23:107–114.
    1956b   The structure of ancient Maya society, evidence from the southern lowlands. *American Anthropologist* **58**:777–782.
    1968   Urban trends of the lowland Maya and the Mexican Highland model. *Proceedings of the 38th International Congress of Americanists* (Stuttgart), pp. 11–16.
    1973   The Altar de Sacrificios excavations: general summary and conclusions. *Papers of the Peabody Museum of Archaeology and Ethnology,* Harvard University, 64(3).

Willey, G. R., and W. Bullard Jr.
    1965   Prehistoric settlement patterns in the Maya lowlands. In *The handbook of Middle American Indians* (Vol. 2), edited by G. R. Willey. Austin: University of Texas Press. Pp. 360–377.

Willey, G. R., W. R. Bullard, Jr., J. B. Glass, and J. C. Gifford
    1965   Prehistoric Maya settlements in the Belize Valley. *Papers of the Peabody Museum of Archaeology and Ethnology,* Harvard University, 54.

Willey, Gordon R., T. Patrick Culbert, and Richard E. W. Adams
    1967   Maya lowlands ceramics: a report from the 1965 Guatemala Conference. *American Antiquity* **32**:289–315.

Willey, G. R., and A. L. Smith
    1969   The ruins of Altar de Sacrificios, Department of Peten, Guatemala: an introduction. *Papers of the Peabody Museum of Archaeology and Ethnology,* Harvard University, 62(1).

Wilson, Eugene M.
    1980   The physical geography of the Yucatan Peninsula. In *Yucatan, a world apart,* edited by E. H. Moseley and E. D. Terry. Alabama: University of Alabama Press.

Winer, B. J.
    1971   *Statistical principles in experimental design.* (2nd ed.). New York: McGraw-Hill.

Winter, Marcus
    1974   Residential patterns at Monte Alban, Oaxaca, Mexico. *Science* **186**:981–986.

Wirth, L.
    1938   Urbanism as a way of life. *American Journal of Sociology* **44**:1–24.

Wisdom, C.
    1940   *The Chorti: Indians of Guatemala.* Chicago: University of Chicago Press.

Wolf, E. R., and A. Palerm
    1957   Ecological potential and cultural development in Mesoamerica. In *Studies in human ecology*. Washington, D.C.: Pan American Union. Pp. 1–37.

Zubrow, Ezra B. W., Margaret C. Fritz, and John M. Fritz
    1974   The romantic vision: introduction. New World archaeology: cultural and theoretical transformations. *Readings from Scientific American*. San Francisco: W. H. Freeman and Company.

INDEX

Page numbers in italics indicate illustrations or maps

A

Abandoned structures, 193, 195, 208
Acanceh, 59
Acropolis, unfinished, 59, 80
Administrators, Maya civic, 55-57, 115, 165,
   166-167
Agent-of-trade cities, 14, *15*
Agriculture, 13, 20, 27, 31, 32, 36, 53, 55, 90,
   91, 102, 106-107, 117, 118, 192, 193,
   211, 212, 214; *see also* Horticulture;
   Kitchen gardens; Milpas; specific crops
   chinampa-type, 107
   swidden-type, 117, 118, 192
Aguada Grande, 90, 91
Aguadas (shallow ponds), 33, 44, *47*, 48
Ahau (rulers), 55, 59
Ahaucan (chief priest), 58, 59
Ah cuch cabob (town officials), 56-57, 61, 166
Ah dzib huun (town clerk), 57, 63
Ah Kin Coba, 12
Ah kin mai (priests), 58, 59, 165, 167-168
Ah Kin Pech, 14
Ah Muzen Cab (Diving God), 12, 78
Akalche (water-filled depression), 34
Aké, 59, 89

Alcoholic drink (*balche*), 37
Almehen (nobles), 55-57, 166; *see also* Class
   structure, Maya; Elite class
Altar de Sacrificios, 14
Altars, communal and domestic, 67-74 *passim*,
   78, 133, 156, 159
Animal pens, 124, 126, 141
Animals, 37-40
Apiculture, *see* Beekeeping; Honey; Wax
Archaeologists in Coba, 3-10; *see also* Coba
   Archaeological Mapping Project; Data
   analysis of Coba; INAH
Architecture, Maya, *see also* Coba architectural
   styles; Pole-and-thatch structures; Vaulted
   architecture
   civic-ceremonial, 51, 59, 145, 65-80, 215;
      see also Temples; specific temples
   residential, *see* Household compounds;
      Residences
   structural shapes (apsidal, rectangular,
      round), 8, 52, 53, 61, 63, 135, 145, 194
Archways, vaulted, 67, 83, 100
Artifacts, *see* Censers; Ceramic artifacts;
   Jewelry; Offerings; Tools
Art work, *see* Ceramic; Codices; Figures; Maya
   use of color; Murals; Stelae; Stone Carvings

243

STUDIES IN ARCHAEOLOGY

Consulting Editor: Stuart Struever

Department of Anthropology
Northwestern University
Evanston, Illinois